D0787789

UNIVERSITY OF WINNIPEG, 515 Portage Ave., Winnipeg, MB R3B 2E9 Canada

T. E. Lawrence
Revised Edition

Twayne's English Authors Series

Kinley Roby, Editor

TEAS 543

T. E. LAWRENCE
Photo credit from Stephen E. Tabachnick and Christopher Matheson's *Images of Lawrence*. By permission of Random House U.K.

PR
6023
A937Z88
1997

T. E. Lawrence

Revised Edition

Stephen Ely Tabachnick

University of Oklahoma

Twayne Publishers
An Imprint of Simon & Schuster Macmillan
New York

Prentice Hall International
London • Mexico City • New Delhi • Singapore • Sydney • Toronto

Twayne's English Authors Series No. 543

T. E. Lawrence, Revised Edition
Stephen Ely Tabachnick

Copyright © 1997 by Twayne Publishers
All rights reserved. No part of this book may be reproduced or transmitted in any form or by any means, electronic or mechanical, including photocopying, recording, or by any information storage and retrieval system, without permission in writing from the Publisher.
Twayne Publishers
An Imprint of Simon & Schuster Macmillan
1633 Broadway
New York, NY 10019

Library of Congress Cataloging-in-Publication Data

Tabachnick, Stephen Ely.
    T.E. Lawrence / Stephen Ely Tabachnick. — Rev. ed.
        p.   cm. — (Twayne's English authors series ; TEAS 543)
    Includes bibliographical references and index.
    ISBN 0-8057-7800-4 (alk. paper)
    1. Lawrence, T. E. (Thomas Edward), 1888–1935—Literary art.
    2. World War, 1914–1918—Campaigns—Middle East—Historiography.
    3. British—Middle East—History—20th century—Historiography.
    4. Soldiers' writings, English—History and criticism.   I. Title
    II. Series.
    PR6023.A937Z88   1997
    828'.91209—dc21   97-21412
                                                                              CIP
The paper used in this publication meets the minimum requirements of American National Standard for Information Sciences—Permanence of Paper for Printed Library Materials. ANSI Z39.48–1984. ∞ ™
10 9 8 7 6 5 4 3 2 1

Printed in the United States of America

To Rex Warner,
the only kind genius I have ever met

Contents

Preface

Some 20 years ago, I wrote in the first edition of this book that although T. E. Lawrence's *Seven Pillars of Wisdom* had been "Extravagantly praised by Thomas Hardy, George Bernard Shaw, and E. M. Forster (upon whose *A Passage to India* it exerted a direct influence)," it suffered from "a lack of critical attention and remains outside the university literature curriculum." In the preface to this new edition, it is appropriate to ask how that situation has changed.

On the positive side, there is far more scholarship about Lawrence now than there was 20 years ago. Then, sensationalist popular biographies by journalists and nonacademics were the dominant genre in Lawrence discussion. Lawrence seemed to have permanently become the popular culture icon that Lowell Thomas had made of him (with his consent) in the 1920s but nothing more than that. Full-length literary criticism of Lawrence's writing, an article about his strategic military theories, or a Ph.D. dissertation of any kind about him was still a rarity. Each serious study was excitedly and rightly welcomed by the Lawrence community as a pioneering advance. But it was difficult to find enough high-quality work on Lawrence as a writer to fill my original edition's secondary bibliography.

Today, although Lawrence remains a fixture of popular culture, academic writers around the world regularly produce doctoral dissertations, articles, and books on his literary, political, or military legacy. Their well-researched works have elevated the tone of the entire international Lawrence discussion, even among nonacademics. Pure speculation and sensationalism will not do any longer. To be taken even half-seriously, a writer on Lawrence must now show that he is familiar with the scholarship on the subject. The writer must also have something to contribute beyond what has already been said.

Moreover, since Lawrence's birth centenary year of 1988, three conferences, a national newsletter, and an international internet discussion group have enhanced the Lawrence dialogue in America. In England, a T. E. Lawrence Society and journal have been instituted. For Lawrence scholars, the heady excitement of working almost alone in a little-explored area has gone, but legitimacy and community have compensated for that. The problem now is how to read all of the high-quality work on Lawrence that is constantly being published.

But as much as we have learned about Lawrence during the past 20 years, we will always have more, it seems, to fathom. We are still not (and may never be) sure about what actually happened when Lawrence was captured by the Turks at Deraa or in the course of the battle of Tafileh or why he joined the R.A.F. as a simple airman after the war. Moreover, Lawrence's self-characterization in *Seven Pillars* remains permanently and tantalizingly contradictory. Despite or because of its fascinating contradictions and mysteries, *Seven Pillars* has gained recognition as one of the finest British autobiographies of the twentieth century. The basic claim of my original edition was that Lawrence was a very important writer who uncannily touches on many of our century's deepest concerns. In recent years, scholars in many fields have discovered that Lawrence is as pertinent to our own period's preoccupation with post-colonialism, terrorism, cultural confusion, problems of sexual identity, and the connection between the personal and the public as he was to an earlier age's obsession with issues of empire, war, and heroism. If recent Lawrence scholarship proves anything, it is that Lawrence is always relevant.

But for all of these positive developments, there remains one negative fact: *Seven Pillars of Wisdom* and *The Mint* are still only rarely taught in university courses. This situation has improved more in America than in England, where one almost never hears that Lawrence is being taught (although several Ph.D. dissertations on him have been produced there recently). Lawrence has been discussed by perhaps a dozen American professors in scattered literary or other courses during the past two decades. But this is not enough: *Seven Pillars* should regularly be considered in courses on modern British literature as well as in those on the literature of British imperialism or postcolonialism. Although it was not explicitly articulated, one important purpose of the original edition of this book was to help make Lawrence available to literature professors who want to teach him, as I myself have done.

Now, with this new edition, I wish to emphasize this pedagogical goal. The scholarly basis for Lawrence studies, although far from complete, has been soundly established. Teaching is the new frontier, a place where great advances in the field can now be made. The distinction of the present, like that of the original, edition of this book is that it subjects *Seven Pillars of Wisdom* and *The Mint* to a formal literary rather than biographical analysis and shifts the emphasis from Lawrence's life to his books and how he appears in them as a character. It shows how these books fit into a tradition, how they are put together, and what they seem to be saying not only about Lawrence himself but also about love, death, heroism, culture, politics, and art. In other words, it attempts to make *Seven Pillars of Wisdom* and *The Mint* available to those who wish to teach them in literature courses.

The original chronology has been simplified, and the biographical and critical review chapter has been updated to take account of recent scholarship (including relevant work on Lawrence's mentor Charles Doughty and on Anglo-Arabian travel writing). So have the original chapters 2–6 (all of which deal with *Seven Pillars*). The result is less of a structuralist and more of a "cultural studies" emphasis than existed in the original volume, but no single critical approach prevails. Errors of fact or typography have been corrected. The chapter on *The Mint* and the final chapter (on Lawrence's influence on other writers) have also been updated. The notes and bibliography have been modified and expanded to include recent scholarship.

But because its original insights remain valid and useful, this edition constitutes an updating and a revision rather than a complete rewriting of the original. Indeed, my basic position remains unchanged: that Lawrence's life should be used to illuminate his books, and not vice versa; that Lawrence is worth reading not only because of the fantastic story (particularly in *Seven Pillars*) that he had to tell but also because of the outstanding way in which he told it; that Lawrence's books must be assessed as autobiographies rather than as fictions or histories; and finally, that Lawrence deserves to be taught in university literature (and other) classrooms because he writes and illuminates important problems of life, art, and politics as well as Rudyard Kipling, Joseph Conrad, and E. M. Forster do.

Acknowledgments

I thank the T. E. Lawrence Trustees for permission to quote from the 1922 Oxford text of *Seven Pillars of Wisdom,* from *The Mint,* and from the letters of Robert Graves to T. E. Lawrence. I also thank the Houghton Library, Harvard University, for permission to quote from the Oxford text and the letters to Graves, and Random House U.K. for permission to quote from *The Mint.* Parts of chapters 2, 5, and 7 originally appeared, in somewhat different form, as articles in the journals *English Literature in Transition: 1880–1920, Studies in the Twentieth Century,* and *Research Studies.*

I would like to express appreciation to all of my colleagues in the Lawrence field for their insights into a subject whose fascination and following grow from year to year. Even our disagreements have the nature of a family squabble over a man, T. E. Lawrence, who sometimes seems like a relative rather than a topic of discussion. I thank Philip O'Brien for his ever willing bibliographical assistance. Edwards Metcalf's enthusiastic support of the Lawrence field has been a source of constant encouragement. I also thank librarians at the Houghton Library, the Huntington Library, the Bodleian Library, Jesus College (Oxford), the British Library, the University of Oklahoma, the Ben-Gurion University of the Negev, and the University of Connecticut, for very gracious treatment.

William Baker, Zev Bar-Lev, and Jay Shir contributed helpful suggestions to the original edition of this book, as did William Moynihan, Joseph Cary, and Paul Alkon. I am grateful for having had the opportunity to discuss Lawrence in various courses at the University of Oklahoma, Tennessee Technological University, UCLA, the Hebrew University, and the Ben-Gurion University.

I thank Kinley E. Roby, the editor of the original and revised editions of this work, for valuable assistance. My wife, Sharon, provided detailed criticism, stylistic corrections, and proofreading for which I am very grateful, while my children, Daphne, Orrin, and Laurie, kept me in touch with reality. I thank my parents for their constant support and regret that my father, Nathaniel Tabachnick, did not live to see that I have corrected the typographical errors that he found in the first edition of this book.

Chronology

1888 T. E. Lawrence born 16 August at Tremadoc, Wales.

1907 Graduates from City of Oxford High School for Boys.

1910 Graduates from Oxford University with First Class Honors in Modern History. B.A. thesis on "The Influence of the Crusades on European Military Architecture—to the End of the XIIth Century" (published as *Crusader Castles*, 1936).

1911 Works on dig at Carchemish, Syria, with D. G. Hogarth and C. Leonard Woolley. Writes *Diary of a Journey across the Euphrates* (published 1937). Translates *Two Arabic Folk Tales* (published 1937).

1914 Finishes work at Carchemish. Joins Geographical Section, War Office; sent to Intelligence Department in Cairo, Egypt.

1915 *The Wilderness of Zin* (coauthor C. Leonard Woolley).

1916 Contributes to intelligence newsletter, *The Arab Bulletin* (Lawrence's contributions published as *Secret Despatches from Arabia*, 1939). Reports on war situation in Mesopotamia. Joins Emir Feisal's forces in the Hejaz.

1917 Captures Akaba; tortured at Deraa; joins General Allenby during official entry into Jerusalem.

1918 Enters Damascus in triumph. Returns to Britain.

1919 Attends Peace Conference in Paris as Feisal's adviser.

1920 Finishes term as Fellow at All Souls College, Oxford.

1921 Attends Cairo Conference as adviser to Winston Churchill in the Colonial Office.

1922 "Oxford text" of *Seven Pillars of Wisdom* printed. Joins Royal Air Force under name John Hume Ross.

1923 Discharged from R.A.F., joins Royal Tank Corps under name T. E. Shaw.

1924 Publishes translation of le Corbeau's *Le Gigantesque (The Forest Giant)*.

1925   Rejoins Royal Air Force.

1926   Privately publishes Subscriber's Edition of *Seven Pillars of Wisdom*. Posted to India.

1927   Publishes *Revolt in the Desert,* an abridgment of *Seven Pillars of Wisdom.*

1928   Completes *The Mint* (published 1955).

1932   Completes "A Handbook to the 37 1/2 Foot Motor Boats of the 200 Class." Publishes his translation of Homer's *Odyssey.*

1935   Retires from the Royal Air Force. 13 May, fatally injured in motorcycle accident near Clouds Hill, Dorset. 19 May, death of T. E. Lawrence.

Chapter One
Introduction

Critical Review

Most travelers to Beersheba, Israel, probably fail to notice the old Hejaz Railway station and companion water tower. They speed by the World War I British military cemetery and do not see its thousand tombstones adorned with romantic and patriotic mottoes like "In God We Trust" and "So Far from Home." If travelers pass through the town center, the old Turkish mosque and administration building look to them like natural aspects of a landscape that contains many old mosques and buildings. Obscured by trees and automobile exhaust, the 12-foot-high obelisk with "ALLENBY 1917–1918" engraved on it is difficult to see from the road. When travelers leave the town and head for Eilat, the old stone railway bridge over Wadi Beersheba is only a blur.

Today's travelers and Beersheba's 170,000 inhabitants have their own wars and their own monuments and no time for the remnants of vanished colonial battles, including the one that took place from 6:00 A.M. to 6:00 P.M. on 31 October 1917 at Beersheba. Involving 40,000 men, it ended only when the 4th and the 12th Australian Light Horse Regiments managed to gallop the Turkish defenses on the Hebron Road in one of the last great cavalry charges.[1] But the sensitive observer gently transcends the present by peering through the windowless eye of the empty water tower and remembering that Beersheba was the first town in Palestine to be captured by the British during World War I. The observer also recalls that, far to the east of General Edmund Allenby's triumphal flank, the man known as "Lawrence of Arabia" made his mark by destroying the same Hejaz Railway (if a different branch from that which ran into Beersheba) and by leaving his literary monuments to these and subsequent adventures, the books known as *Seven Pillars of Wisdom*[2] and *The Mint*.[3] What does the reader of the first, and by far the greatest, of these books find in it?

To the reader encountering *Seven Pillars of Wisdom* for the first time, it appears a unique book that speaks of distant lands and events with an unusual and unsettling power. The uninitiated reader need not feel embarrassed: The more one studies the man and the book that reflects his personality to such a high degree, the more one notices complexities, contradictions, and ambiguities.

Because of a quarter century of scholarly study, Lawrence's book is now less strange and more approachable than at any point since its wide publication in 1935,[4] but still we feel the presence of an essential mystery. We may now be certain that the mysterious "S. A.," to whom Lawrence dedicated his book, was his Arab servant, Dahoum, and that Lawrence was indeed responsible for the military feats that he attributes to himself in *Seven Pillars*, including his secret ride into northern Syria and the capture of Akaba. Yet we are still not sure why he felt that "the citadel of my integrity had been irrevocably lost" after his mortifying experience at Deraa, nor do we know why military victory seems to engender in him the bitterness of defeat. We do not understand the reasons for his abrupt shifts in sympathy toward both the British and the Arabs. And we can never be confident of our comprehension of the character of this erratic, poetic autobiographer who did not always understand himself. Thus it is no wonder that even as *Seven Pillars of Wisdom* has achieved a high position in the canon of twentieth-century British autobiography, the book has continued to excite debate and disagreement.

The continuing controversy would have pleased Lawrence. He reveled in the confusion that he sowed among his contemporary critics and biographers. The following extract is from a letter Lawrence wrote to H. H. Banbury in 1927 after the appearance of the popular abridgment of *Seven Pillars*, entitled *Revolt in the Desert*.[5] The letter testifies to the reigning discord of the critics and Lawrence's delight in that consternation. And it must be remembered that *Revolt in the Desert* relates only the military side of Lawrence's adventures, making it far easier to judge than the more introspective and complex parent work.

> Yes, I was sent the [Leonard] Woolf review: and laughed. Here are the judgements of the great upon my style.
> "So imitative of Doughty as to be near parody." Woolf in the *Nation*.
> "Has none of Doughty's biblical or Elizabethan anachronisms." John Buchan in *Sat. Review*.
> "Gnarled texture twisted with queer adjectives and adverbs." Woolf.
> "Effortless, artless-seeming, adequate prose." Gerald Bullett.
> "Obscure to the point of affectation." *Tatler*.
> "Writing as easy, confident and unselfconscious as a duck's swimming." *Lit. Digest*.

"Style has a straightforward fierceness, an intrepid directness." Ellis Roberts. "Style is like music." C. F. G. Masterman. "A scholar's style, simple, direct, free from ornament." H. W. Nevinson. "Style here and there affectedly abrupt and strenuous, but mostly without affectation." Edw. Shanks. "A cool distinguished prose." Eric Sutton in *Outlook*. "Positively breezy." G. B. Shaw in *Spectator*. There y'are! Take your pick! I wash my hands of the affair: though I protest I am not peevish, as Woolf says.[6]

Until recently, the perplexity has become greater instead of less. For R. P. Blackmur, writing in 1940, "Except Swift, Lawrence is the least abiding writer of magnitude in English."[7] In 1955, Richard Aldington finds in *Seven Pillars* a "kind of verbal dodging" that is "the virtue of a politician and intriguer, not of a writer" and concludes that Lawrence "might have written much better if he had not striven painfully to write too well."[8] Malcolm Muggeridge writes in 1961 that "I found, and find it unreadable, while admiring the care and assiduity with which it has been put together."[9] In 1962, Irving Howe puts *Seven Pillars of Wisdom* in the same class as the works of Melville, Brecht, Kafka, and Pirandello.[10] But only around 1965, 40 years after the book's first appearance, did academic scholars both in America and abroad find it worthy of full-scale treatment and the application of modern analytic tools, producing a series of literary and historical theses and dissertations that continues to the present day.[11]

Since the 1960s, the judgment of the quality of Lawrence's work by serious writers has been unequivocal. Jeffrey Meyers's *Wounded Spirit* (1973), the first book devoted entirely to *Seven Pillars,* classifies it as "essentially and primarily a literary work of genius, beauty and insight . . . a masterpiece of psychological analysis and self-revelation" and "one of the finest books of the modern age."[12] In 1975 Stanley and Rodelle Weintraub rightly claim "That Lawrence's work as a writer is worth serious attention is no longer in doubt,"[13] and in 1979 Thomas J. O'Donnell concludes that the attributes of *Seven Pillars of Wisdom* are "power, universality, and complexity."[14] In 1984 Keith Hull presents Lawrence's book as a masterpiece worthy of comparison with the works of James Joyce and Thomas Pynchon.[15] M. D. Allen, writing in 1991, finds that Lawrence was "not the only modern author, not the only combattant [sic] of 1914–18, to represent his battle as being in the tradition of medieval encounters. But he is probably the only modern author to do so convincingly."[16] And Joel Hodson, the most recent critic, sees "considerable literary merit"[17] in Lawrence's writing and goes on to discuss the influence of *Seven Pillars of Wisdom* on Ernest Hemingway's *For Whom the Bell Tolls.*

In recognizing Lawrence for what he is in *Seven Pillars of Wisdom*—an important, even a great, writer—contemporary critics only second the judgment of the recognized artists (as opposed to litterateurs) of Lawrence's own period. To D. G. Hogarth, Lawrence writes that "Hardy read the thing lately, & made me proud with what he said of it" (*L,* 429).[18] George Bernard Shaw wrote that "it happened that Lawrence's genius included literary genius . . . and the result was a masterpiece of literature."[19] In *Abinger Harvest,* E. M. Forster says about Lawrence and his major book that "he was so modest that he never grasped its greatness, or admitted that he had given something unique to our literature."[20] In *Lawrence and the Arabs,* Robert Graves finds that "*Seven Pillars of Wisdom* is, beyond dispute, a great book."[21] On 6 December 1923 Siegfried Sassoon declares in a letter to Lawrence that "I feel ashamed of all these superlatives, but you've worn me down and swept me away, & I *know* the achievement to be great."[22] And Lawrence's letter of election to the Irish Academy of Letters was written by no one less than W. B. Yeats.[23]

The Mint, which contains the far less exciting story of the Royal Air Force sequel to Lawrence's Arabian adventures and is written in a correspondingly austere style, provoked from the start an even more mixed reaction than the earlier book and provides a much less secure basis for its author's literary reputation. Forster's judgment of 1928 that "*The Mint* is not as great a work as *The Seven Pillars* either in colour or form"[24] has been echoed by later critics. In a 1955 radio talk, L. P. Hartley declared *The Mint* a failed masterpiece whose artistry was constrained by a too strict style.[25] Referring to the fact that *The Mint* was released for general circulation only in 1955, 20 years after its author's death, V. S. Pritchett calls it "one of those time bombs of literature which fail to go off when the hour comes." He finds it "arty" in the bad sense and its author a "word prig." At the same time, he enjoys the third section of the book and admits that "Lawrence wrote spiritedly about action. Another virtue of *The Mint* lies in its honest effort to get to the bottom of his subject."[26] But Jeffrey Meyers, despite his enthusiasm for *Seven Pillars,* calls *The Mint* "incoherent" and "unconvincing."[27]

Yet the book has not been without its admirers, as letters to Lawrence from Forster, Edward Garnett, and David Garnett, among others, show.[28] The anonymous critic for *Kirkus* has summed up the book's ambivalent appeal better perhaps than anyone else: "The imaginative interpretation, poignant, bitter, devastating, suggests a writer's notebook. And yet at times there's the linear, introspective aspect of a modern novel. Now monotonous, now holding, it is a unique reading experience."[29] Although once of the opinion that *The Mint* is merely an exercise in journalism despite some powerful passages, the present writer—after subsequent readings—now agrees with the *Kirkus* reviewer: Although of much slighter spiritual and artistic magnitude than *Seven Pillars,* its sequel constitutes a worthy and original literary experiment and deserves attention as such. And since the third section presents a solution to personal problems raised in *Seven Pillars,* no consideration of Lawrence's mind and art can be complete without it.

Life and Career

Lawrence's life was as unique as his contribution to literature. Thomas Edward Lawrence was born on 16 August 1888 to Thomas Robert Chapman and the former Sarah Madden. Chapman, the lord of a manor, deserted a first wife to elope with Sarah from his home in County Meath, Ireland, and came to England, where he changed his name to Lawrence. T. E., the second of five sons, was born at Tremadoc, Wales. His parents' irregular situation and assumed name caused him distress all his life and partially explains why he found it so easy to change his own name first to Ross and then to Shaw, and why Liddell Hart's biography *"T. E. Lawrence" in Arabia and After* (1934) includes quotation marks around Lawrence's name in the title. The relationship between Lawrence's parents appears to approximate that of Paul Morel's parents in D. H. Lawrence's *Sons and Lovers:* A strongly Calvinistic mother tames and breaks a freer, more Dionysiac, father. No doubt some part of Lawrence's internal civil war and his lifelong celibacy can be traced to this source. On the other hand, D. H. Lawrence's very different path after a similar beginning reveals that we cannot account for T. E.'s complex personality in this simple way. With T. E. Lawrence, there is also the loss of aristocratic privilege owing to his father's elopement, which probably influenced his later willingness to assume the role of an Arabian sheikh.

Despite Lawrence's felt social handicap, his natural gifts brought him success from the start. From 1896 to 1907, he attended the Oxford High School for Boys, where he made rapid academic progress. He reserved his major interests—the typically English pursuits of medieval military archaeology, brass rubbing, and coin collecting—for the hours after school, which bored him. Early on these interests brought him friendship with D. G. Hogarth, Keeper of the great Ashmolean Museum, which today contains not only medieval treasures of the type that attracted the boy Lawrence but also relics of Lawrence's own adventures, including his Arab dagger and robe.

During T. E.'s years at Oxford (1907–1910), Hogarth became a trusted mentor who encouraged his interest in the Arabic language and the Near East. In the summer holidays of 1906, 1907, and 1908, Lawrence toured French castles in order to observe their military design. Always one for testing himself physically, he went on a solo walking tour in the summer of 1909 through parts of what are now Lebanon, Syria, and Israel in order to gather firsthand information on the incredible castles built by the Crusaders in their kingdom. Consolidating the results of all trips, Lawrence produced a beautifully self-illustrated and highly perceptive undergraduate honors thesis, "The Influence of the Crusades on European Military Architecture—to the End of the XIIth Century" (later published as *Crusader Castles*[30]). This thesis presents the unique, if still disputed, theory that the Crusaders brought all of their architectural ideas from the West and were not influenced by Eastern models. Later Lawrence was to learn just how powerful the East's influence could be.

After graduation, Lawrence worked for three years under Hogarth and C. Leonard Woolley (later made famous by his discoveries at the Chaldean city of Ur) at a dig at the ancient Hittite city of Carchemish. From December 1910 to August 1914 he was in Syria for all but seven months. He owed his familiarity with Arab ways to this experience, and it was during this period that he met Dahoum, the Arab servant who is mentioned openly only once in *Seven Pillars* but who is widely agreed to be the elusive "S. A." of the book's introductory poem. Early in 1914 Lawrence and Woolley joined Captain Stewart Newcombe of the Royal Engineers at Beersheba for a survey of the desert, including its biblical, Nabataean, and Byzantine ruins, a stint that resulted in the publication of *The Wilderness of Zin* (1915). Despite its inaccuracies, that book remained the most authoritative source on its subject until the appearance in 1959 of Professor Nelson Glueck's *Rivers in the Desert*. The archaeological value of the book by Lawrence and Woolley was exceeded at the time, however, by its use as a cover for the intelligence work of the British team, who were in fact spying on the Turkish defenses in southern Palestine, about a hundred miles north of the Suez Canal. Another semiliterary result of this period is *Carchemish: Report on the Excavations at Djerabis on Behalf of the British Museum*, which included Lawrence's notes and photos.

World War I began on 4 August 1914; after a brief sojourn in England, Lawrence took his place in the military intelligence service operating out of Cairo, where he made maps and had contact with spies. During this period, although only a young captain, he took part in the attempt to bribe the Turkish commander Khalil Pasha, whose army surrounded 10,000 British troops in Kut, in what is now Iraq. The attempt failed, but Lawrence saw firsthand the military bungling that had earlier resulted in the British catastrophe at Gallipoli. It is not surprising that he later idolized the new commander-in-chief of the British forces in Egypt and Palestine, General Allenby, once the latter had proven his competence, although Lawrence shows a consistent desire to look up to certain father figures throughout his life. Much of Lawrence's thinking during the Cairo period, which lasted until he joined the Arab forces, was directed toward outwitting the French, then in rivalry with the English for future hegemony in the Near East.

Around the time in late 1916 that he transferred to the Arab Bureau, a branch of the intelligence service concerned exclusively with Arab affairs, particularly with the revolt of the Sherif of Mecca against the Turks, Lawrence came into direct contact with the Arab Revolt itself. The "Introduction: Foundations of Arab Revolt" of *Seven Pillars* provides us with the religious and political background of the Sherif's movement and explains how Lawrence got himself transferred to the Arab Bureau in order to become involved with it. The section ends with Lawrence preparing to take a trip down to Jidda with Ronald Storrs, the Oriental Secretary, in order to assess the chances for the revolt's success.

Book 1 of *Seven Pillars* tells of Lawrence's first visit to Arabia, his meeting with the Sherif of Mecca and his three sons, Abdullah, Zeid, and Feisal, and his choice of Feisal as the man to lead the revolt with English backing. His full involvement not yet begun, Lawrence's tone is cool and lighthearted. The second book details Lawrence's appointment as Feisal's adviser, his donning of Arab dress, and his invention of the tactic of railway attack and guerrilla warfare in place of more conventional methods of war. Feisal moves his base from Yenbo up the coast to Wejh. In book 3, particularly the brilliant chapter 33, Lawrence fully develops his theory of guerrilla strategy. Instead of attacking the Turks entrenched at Medina, he advocates wide deployment, raiding tactics, and preaching to the tribes to enlist idealistic support. He tests his tactics on the railroad with partial success. Auda abu Tayi, the Homeric Bedouin desert fighter, enters the picture, and Lawrence devises a brilliant plan of attack on Akaba, far to the north at the end of the Red Sea. The next book, one of the military climaxes of *Seven Pillars,* recounts the epic march through several hundred miles of desert to the final victorious charge on Akaba. Akaba having been taken, book 5 demonstrates the increased importance of the Arab forces on Allenby's right flank. Lawrence polishes his railway techniques, and the book closes with a successful raid. He has gradually progressed from an adviser and observer to one of the principal participants in the revolt, and the tone of his writing begins to darken.

Book 6 constitutes Lawrence's dark night of the soul. Not only does a raid on the bridges over the Yarmuk River fail after the exertion and expectation of a long march, but he is captured by the Turks at Deraa, tortured, and sexually abused. This torture, described graphically in chapter 80, leads him toward nihilism and disillusionment. Yet at the end of book 6, Lawrence is standing by Allenby's side in captured Jerusalem: Personal failure and Allied success form a grim counterpoint. In book 7, a financial misunderstanding with the Emir Zeid convinces Lawrence to abandon the Arab movement altogether, but General Allenby sends him back to Feisal. Book 8 is another "waiting" section, in which Lawrence's forces lay siege to Maan's Turkish garrison and concentrate on cutting the railway. Lawrence receives over two thousand camels from Allenby and prepares for an attack on the Deraa sector, ever closer to the goal of Damascus. Although he acts, he discloses that he wishes to leave the movement entirely. In the next section, plans for the northward thrust continue, and Lawrence cynically discusses himself and the egoistic reality underlying the heroic ideal. By the time Damascus is reached on 1 October 1918, the Arabs' jubilant cries of victory are undercut by Lawrence's estrangement from them and from the British. The whole story closes on this note of triumphant military climax and personal despair.

Liddell Hart praises Lawrence as one of the originators of modern guerrilla warfare, including the doctrine of the indirect attack, high mobility, and firepower; Douglas Orgill, in the *Lawrence* volume of "Ballantine's Illustrated History of the Violent Century" (1973), repeats this praise, if in a modified form. On the other hand, Richard Aldington's debunking of Lawrence extends to his military prowess, which he denies almost completely. In this study we are not concerned with Lawrence's military ability except as it relates to his heroic or antiheroic vision in *Seven Pillars*. Still, it seems worthwhile to consider this aspect because it impinges on the truth content of Lawrence's autobiography. The German military historian Konrad Morsey has documented the widespread use of Lawrence's theories in international conflicts as well as praise of Lawrence by numerous military authorities; he has also unequivocally concluded that Lawrence deserves his fame as a strategist.[31] Whenever guerrilla warfare becomes an important topic, Lawrence is almost automatically discussed; toward the end of the Vietnam War in 1973 and 1974, for instance, at least four papers on his theories were written at the U.S. Army War College.[32] With regard to Lawrence's abilities as a tactician, J. M. Wilson, the authorized biographer, has convincingly shown that Lawrence was indeed responsible for the plan to capture Akaba, the outstanding success of the Arab forces during the war.[33]

In addition to the story of Lawrence's military command, *Seven Pillars* records the severe conflict of roles he experienced during the adventure and his profound bitterness over its spiritual and political outcome. The bitterness stems in part from his position as Feisal's adviser during the Paris Peace Conference of 1919, in which he watched France gain control over Syria despite promises made to Feisal by Lawrence himself and by the British government. As mandatory power, Britain would probably have granted the Arabs a greater degree of independence than France was prepared to give.

The writing of *Seven Pillars* also took its toll. Lawrence began writing the book in Paris in January 1919, lost a first draft, and continued revising it until 1926, taking it through several manuscripts in the process. According to his testimony, during the early years home he wrote at the prodigious rate of 4,000 or 5,000 words a day and once turned out 34,000 words in 24 hours. The strain of reliving his war experiences through his writing may have awakened in him an obsessive need to repeat aspects of the torture he suffered at Deraa, for beginning in 1923 and continuing until his death in 1935, he arranged to have himself whipped at infrequent intervals by John Bruce, a service colleague. Combined with self-imposed physical privation and the possible lasting physical and mental damage resulting from a plane crash in 1919, the struggle against this flagellation compulsion often brought him to the brink of madness. His precarious balance notwithstanding, Lawrence became an adviser to Winston Churchill in the Colonial Office in January 1921; by July 1922, when he resigned, he could declare himself satisfied that England had fulfilled her promises to the Arabs by installing

Abdullah on the throne of Transjordan and by placing Feisal, who had
been evicted from Syria by the French, in control of Iraq.[34]

Ironically, from 1919 on—at the same time that he approached a nervous breakdown—Lawrence became a popular hero due to the efforts of
Lowell Thomas, an American journalist commissioned to broadcast
Allied endeavors during the war. Thomas's exaggerated portrait of
Lawrence, which its subject scorned in comments to friends, was created
with Lawrence's agreement. As Thomas tells us, Lawrence proved only
too eager to play the role of "Lawrence of Arabia" and came, incognito,
to see the show several times. A wish to help Feisal's cause politically may
have been a factor contributing to Lawrence's behavior in this case. But
his behavior points out only one of his many contradictory aspects: a shyness concerning his mental life and yet a powerful desire for the public
spotlight. Lawrence's favorite method of preserving his privacy consisted
of weaving a maze of contradictory stories about himself, a method that
permitted him to realize both his desires at once. At the same time, it
should be noted that he deliberately left behind manuscripts and documents from which a reliable picture of himself and his activities may be
constructed, if with very great difficulty.

As a cure for his undefined spiritual malaise, he joined the Royal Air
Force in August 1922, under the name John Hume Ross. In January
1923, he was discharged upon the discovery by reporters that the famous
Colonel Lawrence of Arabia was serving as a mere airman, or private.
The Mint, composed between 1922 and 1928 and not published until
after his death, offers a detailed account of his life as a recruit. In "Part
One: The Raw Material," the reader follows a nervous Lawrence from
the outside of the recruiting station through the preliminary medical
examination and all the humiliations of drilling, fatigue duty, and fool-
ish officers. The harsh portrait of the wounded commanding officer
given in chapter 20 focuses all of his resentment of basic training. The
only question that remains unanswered is precisely why Lawrence willingly submitted himself to this treatment. "Part Two: In the Mill"
describes the next stage of instruction, the "square," in which the men
are formed into a coherent unit. Lawrence offers close descriptions of the
personalities of his buddies and of their life together but admits in chapter 19 at the end of this section that he is "Odd Man Out," not really
integrated into his company. The final part, "Service," takes place three
years after the ending of "square" duty and finds Lawrence happy and at
ease in the R.A.F. Cadet College. He feels at one with the other men,
with his work, and with nature and life itself. In this section of the book,

Lawrence solves many of the spiritual problems that he had not resolved in *Seven Pillars of Wisdom* or the first two parts of *The Mint*. In *The Mint*, Lawrence's personality is embodied in a new form of autobiography, a unique artistic achievement. During this period Lawrence also found time to translate into English Adrien le Corbeau's *Le Gigantesque (The Forest Giant)*, the story of the growth of a redwood tree, and to write many articles and letters to newspapers and friends. His vast lifetime correspondence, available in thick volumes, reveals a deep sensitivity and real epistolary talent.

A month after being dismissed from the air force, Lawrence reenlisted in the Tank Corps under the name T. E. Shaw. He withstood the harsh life of the "Tanks" for more than two years but in August 1925 succeeded in getting himself retransferred to the R.A.F., where his true passion lay. While serving in the R.A.F. in India, he produced for Bruce Rogers a translation of the *Odyssey* almost as interesting and original as his translator's preface, which attacks Homer as a man and as a writer. The great classics scholar Maurice Bowra, in his own introduction to Lawrence's translation, accepts some of Lawrence's criticisms of the *Odyssey* but sees through them to Lawrence's genuine admiration for the Greek poet and praises Lawrence's special gift:

> But when we set his translation against others, two qualities seem to emerge and give it a special distinction. The first is that he enjoys the story for its own sake and spares nothing to keep it clear and lively, to make the details illuminate and strengthen the whole effect and never to allow the plot to be lost in undue emphasis on the wrong point. The second is that he sees the whole Homeric world with a clear vision as Homer himself saw it.[35]

Lawrence's lifelong interest in Homer's work contributed to his vision of the Bedouin in life and art, and his experience with them in Arabia helped him with his translation. However, even in the relative retirement of India, his scholarly peace was shattered by fantastic newspaper reports of espionage activities, and in January 1929 he was ordered back to England.

From his return until just before his death on 19 May 1935, he remained in the R.A.F., leading a life idyllic in its numbness but becoming a good mechanic in the process, as his "Handbook to the 37 1/2 Foot Motor Boats of the 200 Class" testifies. His brain and erudition never dulled, and to the last he remained sensitive to the arts, particularly literature and classical music, and intimate with some of the best minds in England. He was fatally injured on 13 May 1935, while riding his Brough Superior motorcycle (a gift of the G. B. Shaws), an improvident passion for speed having overtaken his former love of exotic adventure. His life passed permanently into myth and literature, as the Robert Bolt film of 1962 and the Terence Rattigan play *Ross* (1960) demonstrate, and he provided a character type for many literary works written in the 1930s and later, such as W. H. Auden and Christopher Isherwood's *The Ascent of F.6.*

Although we no longer see him as portrayed in the posed photographs of Lowell Thomas's cameraman Harry Chase, that is, as a figure in the Rudolph Valentino "Sheik of Araby" texture of the 1920s, his life remains intriguing as a paradigm of the conflicts experienced by many late romantic, essentially nineteenth-century, intellectuals who had to confront World War I. As a character in his own poetic autobiography, Lawrence also proves one of the first examples in our century of the phenomenon of culture shock, and *Seven Pillars* remains a glaring and unsettling mirror of his plight.

Approximately 50 biographies to date testify to the fascination that his life has held for us in every segment of this century. In the 1920s and 1930s, he was presented by biographers as a hero who had fought selflessly for both Arab and British honor against the "old men" who refused to accept change. In 1954,[36] he was characterized by Richard Aldington as having been too pro-Arab at a time of increasing East-West tension preceding the 1956 Anglo-French invasion of Egypt, which had nationalized the Suez Canal. In the 1960s and beyond, a period of rapid decolonization, some biographers have thought that he served the cause of British imperialism too well. However, this view of Lawrence has also been strenuously opposed during this same period, making for a lively debate.[37] Among the Arabs, Lawrence's reputation has followed a parallel course from early hero-worship to recent accusations of imperialism.[38] We cannot know what the next phase in the estimation of Lawrence's life will be, but judging from the steady output of Lawrence biographies we can safely predict that there will indeed be a next phase.

Our question, however is not whether Lawrence led an interesting life (he did) but whether he produced good literature from it. The literary critic must use Lawrence's life to illuminate his books—not vice versa. Biographers may share with historians the hard task of sifting documentary evidence, but the literary critic has *Seven Pillars* and *The Mint* before him. A cool, impartial, and careful literary analysis of both books inevitably leads to the conclusion that Lawrence the artist speaks to us in a voice different from and greater than that of "Lawrence of Arabia."

Chapter Two

Seven Pillars of Wisdom: Autobiography and Autobiographies of Travel

What is the genre of Lawrence's books? Is *Seven Pillars of Wisdom* a history of the Arab Revolt, an autobiography, a travel book, a fictionalized autobiography, a confession, a romance-confession, or a memoir? It has been called all these names, and *The Mint* has also been difficult for critics to place precisely. This is an important question because our understanding of the nature and quality of Lawrence's work depends upon our answer to it.

Let us place the *memoir* on one end of the spectrum of autobiographical writing, labeling it the history of the external events of a life looked at in retrospect by the person who lived that life, and the *confession* on the other end, labeling it the history of the internal events of a life looked at in retrospect by the person who lived that life. Memoirs are typically written by persons such as military men who have participated in important historical events and who want to leave an explanation of their actions. Confessions, on the other hand, are typically written by religious or intellectual figures such as St. Augustine and Jean-Jacques Rousseau, who want to leave a record of how they arrived at important spiritual decisions.

What do we have in the middle, between the memoir and the confession? *Autobiography:* the history of the relationship between the external and the internal events of a life looked at in retrospect by the person who lived that life. By this definition, both *Seven Pillars* and *The Mint* are clearly autobiographies. The question remains, what kind?

Until William L. Howarth wrote an excellent article distinguishing the three basic types, or subgenres, of autobiography, we had no answer to that question. Howarth calls the first of the three autobiographical types "oratorical autobiography." The foremost example of this kind of autobiography is Henry Adams's *Education of Henry Adams*, and its characteristics are: (1) it is written to prove a point, and ideology motivates and governs all elements; (2) the narrator sympathizes with the protagonist, but from a great distance, and even uses the third person to name the protagonist, for instance, "Adams"; (3) the protagonist relives and learns from his days of sin and error; and (4) a highly rhetorical style of many figures and devices is employed.

Benjamin Franklin's *Autobiography* provides an example of the second type, the "dramatic autobiography." Here the narrator identifies with the protagonist and presents no thesis of character development. The unpretentious and impertinent narrator-protagonist swaggers through picaresque, randomly ordered events changing masks, roles, and identities as he goes along. The shameless writers who fabricate these theatrical autobiographies desire only to portray their own spontaneous minds and characters, rather than to prove a point.

The third type discovered by Howarth, the "poetic autobiography," interests us the most, for Lawrence's work fits clearly into this category, as does Thoreau's *Walden*. Here a narrator who identifies with the protagonist details a tentative, inner journey, frequently making use of the devices of style of the postromantic symbolist poets. Presenting a theory of radical dislocation, the poetic autobiographer displays moodiness, unpredictability, identity problems, and a strongly critical image of himself and others. He provides no answers to the many questions about life that he raises and gives us no clear image of himself: In the end, it is the reader alone who must impose a shape and pattern on the autobiographer's character, who must in fact *create* the autobiographer.[1] As in the case of the other autobiographical types, the personality of the autobiographer is presented in relation to a general framework of historical, social, and political events.

Seven Pillars of Wisdom (as well as *The Mint*) can be definitively named a poetic autobiography. As such, however, *Seven Pillars* presents one unusual problem, which will be discussed in a later chapter in more detail: Lawrence fails to make clear the precise relationship between inner and outer events. Because he does not tell us, we do not always understand why he is at one moment a friend of the Arabs, at the next disgusted with them, why he is one moment exalted and the next depressed. As a result, the book has a tendency to appear as two halves: a triumphant military plot of romantic adventures and a bitter, chaotic personal account of the wounded soul, with no connective tissue. But this problem is less important than it seems. By failing to understand himself and therefore failing to give us a clear picture of the reasons for his spiritual shifts, Lawrence has left his character in *Seven Pillars* open to the reader's imagination. Even more than in most poetic autobiographies, readers must impose their own views to make sense of Lawrence. Both *Seven Pillars* and *The Mint* become, then, truly contemporary reading experiences that would please all critics who believe that the reader must participate in the creation of the story. In form as well as content, Lawrence's autobiographies belong as much to our age as to his. A look at the major influences on Lawrence reveals the full extent to which he was original in developing *Seven Pillars'* poetic autobiography.

Although Lawrence brings a unique sensibility to bear on his reconstruction of Arabian adventures, *Seven Pillars of Wisdom* represents a variation on a literary tradition of which he was fully aware. The particularly fine haze through which he saw the deserts of Arabia and the people who lived there owes much of its seemingly distinctive tint to the literary treatments of a very select group of writers: authors of the nineteenth-century travel books so popular with the English public, particularly those writers who traveled to the Near East, and W. H. Hudson, the fictional and nonfictional romanticizer of the pampas and wastes of South America.

Despite Lawrence's typical and genuine hero worship and modest self-appraisal, his knowledge of his place in the grand tradition of "Arabian" writers becomes apparent in the following quotation from the foreword he wrote for Bertram Thomas's *Arabia Felix* (1932):

> You see, in my day there were real Arabian veterans. Upon each return from the East I would repair to Doughty, a looming giant, white with eighty years, headed and bearded like some renaissance Isaiah. Doughty seemed a past world, in himself; and after him I would visit Wilfred Blunt. An Arab mare drew Blunt's visitors deep within a Sussex wood to his quarried house, stone-flagged and hung with Morris tapestries. There in a great chair he sat, prepared for me like a careless work of art in well-worn Arab robes, his chiselled face framed in silvered, curling hair. Doughty's voice was a caress, his nature sweetness. Blunt was a fire yet flickering over the ashes of old fury.
>
> Such were my Master Arabians, men of forty, fifty years ago. . . .
>
> I suppose no new Sixth Former can help feeling how much his year falls short of the great fellows there when he joined the school. But can the sorry little crowd of us be in a tradition, even? I fear not. Of course the mere wishing to be an Arabian betrays the roots of a quirk; but our predecessors' was a larger day, in which the seeing Arabia was an end in itself. They just wrote a wander-book and the great peninsula made their prose significant. (Incidentally, the readable Arabian books are all in

English, bar one; Jews, Swiss, Irishmen and Whatnots having conspired to help the Englishmen write them. There are some German books of too-sober learning and one Dutch). Its deserts cleaned or enriched Doughty's pen and Palgrave's, Burckhardt's and Blunt's, helped Raunkiaer with his Kuwait, Burton and Wavell in their pilgrimages, and Bury amongst his sun-struck Yemeni hamlets.[2]

Although Lawrence pays homage to almost all of his major predecessors, his real admiration remains restricted to those who achieved the finest literary artistry in their travel accounts, as he makes clear in a letter to Sir Percy Sykes written the year after this foreword: "I hope your review, however brief, will recognize the great merit of Palgrave as explorer and writer. . . . He was in the Philby-Thomas class as explorer and wrote brilliantly" (*L,* 768). In the distinction he makes between St. John Philby (the convert to Islam who was the father of Kim Philby, the Communist spy) and Bertram Thomas as great *explorers* and, on the other hand, W. G. Palgrave as a great explorer *and* writer, we have the point: Lawrence's reaction to these travel accounts is primarily a literary one. To Robert Graves he writes in 1925 that "E. M. Forster's guide book to Alexandria . . . is great literature, and a good guide. Boost it."[3]

This literary sensitivity to, and judgment of, travel books dates from his earliest letters. On 2 August 1909, during his walking tour of Syria and Palestine, Lawrence writes to his mother that the descriptions of the spring at Banias in Eliot Warburton's *Crescent and the Cross* and William Thomson's *Land and the Book* (both nineteenth-century travel works) are "admirable descriptions" but "'purple patches,' both of them" (*L,* 70). When in 1910 he describes D. G. Hogarth's *Wandering Scholar in the Levant* (1896) as "one of the best travel books ever written" (*L,* 87), we can safely assume that his criteria for this judgment are primarily literary. And the surprising lack of references to Richard Burton's famous *Personal Narrative of a Pilgrimage to Al-Madinah and Meccah* (1855) in his letters indicates a disapproving literary rather than scientific conviction. A clue to this opinion appears in a letter of 1922, in which Lawrence prefers Edward Lane's translation of the *Arabian Nights* to Burton's on the basis of style (*L,* 359), although in a letter to Jonathan Cape in the same year, he finds Lane's translation "pompous,"[4] and in another letter he calls Burton's Arab portrayals "pinchbeck."[5]

In the same letter in which he disparages Burton's talent as a translator, Lawrence indicates clearly which of his predecessors' books he likes best, as well as the reason for his preference: "*War and Peace* I thought decently written on the whole. Of course not a miracle of style like *Salammbo* or *Moralités Légendaires:* or like Doughty and *Eothen* and *Idle Days in Patagonia"* (*L,* 359). This letter assumes particular importance because it was written while Lawrence was attempting to revise the Oxford text of *Seven Pillars of Wisdom* and not long before or after that, as were the other sources quoted. The high value he places on style itself, as well as the rank in which he locates Doughty, Kinglake, and Hudson, is clear.

In his introduction to *Travels in Arabia Deserta,* Lawrence writes that "Mr. Doughty was not content till he had made the book justify the journey as much as the journey justified the book, and in the double power, to go and to write, he will not soon find his rival."[6] This quotation provides a clear view into the kind of treatment Lawrence took from the Arabian travel books, particularly Doughty's, which he loved, and applied to *Seven Pillars.* If the travel book is to rely on its merit as writing at least as much as upon its scientific or objective descriptions of people, places, and events for its ultimate value, then certain other points about it become obvious.

First, a subjective and—in the case of the Anglo-Arabian travel tradition—inevitably romanticized account will characterize the author's treatment. Michael Foss explains how and why the Arabian travel book became in the hands of English writers something more than a purely scientific medium:

> Those who followed Burton's guide were likely to enter into a world of subtle unreality designed to satisfy a poet's need. . . . Arabia continued to be illumined by the poet's shifting light. For the rest of the nineteenth century, the men who informed England most successfully of that frontier land were poets all—Palgrave, Blunt and Doughty. In the late nineteenth century, an age of scientific rationalism, the rediscovery of Arabia was not a reflection of scientific investigation, but the distorting mirror of the imagination. Perhaps the English public could accept no other presentation; for whereas explorers of unknown countries started with few preconceptions, the Arabian traveller from Europe took with him the historical memories of over a thousand years of conflict with Islam. He necessarily entered into the "fabled" land of the Arabian Nights.[7]

The elements of historical romance and—in the case of the nineteenth-century traveler—Rousseau's idea of the "noble savage," Victorian hero-worship, and a century of Gilbert and Sullivan stylizing in the popular media enter the relationship between Englishmen and Arabs at a deep level. The result is that these writers could remain sincerely unconscious of their essentially heightened and in some ways unreal view of the desert while transmitting that view to their readers.[8]

At the same moment, the theme of the clash of cultures—the interaction between the personality of the Western traveler and a totally different and for the wayfarer utterly unassimilable environment and set of mores—provides the main drama or action of these books. Although the desire to relive past ages of heroism remains ingrained on the unconscious level, the realities of present discomforts become too intrusive for the traveler to disregard. As a result, Doughty's combination of naturalistic detail and mythologized characters, settings, and dialogue has something in common with Kinglake's blend of Byronic rapture and ironic undercutting. These Arabian travelers *want* to see the heroic and inspiring in the desert from the start but must constantly come down to earth when they behold the reality. This same combination of seemingly heroic characters and unpleasant reality finds its place in *Seven Pillars of Wisdom* as well. But when Jean Béraud Villars decides that "its balance between romanticism and naturalism was the essence of a new form of literature,"[9] he praises the originality of *Seven Pillars* at the expense of other Arabian travelogues in which a traveler's expectations and actual experiences exist side by side in discordance.

Finally, the individual personalities of the authors, expressed through the medium of powerful and individual styles of writing, constitute the most important and striking quality of these works. In Hogarth's phrase, these books are really "autobiographies of travel."[10] The structural cohesion of the travel book relies not on the coherent shaping of incident but on the sensibility of the author-protagonist. It could scarcely be otherwise when travelers as prone to quirks as our "Arabians" recount long, meandering journeys. Depending on the precise type of travel autobiography—oratorical, dramatic, or poetic, to use Howarth's categories—that they write, the authors become the main characters, and their books guessing-games; the reader's role is to explore and shape the authors' indirectly revealed personalities.

When placed against descriptions and analyses of the works of Kinglake, Hudson, and Doughty—all of which Lawrence read before or during the composition of *Seven Pillars*—Lawrence's use of personal revelations, a romantic vision, and an art-prose style becomes an expected and reasonable element of *Seven Pillars*, which still retains its unique form and content.

Kinglake

The Near East has long attracted an eccentric kind of Englishman dissatisfied with the more mundane interests of Continental grand tours and travelogue writing. As Lawrence wrote, "the mere wishing to be an Arabian betrays the roots of a quirk." Beginning with the establishment of the Levant Company in 1581 and its subsequent explorations in this area, the Near Eastern travel account edged its way from purely commercial interest to the status of an organized, highly self-conscious, and artistic literary genre that has included among its practitioners such recognized artists as William Thackeray and E. M. Forster.[11]

The publication in 1844 of Alexander Kinglake's *Eothen*[12] ("From the East") marks the beginning of the artistic period in Anglo-Arabian travel writing. Kinglake's achievement lies in making the writing more important than what he sees in his travels. In the words of Iran Banu Hassani Jewett, Kinglake "used the Near East not as an area, but as a literary theme."[13] He transmits his personality through what is obviously a loosely structured, picaresque dramatic autobiography of travel, replete with dramatic scenes and confrontations, and sets the tone of adventurous quest that Lawrence inherits.

What in the end do we learn of Kinglake's character? Although he constantly attacks false romantic pathos, false religious fervor, and viciousness and prejudice in human affairs, he retains quite consciously the religious and political preconceptions of the English traveler of his times. He makes no attempt to meet people of other cultures on their own terms but always judges them according to standards native to himself. In the end, he clings to a personal, humanistic Christianity, the Greek classics, and British force and moral superiority as Arnoldian "touchstones," however banteringly qualified. Like Doughty and most other nineteenth-century travelers—with the exceptions of the Arabist Burton and the anti-imperialist Blunt—he retains his distance from the alien culture and continues to judge it from on high. He can grant the East only novelty—not moral or cultural equality. Lawrence lacked precisely this certainty, and *Seven Pillars* becomes more complex than either *Eothen* or *Arabia Deserta* as a result, reflecting the price in personal suffering that Lawrence had to pay for his modern, relativistic position. (This point will be investigated more fully in the chapter on the "two veils" of Lawrence's mind.) Here, as in his allowing his journey itself to supply the loose structure of his book, Kinglake exerts an oppositional influence on Lawrence. But—in Kinglake's adventurous view of his travels, his attitude toward Homer, his sometimes guarded use of his personality, and his artistic style—his influence on the later writer can be clearly discerned.

Lawrence rejects Kinglake's imperialism but accepts his romanticism. Referring to Lady Hester Stanhope, that amazing figure who is mentioned in Thackeray's *Vanity Fair* and who once faced down a tribe of charging Bedouin with a raised umbrella and the single word "Avaunt!," Kinglake remarks that he sees in her (and perhaps by extension in himself) a "longing for the East, very commonly felt by proud people when goaded by sorrow." In this tinge of indefinable and inexplicable Byronic pathos, Kinglake touches a chord struck by most Arabian travelers including Lawrence, whose ostensibly inexplicable cause for sorrow at the end of his campaign falls into the category of the common literary effect of the post-Kinglake travel-book writer. And for all Kinglake's spontaneous self-revelation, he tells us that Lady Hester read his character in his face and informed him of the result, but "this, however, I mean to keep hidden." For the most part an open, dramatic autobiographer, Kinglake is not above increasing our interest in his personality by veiling it from us, at least early in the book. Like the later Lawrence, Kinglake also understands the value of self-deprecating humor in an autobiography: Such expressions as "this poor, pale, solitary self that I always carry around with me" and the "eternal Ego that I am" could not fail to endear him to Lawrence.

Kinglake's romantic love of Homer's *Iliad*—and his dislike of the *Odyssey*—parallels Lawrence's own attitudes toward the Greek poet. We must remember that Lawrence had not yet begun his own *Odyssey* translation until he had already finished reading *Eothen*, and that until he worked on that translation his attitude toward Homer was one of complete admiration. Perhaps an echo of Kinglake's dislike of the *Odyssey* remained in his mind.

Most of all, Lawrence appreciated *Eothen* for its style. When Kinglake is not indulging in ecstasies similar to those of Byron's *Manfred*, he resorts to biting irony. This use of irony and dramatic technique shields the reader from the horror of Cairo during the plague of 1835, just as it keeps the reader from too much romanticism at other points. Kinglake's essential mental health resides in his ability to distance himself through humor from his own foibles and from events. The following passage from the climactic Cairo chapter, a certain "miracle of style," proves an excellent example of his ironic distancing technique; the situation is Kinglake's imaginary view of the thoughts of a European in Cairo dying of plague:

Once more the poor fellow is back home in fair Provence, and sees the sundial that stood in his childhood's garden—sees part of his mother, and the long-since-forgotten face of that dear sister (he sees her, he says, on a Sunday morning, for all the church bells are ringing): he looks up and down through the universe, and owns it well piled with bales upon bales of cotton and cotton eternal—so much so, that he feels—he knows, he swears he could make that winning hazard, if the billiard table would not slant upwards, and if the cue were a cue worth playing with; but it is not—it's a cue that won't move—his own arm won't move—in short, there's the devil to pay in the brain of the poor Levantine; and perhaps the next night but one he becomes the "life and soul" of some squalling jackal family, who fish him out by the foot from the shallow and sandy grave. (197)

Kinglake's use of dashes and parentheses allow him to create a surrealistic, cinematic effect of partial views, shifting focuses, and wild dreams. As in this chapter in particular and the book as a whole, he moves with ease from one unrelated scene to the next, his eye (and ear) catching every detail of the dying man's frantic associations, and brings us to a magnificent climax of grim irony. He treats his own bout with the disease with scarcely less irony.

Although Lawrence could never detach himself from his own self or from events as totally as Kinglake, the earlier writer taught him how to combine rapture and irony, romanticism and naturalism, and that fine style in travel writing means the difference between a literary and a nonliterary account.[14] The tortured and involuted Lawrence may have little in common with the spontaneous mind of Kinglake, who is able to place ironic distance between himself and trouble at all times. Nonetheless, Kinglake's errors of weak structure and cultural prejudice and his strength as a stylist, an exploiter of his own personality, and an honest viewer of desert truths under the romance could not have been lost on the later writer.

Hudson

A friend of T. E. and an admirer of Doughty, W. H. Hudson practiced the art of the travel autobiography in *Idle Days in Patagonia*[15] and authored the famous novels *The Purple Land* and *Green Mansions*, to name but a few of his works. Besides the reference to *Idle Days* as a "miracle of style," we have many other signs of Lawrence's pleasure in Hudson's work. On 4 October 1923, he writes to Edward Garnett that

The Hudson's are sumptuous. How well the old man reads in them. *The Shepherd* has found two friendly readers already; yet I like better, much better, the memories of his childhood [in *Far Away and Long Ago*]. Wonderful that one man should have written that and *Patagonia*, and *The Purple Land*, and *Green Mansions*: and I go about thinking that into his first book anyone not a born writer can put all that his spirit holds. Hudson is hardly a born writer, either. Not for him that frenzied aching delight in a pattern of words that happens to run true. (*L,* 433).

By this last comment, Lawrence seems to mean that Hudson is a conscious stylist who must work hard to achieve his effects, like Lawrence himself, but that he is no less a fine writer for that. This idea becomes clearer as the letter, one of the most interesting in the Garnett edition, continues:

Do you know that lately I have been finding my deepest satisfaction in the collocation of words so ordinary and plain that they cannot mean anything to a book-jaded mind: and out of some of such I can draw deep stuff. Is it perhaps that certain sequences of vowels or consonants imply more than others: that writing of this sort has music in it? I don't want to affirm it, and yet I would not deny it: for if writing can have sense (and it has: this letter has) and sound why shouldn't it have something of pattern too? My sequences seem to be independent of ear . . . to impose themselves through the eye alone. Do you think that people ever write *consciously* well? or does that imply an inordinate love for the material, and so ruin the art? I don't see that it should. A sculptor who petted his marbles from sheer joy in their grain and fineness would . . . be better than a mere block-butcher. (*L,* 434)

So in the end Lawrence dismisses the romantic notion, adhered to by Kinglake, who always insists that his pen is not under his control, that style must be an unconsciously directed effusion, and believes that a miracle of style like *Idle Days* can result from conscious art like his own and Hudson's. A further clarification of his opinion on this point of conscious style and on his view of *War and Peace* occurs in a letter of 6 November 1928 to Robert Graves: "A man's a great writer when he can use plain words without baldness. . . . If a fellow isn't big enough he must do the other thing: . . . what you call style:—surface his work. The War-and-Peace plainness is better, perhaps: but one is fonder, often, of the rather less-than-big work. It feels more homelike. That's the reward of secondary writers."[16] Thus, fine style in Lawrence's scheme becomes the tool of the minor writer, in which category he would include himself since he was such a conscious craftsman. We need not take this misconception about style itself and Lawrence's literary position too seriously: It probably arises out of the fact that he read Tolstoy in the bland Constance Garnett translation, the only one available in England at that time.

For the most part, Lawrence acts far from apologetic about his enthusiasm for Hudson's work. When Edward Garnett complained of a lack of forthrightness in the "Myself" chapter of *Seven Pillars* and said that "in his books Hudson does not hide his feelings," Lawrence's reply was "Yes! But Hudson is above us all."[17] And as late as 1933 he declares himself "rather saddened" by the lack of "all Hudson, most Conrad, some Doughty" in his Clouds Hill library (*L, 776*).

An inadvertent clue to what precisely Lawrence liked in Hudson appears in Richard Haymaker's *From Pampas to Hedgerows and Downs* (New York: Bookman Associates, 1954), when Haymaker writes that

> The pampas of La Plata, the plains of Patagonia, the countryside of southern England, with their characteristic flora and fauna, are so fully and freshly depicted that they become new realities in the realm of human experience, analogous to the recreation of Selborne, Walden Pond, and the Catskills by White, Thoreau and Burroughs; Dorset and Devon by Hardy, Llewelyn Powys and Williamson; Morocco and the Arabian desert by Loti, Cunninghame Graham and Doughty. . . . (170).

Haymaker compares Hudson to Charles Doughty, Thomas Hardy, Henry Williamson, and Graham, all of whose work Lawrence admired. Specifically, what appealed to Lawrence is Hudson's method of answering a question originally asked by Charles Darwin in his *Voyage of the Beagle* and quoted in *Idle Days* for its appositeness: "Why, then—and the case is not peculiar to myself—have these arid wastes taken so firm possession of my mind?" (201). With Doughty, who found that if "in truth one live with the Aarab, he will have all his life after a feeling of the desert," Hudson can say of the Patagonian desert that "in spite of accurate knowledge, the old charm still exists in all its freshness; and after all the discomforts and sufferings endured in a desert cursed with eternal barrenness, the returned traveller finds in after years that it still keeps its hold on him, that it shines brighter in memory, and is dearer to him than any other region he may have visited." He heads into the plains of Patagonia drawn by some mysterious force, that common propellant behind most travel books dealing with exotic places: "And yet I had no object in going—no motive which could be put into words; for although

I carried a gun, there was nothing to shoot." Doughty and Lawrence both felt this same mystery, which derives from Kinglake.

Hudson substantiates his love of these plains with a description that undoubtedly moved Lawrence to envy:

> In the scene itself there was nothing to delight the eye. Everywhere through the light, gray mold, gray as ashes and formed by the ashes of myriads of generations of dead trees, where the wind has blown on it, or the rain has washed it away, the underlying yellow sand appeared, and the old ocean-polished pebbles, dull red, and gray, and green, and yellow. On arriving at a hill, I would slowly ride to its summit, and stand there to survey the prospect. On every side it stretched away in great undulations; but the undulations were wild and irregular; the hills were rounded and cone-shaped, they were solitary and in groups and ranges; some sloped gently, others were ridge-like and stretched away in league-long terraces, with other terraces beyond; and all alike were clothed in the gray ever-lasting thorny vegetation. How gray it all was! hardly less so near at hand than on the haze-wrapped horizon, where the hills were dim and the outline blurred by distance. (206–7)

Hudson appears here as the master romanticizer of landscape, who conjures up a purple land of misty campo, complete with "haze-wrapped horizon," but he manages this coloring without recourse to the keyed-up metaphors that Lawrence frequently uses. Where Lawrence focuses on the desert's brilliant aspect, Hudson downplays this, relying on balanced phrases and one exclamation mark to create a striking description. By way of contrast with Hudson's fine haze, we remember the heat of Arabia that "came out like a drawn sword and struck us speechless" as Lawrence approaches Jidda for the first time. Lawrence must have admired Hudson's ability to accomplish dramatic effects with subtle means.

Similarly, he surely admired Hudson's easy use of his personality, his lack of reticence in describing and explaining his emotions, his ability to "let go." In a literary use of the memory that precedes Proust's "Madeline" incident by several years, Hudson in his "Perfume of an Evening Primrose" chapter expands on the meanings that a flower's odor has for him: "The suddenly recovered sensation is more to us for a moment than a mere sensation; it is like a recovery of the irrecoverable past" (244)—*à la recherche du temps perdu*. Hudson continues in a Proustian vein when he finds that "I cannot think of any fragrant flower that grows in my distant home without seeing it, so that its beauty may be always enjoyed—but its fragrance, alas, has vanished and returns not!" (244).

Lawrence may have had Hudson's chapter in mind when he recalls in *Seven Pillars* the time that he and his servant Dahoum went to a desert ruin of clay said to have been kneaded with the "precious essential oils of flowers. My guides, sniffing the air like dogs, led me from crumbling room to room, saying, 'This is jessamine, this violet, this rose.' But at last Dahoum drew me: 'Come and smell the very sweetest scent of all,' and we went into the main lodging, to the gaping window sockets of its eastern face, and there drank with open mouths of the effortless, empty, eddyless wind of the desert, throbbing past. . . . 'This,' they told me, 'is the best: it has no taste' " (*S, 39–40*).

Just as Lawrence must have studied Hudson's ability to use an "alas!" every now and then and get away with it—an impossible task for a postromantic modern writer—so too he must have enviously noted Hudson's ability to emphasize outer rather than inner events in his auto-biography and to be at home with his own personality when he describes it. Although Hudson is a poetic autobiographer who presents life as a never-ending search and never gives us a concise, clear picture of his personality (which appears only obliquely in *Idle Days*), the amount of ego in the book is sharply controlled by its outer, nature framework. As Robert Hamilton puts it, Hudson "combined insight with interest to a remarkable degree, and his work, though always informed by his unique personality, was objective in intent. He was personal without being an egoist; objective without being shallow."[18] Lawrence may have deplored the lack of structure that *Idle Days* shares with other travel books. It begins with a dramatic opening worthy of the deck of the *Patna* in Conrad's *Lord Jim*. Hudson, however, soon diffuses the pressure, and the book comes apart as he gets lost in a myriad of subjects. But Hudson's blend of natural descriptions and analysis of ideas and an unusually sanguine—for a poetic autobiographer—self that shows itself primarily through these ideas and descriptions was beyond Lawrence's very self-conscious ability to achieve. By managing to lose himself in objective events, Hudson could afford to be at ease with himself.

Kinglake's totally detached irony, Hudson's emphasis on external events, and—as we shall see—Doughty's stoic reticence could not have influenced a man unsuited by nature to these devices. Lawrence tried making the Arab Revolt more important than himself in *Seven Pillars* but failed. Yet Hudson's *Idle Days in Patagonia* provided him with a model, with an author who, in Richard Haymaker's words, "possessed fresh and significant material" and was "a master of a style that could be exquisite, vigorous and eloquent, and a poetic personality."

Doughty

Lawrence frequently expressed his esteem for Charles M. Doughty as the greatest of all his predecessors in the Anglo-Arabian travel-book tradition. The introduction Lawrence wrote for *Travels in Arabia Deserta* in 1921 offers direct evidence—in the most specific terms—of the depth of his attachment to Doughty's work during the period in which he was engaged in writing and rewriting *Seven Pillars of Wisdom*. For Lawrence, *Arabia Deserta* will remain a monument for its literary artistry no less than for its contribution to the study of the Arabian Peninsula:

> It is to the outside public willing to read a great prose work, the record of the wanderings of an English poet for two years among the Beduin, that this edition must make its appeal. . . . There is no sentiment, nothing merely picturesque, that most common failing of oriental travel-books. . . . It is a book which begins powerfully, written in a style which apparently has neither father nor son, so closely wrought, so tense, so just in its words and phrases, that it demands a hard reader. . . . Mr. Doughty was not content till he had made the book justify the journey as much as the journey justified the book, and in the double power, to go and to write, he will not soon find his rival. (1:17)

Elsewhere in this introduction, the infusion of Doughty's personality into the book in an indirect manner and the theme of cultural clash figure prominently in the aspects Lawrence singles out for comment, usually to his own self-detriment. Most important, Doughty is "never morbid, never introspective" and triumphed over his body to a degree "none of us" did. Doughty refused "to be the hero of his story," also a pointed reference to Lawrence's own case. Finally, Lawrence is "presumptuous" to put his name near "one of the great prose works in our literature."

But Lawrence was not without his criticism of Doughty's work, especially as he grew older. Lawrence's caveats about Doughty's book reveal a sharp analytical eye and indicate not only Doughty's failings but also those common to the Anglo-Arabian travel-book tradition. Lawrence made special efforts to avoid these very faults when it came to writing his own book but was not always successful. First, Lawrence realized that he could never achieve Doughty's stoic reticence and his distancing from himself as the character Khalil (both traits of the typical oratorical autobiography) simply because Lawrence's personality is involuted, self-conscious, relativistic, and totally lacking in the fixed point of Victorian pride and cultural imperialism. Lawrence rejected Doughty's simplicity

and arrogance of character as well as his imperialistic attitude toward
the Arabs. Second, in his criticism of Barker Fairley's work on Doughty,
Lawrence attacks *Arabia Deserta*'s lack of artistic structure:

> That Barker Fairley book on Doughty spoiled itself, by trying to do too
> much. He maintained that the *form* of *A.D.* and *Dawn in Britain* was sub-
> tle, and designed, and balanced, and cumulative. I think it was accident;
> and a bad accident. Doughty seems wholly to have lacked the strategic
> eye which plans a campaign. . . . *A.D.* is hampered by its lack of form,
> less only than *Dawn*, because there was a basis of fact to follow, and life
> isn't as shapeless as unassisted and undisciplined art. (*L*, 526–27)

Lawrence, who attempted to become a "master architect" (*S*, 192) of
both war and literature, strives for the kind of comprehensive literary
structure that he felt (rightly) that Doughty was unable to attain.
Finally, in the course of a detailed criticism of Herbert Read's review of
Seven Pillars,[19] Lawrence, now in 1927 a member of the R.A.F., elabo-
rates on what he perceives as Doughty's stylistic faults, sounding less
enthusiastic than he had in the 1921 introduction to *Arabia Deserta*:
"These fellows here, with whom I have lived the last five years, are not
so sure in their English as to enjoy *Arabia Deserta*. Doughty uses hard
words for which they would need a dictionary, and his Scandinavian syntax puzzles them. He closed his goodness off from the world by not
being as honest and simple in manner as he was in mind" (*L*, 550). In
much the same spirit is the criticism of Doughty's style that he makes in
Men in Print (London: Golden Cockerel Press, 1940): "This inlay of
strange words into a groundwork of daily English is a mistake. The
effect is fussy, not primitive, more peasant art than peasant." On the
matters of a too simple view of oneself and one's surroundings, of weak
and digressive structure, and of too precious style, Lawrence calls
Doughty to account. But we should note that most of Lawrence's criticism of Doughty follows the completion of *Seven Pillars* (and Doughty's
muted criticism of it[20]), whereas his reference to Doughty's book as a
"miracle of style" dates from the years in which he was engaged in continually recasting his own work. Even the most fleeting reference to
Seven Pillars reveals the extent of Doughty's influence on Lawrence.

In the following passage, drawn from the great ibn Rashid court
scene in *Arabia Deserta* (which Lawrence especially liked), Doughty's use
of archaic style to medievalize, his use of biblical reference, his attempt
to integrate Arabic and English, the projection of his stoic personality,
and the clash of cultures theme, are all brilliantly apparent:

I saluted the Emir, *Salaam aleyk*.—No answer: then I greeted Hamud and Sleyman, now of friendly acquaintance, in the same words, and with *aleykom es salaam* they hailed me smiling comfortably again. One showed me to a place where I should sit down before the Emir, who said shortly "From whence?"—"From my makhzan."—'And what found I there to do all day, ha! and what had I seen in the time of my being at Hayil, was it well?' When the Prince said "Khalil!" I should have responded in their manner *Aunak* or *Labbeyk* or *Tawil el Ummr*, "O Long-of-Age! and what is thy sweet will?" but feeling as an European among these light-tongued Asiatics, and full of mortal weariness, I kept silence. . . . I answered after the pause, "I am lately arrived in this place, but *aghruty*, I suppose it is very well." The Emir opened his great feminine Arab eyes upon me as if he wondered at the not flattering plainness of my speech; and he said. . . . "went you in the pilgrimage to the Holy City (Jerusalem)?" (2:26)

The question is, what does Lawrence owe to this brilliantly multilingual style and vision that combines English, Arabic, and sometimes Turkish and Hebrew phrases into a unique blend unlike the English of any period? Whatever the answer, Doughty's amalgam accurately captures the arabesques common to Arabic and its close cousin, Hebrew (in which even today one says "you find favor in my eyes" for "I'm fond of you").[21]

As much as he attacks Doughty for literary archaism, we frequently find the same linguistic device in Lawrence's book. He transposes contemporary Arabic into archaic English in order to capture the flavor of Arabic, as in his conversation with Tafas: " 'What is upon you, Tafas?' said I" (*S*, 82). And how many heightened descriptions of the desert (such as the passage in which each piece of flint becomes "tipped like a black diamond with flame" [*S*, 607]) owe something to this one sentence of Doughty's?: "The Arabian heaven is burning brass above their heads, and the sand as glowing coals under their weary feet." Albert Cook goes so far as to say of a particular descriptive passage in *Seven Pillars* that "Doughty's style is here being stretched, purged somewhat . . . and dynamized with the account of a constantly purposive action."[22] Lawrence often gives us a leaner, twentieth-century version of Doughty's fin de siècle medievalized prose, but since both men are stylistic geniuses, their writing is of necessity individual and different despite some similarities.

Doughty's spiritual vision also affects Lawrence. *Seven Pillars*, like *Arabia Deserta*, is a book first and foremost about its author's quest for the absolute in the Arabian desert. We no more accept Doughty's explanation that his two-year exposure to hardship and danger was the sim-

ple fruit of his desire to contribute to geography and the English language than we ever fully understand the motives behind Lawrence's
striving for his unstated and apparently unattainable goal. As R. P.
Blackmur points out, the spiritual quest underlying this famous quotation from *Arabia Deserta* (1:95) remains Doughty's major contribution
to Lawrence's view of the desert: "The traveller must be himself, in
men's eyes, a man worthy to live under the bent of God's heaven . . . he
is such who has a clean human heart and long-suffering under his bare
shirt. . . . Here is a dead land, whence, if he die not, he shall bring home
a perpetual weariness in his bones. The Semites are like to man sitting in
a cloaca to the eyes and whose brows touch heaven." That Lawrence
thought this quotation important is revealed when he describes the
Arabs as "petty incarnate Semites who attained heights and depths
beyond our reach" (*S*, 586), which simply rephrases the last sentence in
the quotation.

Doughty's heroic view of the Bedouin influences Lawrence as well.
Lawrence's portraits of Auda and Nasir, for instance, owe much to
Doughty, whose Sheikh Motlog, "a personable, strong man and well pro-
portioned, of the middle stature, of middle age, and with a comely Jewish
visage," who rules his tribe "with a proud humility among the common
people" and commands "with a word the unruly Beduw," appears in several reincarnations in *Seven Pillars*. And Lawrence's description of Tallal
as "the splendid leader, the fine horseman, the courteous and strong
companion of the road" carries in its parallelism the same chivalric ring
as Doughty's description of Motlog. But then, "the Asia of Kinglake
and Lamartine is wholly gone . . . and some of us, the medievalists,
lament it," Lawrence had written in 1920,[23] showing how natural this
kind of romanticizing was to him.

For the heroic, epic view that Lawrence denied himself in life and in
direct statements about his own character in *Seven Pillars* clearly informs
that entire book, despite its author. His artistic self allows, like Doughty's,
the projection of men larger-than-life set against a stark background of
naked desert and searing sun, no matter how many internal debates he
reports, no matter how many cynical presentations of the failings of
himself and others. He could not feel heroic or grand at any moment,
but through his art we see him and his Arab companions as just that.
Thus, as he—like Doughty—can mock men who are "always fond to
believe a romantic tale" (*S*, 562), he can state in a few sentences a contradiction as clear as this: "The epic mode was alien to me, as to my
generation. Memory gave me no clue to the heroic, so that I could not

feel such men as Auda in myself. He seemed fantastic as the hills of Rumm, old as Malory" (*S,* 549). Even in retrospect, his honesty will not allow him to see himself as other than small, unheroic, as modern and disillusioned as Wilfred Owen. At the same time, his artistic self's memory of Doughty's medieval treatment of the desert and of Malory's *Morte d'Arthur* and of the fantastic background of the Wadi Rumm creates a heroic backdrop for understanding the men with whom he worked and whom he consistently and brilliantly led. Despite all of Lawrence's (and Doughty's) naturalistic portrayals of hardships and failures, we retain after reading *Seven Pillars* the same essentially striking view of the desert that Doughty gives us.

Lawrence and Doughty were heroes as disparate as the centuries in which they wrote, the one self-consciously prey to the dragons of a lack of cultural identity and the essential egotism and complexity of the heroic deed and unable to keep silent about these problems; the other so self-confidently aware of what he achieved and his position in the world that he felt no need to speak openly on the subject. But in the end the two men are artists in the same tradition, that of Kinglake and Hudson as well, and Doughty's literary influence on Lawrence is all-pervasive. For it is Doughty among living writers who provided Lawrence with the artistic "clue to the heroic" that he lacked in life and found elsewhere only in the far-removed Homer, Malory, and Crusader castles, and for which we as readers of *Seven Pillars* must be grateful.

Chapter Three
Seven Pillars of Wisdom:
Lawrence as Aesthete and Hero

Despite self-doubts, doubts about his mission, and the knowledge that a true hero in the Homeric sense should not be conscious of his heroism, Lawrence comes across to the reader of *Seven Pillars* as perhaps the last modern hero, the man who successfully achieved his goal in the face of all barriers, internal and external. But Lawrence himself, as the Homer-Achilles of his "introspection epic" (*L, 621*), reveals to us the difficulty of waging heroic war in the modern world, clad only in the armor of Homeric ideals and a fin de siècle, neomedieval chivalry and world-weary longing for death. Like Joseph Conrad and Stephen Crane, who straddle the transition from romanticism's last gasp, the "Death in Venice" of a tradition that sees dying bravely as something good, to the new age of Hemingway's antiheroism, in which death in war is meaningless but to be endured, Lawrence finds himself facing a new situation with outmoded philosophical tools. The result, as in their cases, is that romantic and antiromantic views of death, among other things, exist side by side in *Seven Pillars* in discordance. Just as we can ask whether Lord Jim dies a hero or whether Henry Fleming's encounter with "the great death" in *The Red Badge of Courage* has resulted in true heroism or increased self-delusion, so Lawrence as narrator-protagonist combines heroic and antiheroic elements in his vision. When romanticized high ideals based on classical and medieval study clash with bitter modern experience, Lawrence transmutes late Victorian gilt into the jagged shrapnel of the World War I poets and his personal poetry of radical mental fragmentation. From this grating contrast, he forges the powerful, if mixed, vision that is *Seven Pillars of Wisdom*.

Death in Arabia

As Lawrence lies waiting for the Turks to kill him, having fallen off his charging camel, the lines of Ernest Dowson's "Impenitentia Ultima" come racing through his head: "For Lord I was free of all Thy flowers, but I chose the world's sad roses, / And that is why my feet are torn and mine eyes are blind with sweat" (*S,* 304). This memory is entirely appropriate in a book in which death is very frequently reported in the language of late romantic poetry. In this language, death and love are frequently linked, as in the poem in memory of "S. A.," which opens *Seven Pillars:* "Love, the way-weary, groped to your body, our brief wage / ours for the moment / Before earth's soft hand explored your shape, and the blind / worms grew fat upon / Your substance" (*S,* 5). Ferraj's death becomes a welcome gift in view of the earlier demise of his lover Daud:

> We tried to stop the wide, slow bleeding, which made poppy-splashes in the grass; but it seemed impossible, and after a while he told us to let him alone, as he was dying, and happy to die, since he had no care of life. Indeed, for long he had been so, and men very tired and sorry often fell in love with death, with that triumphal weakness coming home after strength has been vanquished in a last battle. (*S,* 516)

In the chapter on "Strangeness and Pain," the controversial fifth paragraph, which deals with Arab homosexual love and appears to have little connection with preceding or following paragraphs, can be explained by the same romantic linkage of death—discussed in Lawrence's third paragraph ("those tired enough to die")—and love. The poetry of death and love rises to lyrical heights in what is possibly the most famous set piece in the book:

> The dead men looked wonderfully beautiful. The night was shining gently down, softening them into new ivory. Turks were white-skinned on their clothed parts, much whiter than the Arabs; and these soldiers had been very young. Close round them lapped the dark wormwood, now heavy with dew, in which the ends of the moonbeams sparkled like sea spray. The corpses seemed flung so pitifully on the ground, huddled anyhow in low heaps. Surely if straightened they would be comfortable at last. So I put them all in order, one by one, very wearied myself, and longing to be one of these quiet ones, not of the restless, noisy, aching mob up the valley, quarrelling over the plunder, boasting of their speed and strength to endure God knew how many toils and pains of this sort; with death, whether we won or lost, waiting to end the history. (*S,* 308)

Lawrence's own longing for death appears here as it does in many other places in *Seven Pillars.*

This longing places Lawrence clearly in the romantic tradition. Beginning with the Keats of "Ode to a Nightingale," who wishes to merge himself with "easeful Death" and running through the poetry of Tennyson like a bass line, the combination of love and death reaches a height in the late nineteenth-century cult of death felt in the symphonies of Gustav Mahler. H. Rider Haggard's *She,* which traces a journey through a dead land, burial caves, and the veil of life itself, and Conrad's *Heart of Darkness,* with its imaginative anthropology of a voyage into unknown darkness, are both Mahlerian death "trips," in whose Ayesha and Kurtz is also seen the late romantic vision of Faustian supermen. Like Ayesha and Kurtz, Lawrence has been discussed in terms of the late nineteenth-century philosophies of the will and artistic rebellion against societal conventions.[1] Both *She* and *Heart of Darkness* inevitably deal with love as well—Ayesha's for Kallicrates, Kurtz's African and European girlfriends' for him. The influences on, and significance of, Lawrence's connection of love and death, particularly heroic death, remain to be explored more fully.

First, let us look in detail at the literary precedents for this linkage. "The Sword Also Means Cleanness and Death" proclaims the motto on the front cover of *Seven Pillars,* and of course we expect writing about death in a war story. But in fact Lawrence is a late nineteenth-century aesthete, one of "the last romantics" in Yeats's phrase, and war only provides him with an opportunity for shaping death in the image of that philosophy. On the level of literary influence, Lawrence simply adopts the style and mannerisms that he learned from his favorite writers. Who exactly (in addition to the travel writers) were these? This is important to establish in view of Lawrence's many admissions of literary borrowing, one of which appears in a letter to the painter William Rothenstein: "My style is a made-up thing, very thickly encrusted with what seemed to me the tit-bits and wheezes of established authors. . . . There isn't any good, any permanence, in such a derivative effort."[2] Lawrence's borrowings, which in fact add to the rich resonance of his styles despite his disclaimer, derive from classical Greek and Latin authors as well as from medieval chroniclers and modern French and English writers. But although the relatively abstruse philosopher of the mind/body problem—Bernardino Telesio ("Telesius")[3]—and Syrian Greek poets, among others, add an exotic touch to reading that also included the more commonplace Rudyard Kipling and Henry Williamson, the books Lawrence most enjoyed offer few surprises in terms of the period during which he was an undergraduate.

Vyvyan Richards provides the best reconstruction of his friend's taste in literature. In the picture he paints in his excellent *Portrait of T. E. Lawrence,* late Victorians take precedence, with a lesser emphasis on early twentieth-century writers. He stresses the importance of the Morris cult in vogue while he and Lawrence were at Oxford, and its carryover into Lawrence's later life. Lawrence's antiquarian interests fit well into the perfect catalog of Oxford Edwardian tastes that his reading constitutes. What is surprising is that, with few changes, these authors remained Lawrence's favorites throughout his life, although he also came to appreciate the importance of the modernists T. S. Eliot and James Joyce and was astute enough to recognize early and promote the career of future Poet Laureate Cecil Day-Lewis.

Among works that Lawrence favored, Richards mentions specifically Christina Rossetti's "The Martyr," Tennyson's "Palace of Art" and "Dream of Fair Women," Frederick Rolfe's "Don Tarquino" ("favoured especially for its 'fleshliness' "), "Gods and Their Makers" by Housman, and "most of Walter Pater." Aeschylus, a required part of the great Oxford classics course that trained many empire builders, Shakespeare, and Shelley complete this early picture, with Nietzsche and Robert Graves entering later. "Rupert Brooke he compared with Keats for his techniques; but found him much too restrained to be as musical as Keats could be. He admired W. H. Hudson and had most of his writings." Above all, "Morris, Doughty, Aristophanes and Malory went with him from boyhood to his death."[4]

Lawrence's love of the late romantics and censure of antiromantics appears as late as 1928, in a letter to David Garnett: "Really, people are odd. They are writing apologetically of [Dante Gabriel] Rossetti, in the papers, everywhere. He was a magnificent poet. Morris is half-praised. Morris was a giant. Somebody said that Dowson wasn't a great poet; or Flecker. God Almighty! Must everyone be as seven-leagued as Milton and Byron and Hardy?" (*L,* 612). In a list of preferred reading compiled well after the writing of *Seven Pillars,* he lists Morris as his favorite writer.[5]

During the Arabian campaign itself, Lawrence's reading matter consisted of "the *Morte* [*d'Arthur*]: Aristophanes (I read all the *Peace,* very gratefully, & without much technical trouble) and *The Oxford Book of English Verse*" (*L,* 512). Besides Lawrence's 1835 Dinsdorf edition of Aristophanes in the original Greek, the Houghton Library at Harvard holds the 1915 edition of *The Oxford Book of English Verse,* which Lawrence "Bought in Cairo 1916. Carried through Hejaz and Syria 1917–1918" according to the note above his initials in the flyleaf. Graves writes about this book that its influence "on his feelings and actions during the campaign would be well worth studying. The copy survives with marginal annotations, many of these dated."[6] The poems in the index of first lines of this vellum-bound book have been marked in pencil with from one to four dashes, which confirm Lawrence's romantic tastes; all neoclassical poets except Gray are excluded. Lawrence's choice of poems for his own private anthology, *Minorities*,[7] supplements the picture already outlined.

The result of this reading, so different from the tastes of a post–World War I modernist, was noted by Lawrence himself: "It's odd, you know, to be reading these [Eliot's] poems, so full of the future, so far ahead of our time; and then to turn back to my book, whose prose stinks of coffins and ancestors and armorial hatchments. Yet people have the nerve to tell me it's a good book! It would have been, if written a hundred years ago: but to bring it out after [Joyce's] *Ulysses* is an insult to modern letters" (*L*, 488). When we find the captured Turkish musicians in *Seven Pillars* referred to as a "pale crew of bearded, emaciated men with woe-begone faces" (*S*, 74), we catch an unmistakable echo of Keats's "La Belle Dame Sans Merci," which Lawrence includes in *Minorities*. But in addition to hundreds of such allusions in phrases, Lawrence's favorite reading results in "aesthetic" description, medievalizing of characters in the manner of Rossetti, Morris, and the pre-Raphaelites, and the "black romance" of death and homosexual love. Here it should be noted that homosexuality was a common element in the rebellious aesthetic stance of fin de siècle writing and that Lawrence, given his positive references to homosexuality in *Seven Pillars*, obviously found this stance congenial.

We also find everywhere in Lawrence's book that special sensitivity to color that is a pose of the 1890s: "It was pretty to look at the neat, brown men in the sunlit sandy valley, with the turquoise pool of salt water in the midst to set off the crimson banners which two standard bearers carried in the van" (*S*, 163). Joris-Karl Huysmans's des Esseintes (and Lawrence read *À Rebours* [*Against the Grain*] in 1922) or Oscar Wilde's Dorian Gray could have spoken the following: "As we went, the brushwood grouped itself into thickets whose massed leaves took on a stronger tint of green the purer for their contrasted setting in plots of open sand of a cheerful delicate pink" (*S*, 351). Lawrence also demonstrates the sensitivity to dress of a Wildean "dandy": "Fellows were very proud of being in my bodyguard, which developed a professionalism almost flamboyant. They dressed like a bed of tulips, in every colour but white; for that was my constant wear, and they did not wish to presume" (*S*, 465).

Lawrence, as Oxford aesthete, finds himself in a situation almost too good to be true: the leader of a rebellion against established authority amid an exotic people remote from all "civilization." Of course we find his abnormally, deliberately oversensitive, heightened sense of color contributing brightness to a chivalric, medieval blend of warriors who owe more to Doughty, Morris, Malory, and Homer than to any objective vision. Just as Vyvyan Richards claims that the "long beduin tents reminded Lawrence of the Scandinavian halls of the Morris sagas," so A. W. Lawrence finds among the Arabs "a spirit that would appeal to such a lover of the *Morte d'Arthur*."[8] Feisal first appears like a noble Saladin out of the Richard Coeur-de-Lion stories, looking "very tall and pillar-like, very slender, in his long white silk robes and his brown headcloth bound with a brilliant scarlet and gold cord. His eyelids were dropped; and his black beard and colourless face were like a mask against the strange, still watchfulness of his body. His hands were crossed in front of him on his dagger" (*S*, 91). Lawrence constantly uses the words "chivalric" and "heroic," and although he refers to himself at one point as a "theatre knight" and thus undercuts his brilliant backdrop with personal ironies—much in the manner of Kinglake, who is always willing to go from the sublime to the ridiculous—his main characters remain epic, larger-than-life in our minds. Auda, for instance, enters like a "knight-errant" of the desert and "saw life as a saga. All the events in it were significant: all personages in contact with the heroic. His mind was stored with poems of old raids and epic tales of fights, and he overflowed with them on the nearest listener" (*S*, 223). Lawrence himself wrote on the last page of the 1922 Oxford text of *Seven Pillars* that "The Arabs made a chivalrous appeal to my young instinct." As Malcolm Allen has shown in detail, *Seven Pillars* "can be regarded in the light cast by medieval and neomedieval romance."[9]

Although Lawrence translated the *Odyssey* long after he completed *Seven Pillars*, Homer's vision also plays a major role in the character of Lawrence as we see him in his book and influences the view that Lawrence as author takes of his characters. In the words of James A. Notopoulos, Lawrence's "splendor as a human being and a writer cannot be understood without the metaphors of the *Odyssey* and the *Iliad*. Both of these poems enter into his experiences, his writing, and into shaping his outlook. Homer was a lifelong study with Lawrence and he emerges as one of his finest translators. That he read him as part of his schooling in England is taken for granted. Homer followed him to the dig of Car-chemish by the Euphrates. . . . He discusses the *Iliad* with Thomas Hardy for whom Homer was also a companion. Homer follows him to Karachi where he spent all his off-duty hours in translating the *Odyssey.*"[10] Maren Cohn finds that Lawrence was able to translate the *Odyssey* so well because his wartime Arabian experience prepared him for "moving back and forth between vastly different, foreign spheres,"[11] and she goes on to draw detailed parallels between Lawrence and Odysseus.

As Notopoulos points out, "The Arab had the very characteristics of Homer's warriors: individualism, family pride in the heroic code of honor, revenge, joy in arms, in booty, and as Lawrence observed, 'to an Arab an essential part of the triumph was to wear the clothes of an enemy' " (340). Not only did the Arabs offer Lawrence "a theme ready and epic" (*S,* 549) for Homeric glorification in literature, but as Avra-ham Feinglass claims,[12] Lawrence's reading of Homer actually allowed him to act out the role of the primitive hero whom the Bedouin would respect. Lawrence mentions the "Beersheba Beduin" (*S,* 484). In the early 1970s, I interviewed two older members of the tribe settled at Tel Sheva, just a few miles outside of modern Beersheba (and an archaeolog-ical site discussed by Woolley and Lawrence in *The Wilderness of Zin*), to find out if they knew anything of Lawrence. One answered immediately, "Sure—I've seen the movie!" referring to the 1962 David Lean/Robert Bolt production.[13] The second claimed that she had heard stories that Lawrence had slept in her father's tent, a tale equivalent to a Near East-ern "Washington Slept Here" declaration. Feinglass, then the member of a kibbutz in the Beersheba area, had only slightly better luck. Although he learned nothing directly of Lawrence, he turned to Elihu Nawi, a former mayor of Beersheba and the compiler of an anthology of folk tales, *Stories of the Arabs* (1972), who recommended to him Aref el-Aref's *Bedouin Love, Law and Legend* (1944) as a source of factual infor-mation about Bedouin customs. Aref el-Aref's comments on the Bedouin way of life, quoted by Feinglass, prove that Lawrence had some solid basis for his view of the Bedouin as Homeric heroes who in his time still lived according to a very harsh code that he practiced with diffi-culty: "When the Badawi complains it may be accepted readily that he has a very real cause and that he has suffered beyond bearing. He is a patient soul, almost stoic in his forbearance. He will face extremes of heat and cold without a murmur, go for two days without food or drink should the need arise, and undergo great feats of physical endurance to complete a task or keep a promise."[14] Lawrence is not remembered by

UNIVERSITY OF WINNIPEG, 515 Portage Ave., Winnipeg, MB, R3B 2E9 Canada

DISCARDED

the Bedouin of the Beersheba area whom Feinglass and I have interviewed because his major contact with the Bedouin was restricted to the tribes farther east, among them the Beni Sakhr and Howeitat, who even today form the backbone of King Hussein's Jordan Arab Legion.[15] But when Lawrence describes them as tough warriors, superimposes Homeric phrases on them, and speaks of his own difficulty in imitating their mores, we can now understand why. Like Auda and like the Beersheba Bedouin to whom I have talked, we may well believe that, at least in terms of physical endurance, "The world is greater as we go back."

Notopoulos offers about Lawrence's *Odyssey* the interesting opinion that "As one who had lived with Arab oral bards, to such an extent that he even made an amusing parody of the formulaic style in a story to parody Auda's incorrigible epic addiction, Lawrence failed to perceive the oral style of the *Odyssey*" (339). But in writing *Seven Pillars,* Lawrence remembered well the epic vision that the desert had allowed him to glimpse, the old heroism that could laugh at death. As Notopoulos points out, "Lawrence's chief fascination with Auda . . . was the warrior's delight in war and the delirium of the brave. The crescendo of the epic action of the book coincides with Auda's exhibition of the delirium of the brave. . . . Lawrence's description of Auda's furious charge at Aba el Lissan . . . is sheer Homeric."

Lawrence himself undergoes the stages necessary to the creation of all literary heroes: separation (his lone mission among the Arabs); initiation (his tutelage in Arab ways under Feisal); confrontation (his touching "the great death," in Stephen Crane's words, in battle); and return to society, after having paid for and exorcised its sins (this return occurs only in part 3 of *The Mint*). But as we shall see, his dual role as Homer and Achilles caused problems unknown to Homer himself, who wrote fiction and not autobiography. In any case, both his late romanticism and the Homeric tradition, in which heroic death and homosexual love are also linked (as in the death of Achilles' lover Patroclus in the *Iliad*), unite to produce, on the literary level, Lawrence's fin de siècle treatment of love and death in *Seven Pillars.*

However, the real reason for Lawrence's linkage of love and death throughout *Seven Pillars* finds no direct expression there or in any other source: According to Tom Beaumont, a British machine gunner who served with Lawrence, it was during September, 1918, at Umtaiye that Lawrence told him of the death of Salim Achmed, "S. A.," or Dahoum, Lawrence's Arab servant.[16] At the very moment that the campaign was reaching its victorious conclusion, Salim Achmed, whom Lawrence employed as a spy behind enemy lines, was dying of typhoid. When we make the connection between "S. A." and Salim Achmed, the tactile feeling of the "S. A." poem becomes important: "Love, the way-weary, groped to your body, our brief wage / ours for the moment / Before earth's soft hand explored your shape, and the blind / worms grew fat upon / Your substance." How are we to take this very sensual statement?

The issue of whether Lawrence was a practicing homosexual, with Dahoum or others, remains controversial. On the one hand, Lawrence sometimes called homosexual love "beastly" and stated at least twice that he had never had voluntary sexual experience.[17] Jeremy Wilson disputes insinuations by C. Leonard Woolley of homosexuality between Lawrence and Dahoum at Carchemish and denies that Lawrence was a homosexual.[18] John Mack, a psychiatrist, concludes that Lawrence's

> literary candor concerning sexual activities and other body functions also reflects a fundamental intellectual honesty and integrity which must not be confused, as it has often been, with what Lawrence would or could tolerate in himself. His candid descriptions of the homosexual practices of Bedouin youth in the desert in *Seven Pillars of Wisdom* have, in my opinion, been mistakenly offered as evidence of his own participation in these activities. The evidence is strongly to the contrary, however sympathetic Lawrence may have been to the intimacy of these youths.[19]

However, several other commentators, including Richard Aldington, Jeffrey Meyers, and Daniel Wolfe, have been convinced of, or have strongly suspected, that Lawrence was either a practicing homosexual or very inclined toward homosexuality.[20]

There is at this time no convincing evidence of Lawrence's ever having committed any homosexual acts voluntarily. However, Mack's complete separation between writing and life is unconvincing, especially because Lawrence wrote autobiography and not fiction. Stephen Spender's comment that Lawrence "surely must have been at any rate a repressed homosexual. Remember his very sympathetic account of the two Arab boys who are lovers"[21] is a writer's recognition of the connection between art and life. Lawrence's very sympathetic treatment of Ferraj and Daud, his positive description of Sherif Ali, his favorable portrayal of Arab male "friends quivering together in the yielding sand with intimate hot limbs in supreme embrace" (*S,* 30), and the sensual content of the "S. A." poem indicate that at the least he himself longed for a breaking down of the prison walls of puritanical restrictions on sensuality and a puritanical overconscientiousness and that he possibly experienced this himself to some degree. Most likely, given Lawrence's inhibitions, his relationship with Dahoum was idealized and included some limited excursion into the sense of touch but nothing more.

By part 3 of *The Mint* Lawrence indicates that he can touch and be touched, if not in a sexual manner; he seems able to achieve some reorientation of the senses toward the tactile East, as Whitman advocates in *Leaves of Grass,* one of Lawrence's favorite books. Although the precise nature of Lawrence's sexual inclination remains speculative, what is clear is that he links death, love, and heroism in many parts of *Seven Pillars* because death, the heroic frenzy, and the love he experienced with Dahoum all contribute to the loss of self-consciousness and to the opening of the self to the world spirit. For Lawrence, the merging of the self with the universe remains the ultimate, absolute goal.

The Other Side of the Coin

If *Seven Pillars* offers a romantic view of death, love, and heroism, it also presents antiheroic scenes and opinions worthy of Wilfred Owen and Ernest Hemingway. In 1934 Lawrence wrote to a young writer that "The very young often are half in love with Death—and half afraid of him. Later, when Death is nearer, you will be reluctant to think so closely of him."[22] In fact, the close reader of *Seven Pillars* detects clearly the harsh and repulsive reality under the romantic veil. Lawrence dreamed of a world of heroic glory that he glimpsed sometimes among the Bedouin; but as a modern man and despite the force of his will to push his body to the breaking point, he suffers the fate of the sensitive intellectual forced to participate in brutal and bloody deeds and almost breaks down as a result. As James Notopoulos correctly writes, "He exhibits the dilemma of a modern figure who experienced the Homeric delirium of the brave and wrote of it with the requisite magic of literature, yet was condemned to tragic frustration by the anachronism of the heroic act in our times. . . . Lawrence could not write the simple direct kind of epic. It had to be an epic fashioned out of complex factors."

Some of these factors are (1) the knowledge that he is working for Britain as well as for the Arabs and is therefore not the true leader of a national liberation movement that he would like to be; (2) constant self-consciousness of his role as a "hero" who must imitate and parody Auda rather than experience the simple directness of Auda's emotions; and (3) a repulsion from brutality and cruelty and a too hard physical and mental test.

Throughout *Seven Pillars*, Lawrence makes no attempt to hide the reality of the revolt under the glory:

> The mud roof dripped water all the day long, and the fleas on the stone floor sang together nightly, for praise of the new meats given them. We were twenty-eight in the two tiny rooms, which reeked with the sour smell of our crowd.
> In my saddle-bags was a *Morte d'Arthur*. It relieved my disgust. The men had only physical resources; and in the confined misery their tempers roughened. Their oddnesses, which ordinary time packed with a saving film of distance, now jostled me angrily; while a grazed wound in my hip had frozen, and irritated me with painful throbbing. Day by day, the tension among us grew, as our state became more sordid, more animal. (*S*, 485–86)

Lawrence escapes into romance as a character; as author, he reveals both reality and escape, both the sordid conditions and his reading of the *Morte d'Arthur*. When one of his men must be whipped for an infraction of discipline, Lawrence feels "sorry for Awad; his hardness put me to shame" (*S*, 486). Bedouin life was indeed hard, and however many literary allusions it caused to spring into the mind of a romantic temperament, we feel a revulsion lurking under the Homeric glory:

> The valley was a weird sight. The Arabs, gone raving mad, were rushing about at top speed bareheaded and half-naked, screaming, shooting into the air, clawing one another nail and fist, while they burst open trucks and staggered back and forward with immense bales, which they ripped by the rail-side, and tossed through, smashing what they did not want. . . . To one side stood thirty or forty hysterical women, unveiled, tearing their clothes and hair; shrieking themselves distracted. The Arabs without regard to them went on wrecking the household goods; looting their absolute fill. . . .
> Seeing me tolerably unemployed, the women rushed, and caught at me with howls for mercy. I assured them that all was going well: but they would not get away till some husbands delivered me. These knocked their wives off and seized my feet in a very agony of terror of instant death. A Turk so broken down was a nasty spectacle: I kicked them off as well as I could with bare feet, and finally broke free. (*S*, 369)

Primitive epics certainly contain rushes for spoils and occasionally a cowardice that is despised, but they are narrated by primitive poets contemporary with these events. The irony with which Lawrence narrates this episode ("I assured them that all was going well"; "till some husbands delivered me") indicates that the whole scene appears sordid to him, however Homeric it might be. Lawrence's life as leader of a "Homeric" band certainly was not easy, either with the men or with other leaders: In chapter 90, Lawrence reports Zeid's irresponsible squandering of the gold necessary for further action, which "meant the complete ruin of my plans and hopes, the collapse of our effort to keep faith with Allenby" (*S*, 500), and results in Lawrence's only attempt to quit the revolt altogether; and even Feisal "showed himself hot-tempered and sensitive, even unreasonable, and he ran off soon on tangents" very early in the adventure (*S*, 97).

As difficult as it was for a modern, highly educated Englishman to witness such events as the hunting of defeated men ("The Arabs on their track rose against them and shot them ignobly as they ran" [*S*, 482]), even brutal enemies, it was much more difficult when the detached viewing gave way to involvement and participation:

> I made him enter a narrow gully of the spur, a dank twilight place overgrown with weeds. Its sandy bed had been pitted by trickles of water down the cliffs in the late rain. At the end it shrank to a crack a few inches wide. The walls were vertical. I stood in the entrance and gave him a few moments' delay which he spent crying on the ground. Then I made him rise and shot him through the chest. He fell down on the weeds shrieking, with the blood coming out in spurts over his clothes, and jerked about till he rolled nearly to where I was. I fired again, but was shaking so that I only broke his wrist. He went on calling out, less loudly, now lying on his back with his feet towards me, and I leant forward and shot him for the last time in the thick of his neck under the jaw. His body shivered a little, and I called the Ageyl; who buried him in the gully where he was. Afterwards the wakeful night dragged over me, till, hours before dawn, I had the men up and made them load, in my longing to be free of Wadi Kitan. They had to lift me into the saddle. (*S*, 181–82)

As Andrew Rutherford has pointed out, Lawrence's "meticulous recording of every detail of the incident suggests an obsessive recollection, which he is now perhaps trying to exorcise."[23] Lawrence's hand shakes, and the act of killing makes him physically and morally sick. Instead of the poetry of mortality and the oversensitive painting of colors that typifies Ferraj's brave death, here we have only the stark reportage of horror. Neither Auda's nor Odysseus's hands would have shaken. When

Lawrence deals with brave and noble death or with justified revenge killing (as of the Turks at Deraa for their torture of him a year earlier and their brutality toward the villagers of Tafas, in chapter 117), he assumes the Homeric tone; but in an instance such as the one just related, he can find no flicker of grandeur, and his soft modernity betrays the epic pose. In the course of the revolt, Lawrence had to do—and witness—many deeds that could never be called heroic.

For this and other reasons, Lawrence had great difficulty in seeing himself as a hero, as he tells us in chapters 99 and 100. Written in the difficult, opaque prose to which Lawrence always resorts when describing his thoughts, these chapters actually contain an honest and brilliant, if sometimes confused, statement on modern heroism (or antiheroism). In them we find that Lawrence is a Homer who sees some old-time heroes like Auda and Tallal but who cannot himself participate in their mentality. Although Auda fights for the cause of Arab freedom, Lawrence only parodies him as he parodies his epic style of oral poetry in chapter 48. In fact, Lawrence feels that he is a British agent, sent to live "my outcast life among these Arabs, while I exploited their highest ideals and made their love of freedom one more tool to help England win" (S, 544). As such, "the stranger, the godless fraud inspiring an alien nationality" (S, 548), Lawrence feels that he did too good a job: As he tells us in chapter 1, a man following his model among the Arabs "may imitate them so well that they spuriously imitate him back again" (S, 31). Thus any heroism Lawrence may display is only an act and a tool of the British government, which he felt betrayed promises of independence that he made to the Arabs: "If I did not hesitate to risk my life, why fuss to dirty it? Yet life and honour seemed in different categories, not able to be sold one for another: and for honour, had I not lost that a year ago when I assured the Arabs that England kept her plighted word?" (S, 545). But in fact the problem of heroism that Lawrence raises goes far beyond one specific case of dual loyalties:

> With man-instinctive, anything believed by two or three had a miraculous sanction to which individual ease and life might honestly be sacrificed. To man-rational, wars of nationality were as much a cheat as religious wars, and nothing was worth fighting for: nor could fighting, the act of fighting, hold any meed of intrinsic virtue. Life was so deliberately private that no circumstances could justify one man laying violent hands upon another's: though a man's own death was his last free will, a saving grace and measure of intolerable pain. (S, 548)

When watching Auda or imitating very well and deeply the Arabs' fervor, Lawrence could be "man-instinctive"; but in "man-rational" the Hemingway note of total disillusionment enters. "Among the Arabs I was the disillusioned, the sceptic, who envied their cheap belief" (*S,* 549). Lawrence would like to believe fully in the idea of a national war but simply cannot.

Now Lawrence discusses the rationalizations that he practiced on himself in order to get through the revolt—and dismisses them; the most enticing of these is the idea that "our endurance might win redemption, perhaps for all a race" (*S,* 550). Instead of simply accepting this possibility, Lawrence admits the truth of the matter:

> Yet in reality we had borne the vicarious for our own sakes, or at least because it was pointed for our benefit: and could escape from this knowledge only by a make-belief in sense as well as motive.
>
> The self-immolated victim took for his own the rare gift of sacrifice; and no pride and few pleasures in the world were so joyful, so rich as this choosing voluntarily another's evil to perfect the self. There was a hidden selfishness in it, as in all perfections. To each opportunity there could be only one vicar, and the snatching of it robbed the fellows of their due hurt. . . .
>
> To endure for another in simplicity gave a sense of greatness. There was nothing loftier than a cross, from which to contemplate the world. The pride and exhilaration of it were beyond conceit. (*S,* 550–51)

In other words, it would be nice to ascribe glorious motives to one's actions, even the sacrificing of one's honor, but in the end one has to admit that all sacrifices are selfish. Ideally Arabs alone should have led this revolt, and Lawrence feels that he is indulging his need for adulation by taking the place of a real Arab leader.

Most of all, "Honest redemption must have been free and childminded. When the expiator was conscious of the under-motives and the after-glory of his act, both were wasted on him" (*S,* 551). As a "modern man" who is "thought-riddled" (*S,* 551), Lawrence must analyze the heroic act instead of simply accepting it. Once the act is analyzed, the magic is gone. As Eugene Goodheart writes, "Heroism may be possible only to an unreflective person. The very need to reflect may render heroism not only problematic, but finally impossible."[24] With such an overactive conscience and analytical faculty, Lawrence had to feel that "There seemed no straight walking for us leaders in this crooked lane of conduct, ring after ring of unknown, shamefaced motives cancelling or double-charging their precedents" (*S*, 551–52).

As the revolt continues, Lawrence's involvement in it grows, and so does his self-consciousness and guilt, although these are never fully explained to us:

> I had had no concern with the Arab Revolt in the beginning. In the end I was responsible for its being an embarrassment to its inventors. Where exactly in the interim my guilt passed from accessory to principal, upon what headings I should be condemned, were not for me to say. Suffice it that since the march to Akaba I bitterly repented my entanglement in the movement, with a bitterness sufficient to corrode my inactive hours, but insufficient to make me cut myself clear of it. Hence the wobbling of my will, and endless, vapid complainings. (*S*, 552)

Lawrence's personal eccentricities have been stressed by biographers and critics as reasons for his feelings, but in these two chapters he has said things that Crane and Conrad and Hemingway have also said: He has explained why it is hard to be a hero in the modern world. When he thinks that "Death in the air would be a clean escape" (*S*, 545) from the guilt of a man who cannot rationalize his actions, no matter how heroic they seem to the crowd, he speaks beyond all romantic poses as someone truly sick of life. If in the end we take away with us a heroic view of Lawrence as one who succeeded in the face of all difficulties in getting to Damascus, we do so despite Lawrence's own view of himself.

If we look at the portrayal of love and death through Lawrence's realistic veil, we find a view that totally contradicts the idealism of the romantic veil, causing a discordance throughout the book. In the realistic view, death is presented as the last resort of a man pressed too far, or a brutal, savage, and meaningless event caused by the primitive instincts aroused by war. When practiced by the Bey at Deraa, who uses compulsion rather than the free choice offered by the Arabs, homosexual love is anything but beautiful and becomes instead an involuntary, violent, and destructive assault on the citadel of self. War and the arbitrary power afforded by war become excuses for the rape of the integrity of the individual and of all civilized moral values.

Lawrence fuses the reality and the romance wonderfully in the symbolism of the Turkish hospital in chapter 121. As Lawrence enters, he meets the "sickening stench" and "sight" (*S*, 656) of rotting and dying bodies that have been totally neglected. This is the underside of glory, the dirt swept under the rug of war. "I picked forward a little between their lines, holding my white skirts about me, not to dip my bare feet in their puddled running" (*S*, 656). The white purity of the heroic ideal can barely escape the contamination of the reality of war. When a medical major, wrongly assuming that Lawrence is responsible for the wretched state of the hospital, unjustly slaps Lawrence in the face, we understand Lawrence's sense that he to some degree deserved this treatment, for "anyone who pushed through to success a rebellion of the weak against their masters must come out of it so stained in estimation that afterward nothing in the world would make him feel clean" (*S*, 659). Lawrence feels that the Arab Revolt demanded too many physical and mental compromises from him. If we see Lawrence as a hero at the end, we also see the price that such heroism exacts from a modern, sensitive intellectual. Lawrence writes as a Homer whose *Iliad* has absorbed into it the bitterness of Shakespeare's *Troilus and Cressida* or Hemingway's *The Sun Also Rises*. Do we cynically mock his Achilles as a man who should have known better or sympathize with the tragedy of a romantic who had to learn too much?

Chapter Four
Seven Pillars of Wisdom: Dramatized Truth in Autobiography

Texts of Seven Pillars

In *Abinger Harvest,* E. M. Forster comments with antischolarly irony that the profusion of variant manuscripts has made *Seven Pillars* a "joy" for students of the book.[1] The story of the composition and revision of *Seven Pillars* has been told thoroughly by Jeffrey Meyers and Thomas O'Donnell,[2] but the relative literary quality of some of the various manuscripts will perhaps always be debated. My purpose now is simply to label the texts for the reader's convenience, using Lawrence's own testimony to do so: (1) Text 1: Begun 10 January 1919 in Paris, and finished 25 July 1919. The whole text, except for the introduction, was lost at Reading Station in November 1919. (2) Text 2: Begun 2 December 1919 at Oxford and then dropped until January-February 1920, when 95 percent was written at Barton Street in 30 days. Finished 11 May 1920 at Barton Street and corrected and added to slowly for nearly two years. Destroyed by Lawrence on 10 May 1922, except for one single specimen page that is inserted after the Epilogue of text 3. (3) Text 3: This is the manuscript in the Bodleian Library, Oxford University. Begun 1 September 1920 and finished 9 May 1922 at 14 Barton Street, with parts written in Jidda and Amman. (4) Text 4: The Oxford text. This is text 3 printed up in eight copies on the press of the Oxford *Times* from 20 January 1922 to 24 June 1922. I have examined the copy of this text at the Houghton Library, Harvard. Except for front and end matter, it is essentially the same as the Bodleian manuscript but the length of both texts (approximately 330,000 words) makes it very difficult to compare more than selected passages. (5) The Subscriber's Edition of 1926: This is what I refer to as the "final edition" and is the same as the Garden City, Dell, and Penguin editions except for very minor details.[3] The Penguin edition contains an introductory chapter of the Subscriber's Edition absent from some American editions. The Subscriber's Edition was painstakingly self-published by Lawrence[4] and includes work by some of the most famous artists of the period;[5] it was distributed to a select group of either 211 or 217 persons.[6] It is approximately 280,000 words long. (6) *Revolt in the Desert* (1927): This is an abridged, 130,000 word version of *Seven Pillars* issued for popular consumption and is a memoir rather than an autobiography because all personal, introspective passages have been eliminated.

The manuscript history of *Seven Pillars* is even more detailed and complicated than appears here, but this outline will do for our purposes. When we discuss Lawrence's different self-portraits, we will be discussing variations between text 3 (the Bodleian manuscript) and text 4 (the Oxford text) on the one hand, and the final edition, in my case that put out by the Garden City Publishing Company and almost identical with the 1926 edition, on the other.

In the course of his many revisions, Lawrence published material from his manuscripts in article form in various journals. Some of these have been made available by Stanley and Rodelle Weintraub, under the title *Evolution of a Revolt* (1967). And as noted in my last chapter, we have in *Secret Despatches from Arabia* the intelligence reports that Lawrence sent to his superiors in the Arab Bureau in Cairo during the revolt, and that he originally published in the Bureau's secret *Arab Bulletin*[7] newsletter for intelligence purposes. Lawrence's letters and reviews dating from 1919–1926 (when he was writing *Seven Pillars*) as well as from earlier and later periods offer important insight into his literary opinions.[8]

Dramatized Truth

One very important factor distinguishing autobiography from fiction is the expectation of literal factual and historical truth that the reader of an autobiography brings to his text. He wants to feel that the writer actually experienced both the inner and outer events that he narrates, and if it transpires that the writer has invented some or all of these events, the reader will take the work less seriously than he would otherwise. Yet anyone who has studied the genre of autobiography knows that a certain tension inevitably exists between the bare, factual, chronological internal and external events of a life, and the form in which they are expressed in the autobiography itself. Moreover, if the autobiographer recounts embarrassing or traumatic events, he may be unable to recall those events precisely as they happened, or may exercise a certain amount of

discretion in revealing details. In the various acts of remembering, select-
ing, arranging, and basically making readable the raw material of his life,
or a portion of his life, the autobiographer puts together a self-portrait
that, like a painted self portrait,[9] may closely resemble or differ greatly
from a mirror image. In this chapter, we will be concerned with the extent
and logic of Lawrence's departures from a mirror image of the external
events, the changing backdrop of his life in Arabia, and with the comparative effectiveness of the two different major self-portraits, or texts of
Seven Pillars, that he has left us. In other words, we will attempt to deter-
mine if and why Lawrence departed from strict historical truth in his
account of the men and events of the Arab Revolt, and whether the 1922
or the 1926 text of *Seven Pillars* makes more powerful and moving reading, particularly in terms of his own character. Numerous writers, among
them Graves, Aldington, Weintraub, Meyers, Mack, Kedourie, O'Donnell, and Wilson have commented on these problems in detail, and it
remains for me now only to indicate agreement or disagreement with
some of their conclusions and to sum up the situation, using my own
reading of the Houghton, Bodleian, and British Library manuscript
material as a firm basis for judgment.

The attempt to impugn Lawrence's historical accuracy in recounting
the facts of the Arab Revolt in *Seven Pillars* crystallizes in Richard Aldington's savage attack on Lawrence's whole life, including the "Lawrence
legend" created by Lowell Thomas.[10] Aldington charges that in *Seven Pillars of Wisdom* Lawrence told outright lies about almost every facet of the
revolt and his role in it. But although some incidents like the battle of
Tafileh still need more attention, a preponderance of the research of the
past quarter century and more has increasingly shown that Lawrence told
the truth about the events of the revolt and his activities during it. For
instance, in chapter 48 of *Seven Pillars,* Lawrence writes that he went on a
"long, dangerous ride" behind enemy lines into Syria "to see the more
important of Feisal's secret friends, and to study key-positions of our
future campaigns" (*S, 276*). Several earlier biographers doubted that
Lawrence undertook this ride, but as Gideon Gera wrote in 1984,
"Today, with many British archives—public and private—open, there
can be no doubt that this outstanding feat was actually performed."[11]
Gera explains that in *Seven Pillars* Lawrence could not reveal the details of
the trip because of important intelligence considerations, including the
fact that some of the British operatives in the area were probably still
active even when Lawrence was writing his book years after the war was
over. Elie Kedourie has charged that in *Seven Pillars* Lawrence did not

state the fact that the Australians had reached Damascus before the Arabs but were ordered by General Allenby to let the Arabs enter first, on 1 October 1918. However, J. M. Wilson has explained that when the Arabs had been in a position to enter first on September 20, they were not allowed to do so. As compensation for that, they were allowed to enter the city first on 1 October. So Lawrence's account in *Seven Pillars,* which does not go into all these details, is truthful.[12]

Perhaps the best answer to the question of Lawrence's accuracy is one that Robert Graves had already stated in 1927, namely that very few witnesses have challenged Lawrence's account, although the text was widely circulated among Lawrence's war comrades before (and after) publication.[13] Another point in Lawrence's favor is that he left behind and made available even during his lifetime the various texts of *Seven Pillars* as well as numerous documents through which his story can be checked.

The differences between some of these materials and *Seven Pillars* have been exaggerated. Robert Payne, for instance, points out that Lawrence's *Seven Pillars* description of his first meeting with Feisal is dramatic and glorious, whereas Lawrence's *Arab Bulletin* report of 18 November 1916 concerning his first view of Feisal reveals only disappointment with Feisal's unreasonableness.[14] In fact, the 18 November despatch does state only that Lawrence slept well "after dining and arguing with Feisal (who was most unreasonable) for hours and hours."[15] What then of the dramatic description of Feisal as a Saladin quoted in my last chapter, and the conversation that reads almost too well to be true?: "[Feisal:] 'And how do you like our place here in Wadi Safra?' [Lawrence:] 'Well, but it is far from Damascus' " (*S,* 91). If we consult an *Arab Bulletin* despatch of 26 November 1916, we find Feisal described there by Lawrence as "tall, graceful, vigorous, almost regal in appearance. . . . very like the monument of Richard I, at Fontevraud. He is hot tempered, proud, and impatient, sometimes unreasonable, and runs off easily at tangents."[16] Here we have clear evidence that Lawrence, very soon after meeting Feisal (and the chronological order of the despatches does not necessarily reflect the order of Lawrence's view of Feisal), saw him in the same heroic light that he felt while viewing Richard I's statue on one of his bicycle trips to France in 1907 (*L,* 50–51), and that fully merits the description and conversation given in *Seven Pillars* (*S,* 91). At the very same moment, he sees the negative side of Feisal's character and reports it in the verbatim language that he uses in *Seven Pillars:* "He showed himself hot-tempered and sensitive, even unreasonable, and he ran off soon on tangents" (S, 97). At the very worst, Lawrence is exercising the autobiographer's right to rearrange his material, not lying. More important, Lawrence's critics do not give him credit for Keats's "negative capability," the ability to hold two contradictory ideas (in this case, that Feisal is both unreasonable and noble) in his mind at the same moment, and to credit each of them equally, although this is one of the keys to his character. As we have already seen, Lawrence is sincerely divided about the heroic and antiheroic aspects of his adventures.

Some writers have claimed that in the final edition Lawrence suppressed negative feelings about Feisal that had been obvious in the Oxford edition.[17] It is true that Lawrence grew more disenchanted with Feisal as the revolt progressed, and as he himself grew more unhappy with his role in it. But here again we find an overt stripping of the veil of romance in the final edition of Seven Pillars itself, in which Feisal appears as "a brave, weak, ignorant spirit, trying to do work for which only a genius, a prophet or a great criminal, was fitted" and whom Lawrence served "out of pity, a motive which degraded us both" (S, 565). Just as Lawrence dissects his own heroic image, so he reassesses Feisal's in the same piercing light, and despite his own romantic desire to see only the appearance, ends up reporting the reality. So the truth is reported in the final edition of Seven Pillars itself, which does not differ from the Secret Despatches or the earlier texts of Seven Pillars as much as some critics have maintained. Although the earlier texts provide some helpful supplemental information, the careful reader finds in the final edition an accurate expression not only of the facts of the revolt but also of Lawrence's feelings about Feisal, Bedouin ways, and blundering Englishmen. The more one reads Lawrence, the more one is convinced that at least as far as the facts of the revolt go, Lawrence wrote as a literary autobiographer rather than the master huckster that Aldington tried to make of him. The reader of Seven Pillars receives a sincere account of the revolt through the eyes of a man whose "negative capability" allowed him to believe and present contradictory ideas all at once.

In the manner of Doughty, Lawrence as artistic autobiographer has selected, embroidered, and heightened true events to make them dramatic. He gives clear testimony to a view of historical writing that would permit such emphasis in a letter of December 1927 to Lionel Curtis:

> One of the ominous signs of the time is that the public can no longer read history. The historian is retired into a shell to study the whole truth;

which means that he learns to attach insensate importance to documents. The documents are liars. No man ever yet tried to write down the entire truth of any action in which he has been engaged. All narrative is parti pris. . . . We know too much, and use too little knowledge. (*L*, 559)

And to George Bernard Shaw he wrote in 1928 that *"The Seven Pillars* was an effort to make history an imaginative thing. It was my second try at dramatizing reality" (*L*, 603). (According to Lawrence, the first try was a projected work bearing the same title as *Seven Pillars* and whose subject was seven cities of the Near East. Lawrence destroyed it in 1914.) Ronald Storrs gives us a clue to precisely what Lawrence meant by dramatizing reality in a footnote to his memoirs, *Orientations:* "Lawrence's account of the voyage, particularly of our conversations, is heightened by the use of what *The Thousand Nights and a Night* calls *Lisan al-hal,* the 'tongue, of the state or occasion;' i.e., the language deemed appropriate to the characters or circumstances."[18] Thucydides, probably the greatest historian who ever lived, makes use of a similar expression to describe the speeches he puts into the mouths of political and military figures in his *Peloponnesian War,* and yet no one has taxed him with inaccuracy. In 1955 Storrs went even farther in vouching for Lawrence's accuracy while describing his dramatic method: "I turned to chapter 8 and found the description of Lawrence's journey with me down the Red Sea startlingly exact, except that Storrs' share of the conversation is rather puckishly tuned up. . . . I found him a touchstone and standard of reality."[19] When departures from strict political or military truth occur in *Seven Pillars,* they stem either from Lawrence's concern with the immediate political situation in the Near East, including the position of Feisal, or more often from the fact that he was an autobiographical artist rather than a document-oriented historian.

Lawrence always worked toward heightened literary effectiveness within the framework of a basic fidelity to fact. Comparison of a passage that appeared in *The World's Work* for September 1921, the Oxford text, and the final version reveals Lawrence's progressive growth as an artist, particularly in the writing of the many "set pieces" that appear in *Seven Pillars.* Here is the passage as it appears in *The World's Work:*

> The dead lay naked under the moon, Turks are much whiter-skinned than the Arabs among whom I had been living, and these were mere boys. Close around them lapped the dark wormwood, now heavy with dew and sparkling like sea spray. Wearied in mind and body, I felt that I would rather be of this quiet company than with the shouting, restless

mob farther up the valley, boasting of their speed and strength, and quarrelling over the plunder. For, however this campaign might go with its unforeseen toils and pains, death must be the last chapter in the history of every man of us. (520)

This is the passage as it appears in the Houghton Library Oxford text, including corrections written on the page in Lawrence's handwriting:

> The dead men looked wonderfully beautiful. The night was shining gently down, softening them into new ivory. Turks were white on the clothed parts of their bodies, much whiter than the Arabs among whom I was living, and these soldiers had been very young. Close round them lapped the dark wormwood, now heavy with dew, in which the ends of the moonbeams sparkled like sea-spray. They lay so pitifully on the ground, huddled anyhow in low heaps, that it seemed needful to straighten them comfortably at last. So I put them all in order, one by one, very wearied myself in mind and body, and longing to be of their quiet, not of the restless, noisy, aching mob up the valley, quarrelling over the plunder, boasting of their speed and strength to endure God knew how many toils and pains of this sort: till death, whether we succeeded or failed, wrote the last chapter in our history. (111)

Finally, the same passage as it appears in the final edition:

> The dead men looked wonderfully beautiful. The night was shining gently down, softening them into new ivory. Turks were white-skinned on their clothed parts, much whiter than the Arabs; and these soldiers had been very young. Close round them lapped the dark wormwood, now heavy with dew, in which the ends of the moonbeams sparkled like sea-spray. The corpses seemed flung so pitifully on the ground, huddled anyhow in low heaps. Surely if straightened they would be comfortable at last. So I put them all in order, one by one, very wearied myself, and longing to be one of these quiet ones, not of the restless, noisy, aching mob up the valley, quarrelling over the plunder, boasting of their speed and strength to endure God knew how many toils and pains of this sort; with death, whether we won or lost, waiting to end the history. (S, 308)

Although the literary improvement from the first passage to the second is quite marked, we might well ask whether the changes between the Oxford text passage and the final edition are at all significant. What of the differences among these texts on the whole? Which is "best"?

Early and Late Rembrandt

If we extend Howarth's analogy of painting and autobiography, the Bodleian-Oxford self-portrait compares with the final version in the following way: The early portrait lacks the sureness of touch and arrangement of the later one and contains many additional details, some enlightening, some extraneous. Because of the extra detail, both the face and the background in this early painting appear more sharply delineated and lit, and the face stands out more clearly from the background. However, the sharpness of the face is only relative, and it retains a certain lack of clarity. The later, final, self-portrait reveals an improvement in technique, but this new control is used to execute a deliberately more shadowy face and background that merge in a more ambiguous and symbolic chiaroscuro effect. The question is, does the perceiver prefer the sharper, blunter, more detailed but less polished and arranged early Rembrandt, or the more perfect and mysterious later one? In either case, it is evident that the observer will never fully know the poetic self-portraitist Rembrandt—or the poetic autobiographer Lawrence.

For instance, despite all of the attention that has been paid to the differences between the two textual self-portraits of Lawrence, the fact remains that S. A.'s identity is not revealed in either of them and that the account of the famous Deraa incident (chapter 80) as given in both versions conceals at least one important point. In both the early and final versions, Lawrence explicitly denies that he was recognized by the Bey. But if the Bey himself was a Circassian, as Lawrence states that he may have been (*S,* 442), he would easily have seen through Lawrence's claim to be a Circassian, too. In a secret report Lawrence sent to the Chief Political Officer at General Headquarters in Cairo in 1919, Lawrence writes that he was betrayed by Abd el Kader (whom Lawrence calls "my old enemy" when he meets him again in Damascus; *S,* 645) and that the Bey definitely identified him as Lawrence.[20] Why Lawrence chose to conceal in both versions of *Seven Pillars* the almost definite fact that he was identified has not been satisfactorily explained.[21] So the Bey's statement that "You must understand that I know: and it will be easier if you do as I wish" (about which Lawrence writes that "it was evidently a chance shot, by which he himself did not, or would not, mean what I feared" [*S,* 443]) remains mysterious. Among other possibilities, it could mean (as Jeffrey Meyers has claimed) that the Bey recognized that Lawrence was a homosexual or (as I propose) that the Bey thought that Lawrence was not as strong as he pretended to be and would break down and submit, although unwillingly, under torture. Since Lawrence writes that the Bey "did not, *or would not,* mean what I feared" (*S,* 443; italics mine), it may be that during the torture the Bey concealed his full knowledge of Lawrence's true identity, so Lawrence did not know at that time that the Bey knew who he was and realized that only later. Lawrence was able to escape because he was tougher and not as badly hurt as the Turks thought.

The question of the Bey's identifying Lawrence admittedly remains obscure and ambiguous. But, aside from this one issue, Lawrence is searingly honest in the earlier and later versions of *Seven Pillars* about the fact that he was tortured and raped and even that he experienced masochistic feelings. In both versions, he writes for instance that "I remembered smiling idly at him, for a delicious warmth, probably sexual, was swelling through me" (*S,* 445) during the beating. But in the final version only, he also states that "Pain of the slightest had been my obsession and secret terror, from a boy," asks "Had I now been drugged with it, into bewilderment?" (*S,* 446), and ends the chapter by writing that "in Deraa that night the citadel of my integrity had been irrevocably lost" (*S,* 447). In the Oxford text, however, he adds sentences not in the final version: "I was feeling very ill, as though some part of me had gone dead that night in Deraa, leaving me maimed, imperfect, only half myself. It could not have been the defilement, for no one ever held the body in less honour than I did myself. Probably it had been the breaking of the spirit by that frenzied nerve-shattering pain which had degraded me to beast level when it made me grovel to it, and which had journeyed with me since, a fascination and terror and morbid desire, lascivious and vicious, perhaps, but like the striving of a moth towards the flame."[22]

The literary difference between the Oxford and the final versions can be summed up by a comparison of the sentence about striving toward pain like a moth (possibly based on Doughty's sentence "As moths will beat to an appearing of light in darkness; so it is in the preaching of a new doctrine")[23] and the sentence from the final version about "the citadel of my integrity." The Oxford text sentence is more blunt and sensational in admitting Lawrence's continuing masochistic desires (although not his actual practice of flagellation, begun in the early 1920s, which he never revealed). But the sentence from the final edition is more beautiful rhythmically, more universal, more ambiguous, and more symbolic. Taken with the other sentences from the final version, it too reveals Lawrence's masochism but places it in a wider context. It speaks not only of a single repulsive incident but also of the loss of integrity involved in the whole game of war, politics, imposture, and cultural clash—which required Lawrence to suffer too great physical and mental torture in order to find the hidden road to be used later for an attack on Deraa and to carry through to victory a revolt that ultimately achieved less in almost every way than Lawrence had hoped.

The final version makes up in literary sureness of touch and greater universality what it may lack in bluntness. A simple narrative passage, the only one surviving from the destroyed text 2, reveals in its metamorphoses Lawrence's technical advance in writing:

> The repeated naval bombardments had degraded the place to its original rubbish, & the contemptible remains of the dirty houses stood about in a litter lacking all the dignity of an ancient ruin: not theirs the great defiant gesture of human building facing that inevitable time whose advance years have already hacked off all the doors. (Single surviving sheet of text 2, inserted after epilogue of text 3.)

> The repeated naval bombardments had degraded the place to its original rubbish, and the poor remains of the houses stood about in a litter with none of the dignity of ancient buildings, of which durable bones face with a great defiant gesture that inevitable Time whose advancing years have already devoured their accidents. Akaba was dirty and contemptible, and the wind howled miserably across it. (text 3, Bodleian manuscript, folio 209.)

> Repeated bombardments by French and English warships had degraded the place to its original rubbish, and the poor remains of the houses stood about in a litter, with none of the dignity of ancient buildings, of which the durable bones face with a great defiant gesture that inevitable Time whose advancing years have already devoured their accidents. (text 4, Oxford text, 115.)

This becomes the considerably smoother statement of the final edition:

> Repeated bombardments by French and English warships had degraded the place to its original rubbish. The poor houses stood about in a litter, dirty and contemptible, lacking entirely that dignity which the durability of their time-challenging bones had conferred on ancient remains. (*S*, 314)

On the whole, although the 1922 text offers some interesting statements omitted from the final text, Lawrence's prediction of 1923 that the final text would be "better" (*L*, 438) has been borne out. After the publication of the final version, Lawrence was never in any doubt that it surpassed artistically the Oxford text, as he wrote to Mrs. Thomas Hardy in 1927: "I'm grateful for your kindly judgement of *The Seven Pillars*. It is inevitable that people should call it less good than the 'Oxford' text, in which I first lent it you: but their judgement leaves me cold. Only I have read the two so closely as really to see the differences: and my taste in every case approved the changes" (*L*, 515). With some help from George Bernard Shaw's reading of the Oxford text, Lawrence cut verbosity and useless description. He juggled paragraphs and chapter beginnings. Many tales of the different tribes and individuals among the tribes have been dropped, along with a long personal description of Vickery and a homosexual incident between a British soldier and a Bedouin (which Lawrence called "beastly" but excused). The final version is thus much tighter, as Lawrence himself pointed out: "It is swifter and more pungent than the Oxford text; and it would have been improved yet more if I had had the leisure to carry the process of revision further" (*S*, 23). Robert Graves's mixed feelings probably come closest to an accurate description of the difficulty of making a final decision between the early and later texts:

> On the whole I prefer the earliest surviving version, the so-called Oxford text, to the final printed book which was the version I first read consecutively. This is a physical rather than a critical reaction. The earlier version is 330,000 words long instead of 280,000 and the greater looseness of the writing makes it easier to read. From a critical point of view no doubt the revised version is better. It is impossible that a man like Lawrence would spend four years on polishing the text without improving it, but the nervous rigor that the revised book gave me has seemingly dulled my critical judgement.[24]

In addition to rounding off the bluntness of some observations on himself and other characters in the revolt in order to make the entire experience more symbolic and mysterious in the manner of Kinglake, Hudson, and Doughty, all of whom mask their personalities in one way or another, Lawrence in the final edition rightly cut down on self-conscious references to the making of a book, but these are interesting nonetheless. The passage in the final edition that begins by noting Lawrence's craving "for the power of self-expression in some imaginative form" (*S*, 549) is amplified in the Oxford text:

At last accident, with perverted humour, had cast me as a man of action—and in the very height of doing I would momentarily forget my wished nature: yet always after such a crisis consciousness returned asking, how had that been done?

Then I would look back at my intention, trying to find a key-word for it, in laboured sentences like these, which hid the reality, unless, perhaps, here and there, it peeped out between the lines. Chance had given me a place in the Arab Revolt, a theme epic to a direct eye and hand—and had given me a taste for the subjective, for the words to mirror our motives or feelings of the time. Whence came the indirection of my diary, and of this book built over it. (Oxford text, 231)

The first paragraph is one of many passages that shows Lawrence's ability to escape the intellect and self-consciousness during moments of action; the second reveals his painful, intense intellectual search for the right words to match his experience once thought had returned and Lawrence's fear that he was not able to find that perfect expression.

To the first paragraph on page 563 of the final edition, which deals with notes Lawrence wrote while on the march, the Oxford text adds: "The narrative hid in faint sentences, scattered through pages of opinion. Of course, my diary had to be something not harmful to others if it fell into enemy hands, but, even making this allowance, it showed clearly that my interest lay in myself, not in my activities, and four-fifths of it were useless for this re-writing" (Oxford text, 239).

After Lawrence's declaration in the final edition that "I could not approve creation" (*S*, 565), apparently referring to military as well as artistic creation, the Oxford text contradicts this with the additional "Nor did I ever work my fullest, except perhaps upon some pages of this book."

In these excised passages, we see the poetic autobiographer's distress when realizing that he is more concerned with his own personality than with the external events through which he passed. He declares his intention of trying to bring his inner and outer history into more equal focus by rejecting much personal revelation in favor of outside events. And we see the degree to which he regarded himself as a creative artist who labors to bring order and balance into his autobiography. Lawrence did not quite succeed in making his inner reactions understandable in relation to the outer, public events of the revolt. Especially after the taking of Akaba, Lawrence's personal reactions do not always follow logically from the events of the revolt as he relates them to us. The personal element clashes with the pure epic. As a poetic autobiographer, Lawrence did not understand himself and could present himself only on the move, in process as it were. He leaves it to the reader to create Lawrence and personally to understand exactly why Lawrence felt as he did when he did. However, by placing the narrator-protagonist Lawrence in the context of other twentieth-century characters in the literature of British imperialism, we can illuminate and re-create his experience. We can understand the spiritual meaning of all of Lawrence's unfocused self-portraits only by placing them on a wall with other portraits and self-portraits of his own and earlier periods.

Chapter Five

Seven Pillars of Wisdom: The Two Veils

The Problem

As narrator-protagonist in his own work, Lawrence travels the long road from Yenbo on the remote Arabian coast to the throne of Damascus, growing progressively more depressed and nerve wracked as the military action in *Seven Pillars* swells and culminates in a successful climax. Impelled by a mysterious personal urge (his love of S. A., his rebelliousness, and his absolutism) to overcome this citadel of Turkish power, suffering mental and physical privation on the way, Lawrence finds his nerve and motive for action gone long before he takes Damascus and carries on only out of "historical ambition, insubstantial as a motive by itself" (*S*, 661), tasting personal defeat in military victory. The division between two political and cultural consciousnesses tears at his mind until he loses belief in English methods and honor and finally in his own capacity to control body and mind. He struggles to retain his Western, British ego in the vast ocean of the Moslem desert, loses that battle, and awakens at the end of the adventure to find himself a stranger to English and Arab alike. Where Charles Doughty and Alexander Kinglake as Victorians were able to maintain their Christian and colonial distance from the Arabs—a distance Lawrence admires from afar—and thus preserve their integrity and stability, Lawrence was considerably less successful.

To other British writers of the early twentieth century, Lawrence's was not a new story. As the product of a modern outsider in an alien and primitive environment that ultimately destroys him as a complete Englishman as well, *Seven Pillars* carries a message strikingly similar to Joseph Conrad's *Heart of Darkness,* E. M. Forster's *Passage to India,* George Orwell's *Burmese Days,* Joyce Cary's *Mister Johnson,* and other British colonial literature of our century. The process undergone by the Westerner confronting an alien environment and described in these works is roughly the following: Unless the Westerner maintains his role as Sahib, or colonial ruler, he becomes involved in the other culture to the point of losing his Western identity. He returns home unable to "focus anything," in the words of Mrs. Mallowe in Rudyard Kipling's "The Education of Otis Yeere," his ego destroyed. At home he reacts violently to the truths he has learned about himself through exposure to the other culture and becomes convinced that he has "prostituted" himself to a "brute race" (in the words of both Lawrence and Marlow in Conrad's *Lord Jim*).[1] In his turn, he has imposed upon the non-Westerner his own mores, debilitating the non-Western culture in the process. The final message of all these works is that conflicts of alien cultures and political needs cannot be bridged at will and that those who make the attempt are eliminated or maimed. In the condensed formula closing *A Passage to India,* the horses, the earth, and the rocks said " 'No, not yet,' and the sky said, 'no, not here.' "[2]

No one states the precise nature of the shock of cultures and its effect on sensitive twentieth-century Westerners who experience it better than Lawrence himself in the highly tensed "Strangeness and Pain" chapter of *Seven Pillars:*

> In my case, the effort for these years to live in the dress of Arabs, and to imitate their mental foundation, quitted me of my English self, and let me look at the West with new eyes: they destroyed it all for me. At the same time I could not sincerely take on the Arab skin: it was an affectation only. . . . Such detachment came at times to a man exhausted by prolonged physical effort and isolation. His body plodded on mechanically, while his reasonable mind left him, and from without looked down critically on him, wondering what that futile lumber did and why. Sometimes these selves would converse in the void; and then madness was very near, as I believe it would be near the man who could see things through the veils at once of two customs, two educations, two environments. (*S, 31–32*)

Because Lawrence's Arab and British veils alternate constantly, allowing him to see now through one, now through the other, he escapes madness but becomes isolated from other men and from a sense of who he is. The double pull of two cultures, combined with his fear of and contempt for the body, with its feelings of pain and touch, serves to remove Lawrence's inner self from the normal spheres of human contact. He can be sure only of his control of that inner self and his absolute subordination of his body to his will—until he finds at Deraa that he does not have even this certainty.

Lacking from the start a stable belief in the cultural and moral superiority of the British Raj because of his own psychological attraction to
the Arabs and his feeling of British dishonesty toward them; lacking any
religious faith (as he confessed to Liddell Hart); wearing always "doubt,
our modern crown of thorns" (*S,* 38), he could believe only in his own
will and ability to straddle the fence of an increasingly dual loyalty and
still remain whole mentally. Seeking to attain the simple Arab ability to
believe in the revolt, he fails here, too. He could satisfy his absolutist
striving among neither British nor Arabs. When this search failed him,
depriving him of his identity as well, he resigned control of his life to the
British army and the Royal Air Force, as recorded in *The Mint.*
    Alec Dixon, a friend in the R.A.F., confirms this reading of Lawrence
as a casualty of the shock of cultures; he recalls that Lawrence "talked to
me of Arabia and particularly of its effect on him. Frequently he
impressed on me the folly of prostituting oneself to an alien cause. (His
conversation on this theme followed very closely along the lines of his
preface to Doughty's *Arabia Deserta.*) He had, he said, learned so well to
play the Arab that he found it extremely difficult, if not painful, to
return to an outlook and frame of mind that was unaffectedly Anglo-
Saxon . . . During those two years at Bovington he seemed strained and,
in some moods, ten or fifteen years older than he really was: Arabia
seemed to cling to him like Sinbad's old man of the sea."[3]
    Of course, this was not the only conflict from which Lawrence suf-
fered in Arabia. But when he sums up all the conflicting motives and
torments of the will, as he does in the following document that he wrote
in 1919, he always lays greatest stress on the difficulty of seeing through
two cultural veils:

> I'm going to tell you exactly what my motives in the Arab affair were, in
> order of strength:
>   (i) Personal. I liked a particular Arab very much, and I thought that
> freedom for the race would be an acceptable present.
>   (ii) Patriotic. I wanted to help win the war, and Arab help reduced
> Allenby's losses by thousands.
>   (iii) Intellectual Curiosity. I wanted to feel what it was like to be the
> mainspring of a national movement, and to have some millions of people
> expressing themselves through me: and being a half-poet, I don't value
> material things much. Sensation and mind seem to me much greater, and
> the ideal, such a thing as the impulse that took us into Damascus, the
> only thing worth doing.

(iv) Ambition. You know how Lionel Curtis has made his conception of the Empire—a Commonwealth of free peoples— generally accepted. I wanted to widen that idea beyond the Anglo-Saxon shape, and form a new nation of thinking people, all acclaiming our freedom, and demanding admittance into our Empire. There is, to my eyes, no other road for Egypt and India in the end, and I would have made their path easier, by creating an Arab Dominion in the Empire. . . . The process intended was to take Damascus, and run it . . . as an independent ally of G[reat] B[ritain]. . . .

. . . I'm not conscious of having done a crooked thing to anyone since I began to push the Arab Movement, though I prostituted myself in Arab Service. For an Englishman to put himself at the disposal of a red race is to sell himself to a brute, like Swift's Houhynyms [sic]. However, my body and soul were my own, and no one can reproach me for what I do to them: and to all the rest of you I'm clean.[4]

Motives (i) and (iii)—Lawrence's Arab veil—balance motives (ii) and (iv)—his British veil. Lawrence writes further that motive (i)—Dahoum—had died some weeks before he entered Damascus, "so my gift was wasted." Sounding much like Oscar Wilde's Lord Henry Wotton, he adds that motive (iii) was "romantic mainly, and one never repeats a sensation. When I rode into Damascus the whole countryside was on fire with enthusiasm, and in the town a hundred thousand people shouted my name. Success always kills the hope by surfeit." Motive (iv), which he hoped would serve British and Arabs both, also failed in realization when France was awarded the mandate over Syria as a result of the Peace Conference in 1919. Of all the motives, only number (ii) was realized and was clearly insufficient to erase the feeling of failure Lawrence experienced.

Any reader of *Seven Pillars* finds nothing remarkable in this list of motives: They appear in exactly this order on the last page of the book. The "Strangeness and Pain" chapter of the final edition repeats his conclusion about prostitution in Arab service. And throughout the book, his Arab and British sensibilities continually conflict with one another.

Despite Knightley and Simpson's attempt to portray Lawrence as a cold-blooded British agent who cared only for "biffing the French out of Syria" (as he wrote in a letter of 1915) and not about Arab independence or his own honor, the evidence they provide inadvertently refutes their point. They accept the document just quoted as genuine. In it, we read clearly that only one of Lawrence's four stated motives directly and unqualifiedly involves purely British interests; he also appears to have had more on his mind than simple hatred of the French.

Several recent writers in addition to Knightley and Simpson have charged Lawrence with British imperialism.[5] Conversely, Richard Aldington, writing at a time of growing British-Arab political tension in the early 1950s, blamed Lawrence for having favored the Arabs over the British and French. These contradictory charges demonstrate that Lawrence was so divided between British and Arab political loyalties that his career can be seen in both ways. Lawrence was concerned with winning the war for the British, but the charge of simple imperialism is difficult to sustain against him. Here, as in his openness to other cultures despite his residual use of some stereotypes, Lawrence represents a position between the old imperialism and what is often called Britain's postcolonial age. For his period, he is very progressive, but seen with post-World War II hindsight, he may not appear to be so. It is important, therefore, always to view him in the context of his own period in order to avoid judging him unfairly. It is as inaccurate to accuse Lawrence of imperialism as it is to claim that Mark Twain in *Huckleberry Finn* was a racist; Lawrence's and Twain's ideas on these respective subjects may not always match our present expectations but were nonetheless very advanced and positive for their eras.

The Arabs' postwar political status, as Lawrence envisioned it during the war, although not independence in the absolute sense, represents as much independence as could practically be achieved in view of great power interests in the area that, as Lawrence knew, would not simply evaporate.[6] He hoped that the British would give more to the Arabs than would the French, and his idea of including an Arab part of the so-called "Coloured Empire" (as opposed to those areas of the British Empire settled by Europeans) in a final commonwealth scheme is advanced for his time. His letter to D. G. Pearman, written two years after the war, shows that Lawrence (unlike many people in the British and French governments) knew that the age of European imperialism was gone forever: "Do make clear to your lads, whoever they are, that my objects were to save England & France too, from the follies of the imperialists, who would have us, in 1920, repeat the exploits of Clive and Rhodes. The world has passed by that point. I think, though, there's a great future for the British Empire as a voluntary association" (*L*, 578). This is only one of many such expressions of anti-imperialism emanating from Lawrence. A passage from his war diary addressed to his superior, Gilbert Clayton, confirms his concern over his position as a man of

honor vis-à-vis the Arabs: "We are calling them to fight for us on a lie
and I can't stand it."[7] That is not the declaration of a cold-blooded
imperialist agent. It was difficult to want the best for both the British
and the Arabs, and often those positions could not be reconciled despite
Lawrence's best efforts.

Both *Crusader Castles* and his 1911 *Diary of a Journey across the
Euphrates* (1937), a companion volume that records details of a Meso-
potamian hike, reveal his deep interest in Syria and the relations
between East and West. His letters of the prewar period show a romantic pleasure in Syria as well as hope for the Arabs. In 1912 he writes: "I
am very glad you got to Baalbek and Tiberias and Damascus. All very
good: but if you could have drunk rose sherbert with snow and eaten
grapes in the bazaars of Aleppo in the heat! You know you have been a
long time in Syria, but not with Arabs: those are people you have not
met, and should" (*L,* 138). The war of 1913 between Turkey and the
Balkan states draws his condemnation of Turkey as an imperial oppres-
sor of the Arabs: "As for Turkey, down with the Turks! Their disappear-
ance would mean a change for the Arabs, who were at any rate once not
incapable of good government. One must debit them with algebra
though" (*L,* 152).

In these letters and the diary, we have a Lawrence not far removed
from the young and easy Kinglake. But the depth of Lawrence's experience transcends Kinglake's on many levels: For one thing, between
Kinglake and Lawrence stands World War I, which, like the khaki-clad
policeman at the end of Hemingway's *The Sun Also Rises,* puts a total halt
to romantic hopes and dreams. As one both willingly and unwillingly
involved in the deceptions attendant on the policy of the great powers,
Lawrence like a Kipling Kim who has grown up to realize what he has
been doing, attempts at least tactical rationalizations of his role when it
comes to writing *Seven Pillars,* his prewar romanticism submerged in the
dust of the Peace Conference. On the whole, however, we can agree with
Hannah Arendt's estimation of Lawrence: "Never again was the experiment of secret politics made more purely by a more decent man."[8]

The political situation of divided aims and loyalties was only a symptom, a tangible focus of the strain of having to see through "the veils at
once of two customs, two educations, two environments," to which
Lawrence attributes his occasional feeling of madness. But the political
situation was spiritually difficult in itself, with Lawrence having constantly to choose between two loyalties:

Not for the first or last time service to two masters irked me. I was one of Allenby's officers, and in his confidence: in return, he expected me to do the best I could for him. I was Feisal's adviser, and Feisal relied on the honesty and competence of my advice so far as often to take it without argument. Yet I could not explain to Allenby the whole Arab situation, nor disclose the whole British plan to Feisal. (*S*, 386)

Why, one asks, must this be so, since both Allenby and Feisal, at least in Lawrence's presentation, were honorable men? Lawrence gives legitimate political reasons at this juncture. If Feisal were to take Damascus and lose it, as Lawrence fears he would, his tribes would lose confidence and the revolt would come to a halt. To have told this to Allenby, for whom even a brief occupation of Damascus by the Arabs would have been a tangible help, would have seemed foot-dragging or open partiality to the Arabs. In this case, Lawrence "decided to postpone the hazard for the Arabs' sake" (*S*, 386).

This situation occurred not once but many times, with Lawrence sometimes keeping Allenby in the dark, and sometimes Feisal. But more corrosive than any tactical political or military skepticism is Lawrence's clear suspicion—justified by the adoption of the Sykes-Picot treaty of 1916 and Lawrence's indirect knowledge of it—that the Arabs are sacrificing for nothing, since France would receive the mandate over Syria:

The Arab Revolt had begun on false pretences. To gain the Sherif's help our Cabinet had offered, through Sir Henry McMahon, to support the establishment of native governments in parts of Syria and Mesopotamia, 'saving the interests of our ally, France.' The last modest clause concealed a treaty (kept secret, till too late, from McMahon, and therefore from the Sherif) by which France, England, and Russia agreed to annex some of these promised areas, and to establish their respective spheres of influence over all the rest. (*S*, 275)

Historians argue the facts of the Sykes-Picot treaty and Lawrence's claims about it even today, with inconclusive results. Since we are explicating Lawrence the narrator-protagonist as he appears between the covers of *Seven Pillars,* that is, as a literary character, we are not interested in or concerned with settling these disputes. However, it should be pointed out that his arguments make perfect sense within the context of *Seven Pillars* itself and are not contradictory concerning the Sykes-Picot treaty. Although Lawrence "had early betrayed the treaty's existence to

Feisal" (*S,* 555), he could not tell him the full depth of his feeling that in the end, despite his best efforts, the French and not the Arabs (as "an independent ally of Great Britain") would rule Damascus: That would have ended the Arab Revolt at once and with it Lawrence's entire bag of goals, Arab and British. Rather, he continued to hope that Feisal's "escape was to help the British so much that after peace they would not be able, for shame, to shoot him down in its fulfilment" (*S,* 555). Needless to say, the necessity for half-truths was excruciating to an over-conscientious man like Lawrence:

> Rumours of the fraud reached Arab ears, from Turkey. In the East persons were more trusted than institutions. So the Arabs, having tested my friendliness and sincerity under fire, asked me, as a free agent, to endorse the promises of the British government. I had had no previous or inner knowledge of the McMahon pledges and the Sykes-Picot treaty, which were both framed by war-time branches of the Foreign Office. But, not being a perfect fool, I could see that if we won the war the promises to the Arabs were dead paper. Had I been an honourable adviser I would have sent my men home, and not let them risk their lives for such stuff. Yet the Arab inspiration was our main tool in winning the Eastern war. So I assured them that England kept her word in letter and spirit. In this comfort they performed their fine things: but, of course, instead of being proud of what we did together, I was continually and bitterly ashamed. . . . Clearly I had no shadow of leave to engage the Arabs, unknowing, in a gamble of life and death. Inevitably and justly we should reap bitterness, a sorry fruit of heroic endeavour. (*S,* 275–76)

Lawrence's two veils come to the fore here: On the one hand, he is not a "free agent" but a British agent, and he cares most about motive (ii), winning the war against Britain's enemies. This is the same Lawrence who concedes that "for victory everything material and moral might be pawned" (*S,* 337), referring to a purely British victory. At the same moment, he sees the Arab Revolt as "heroic endeavour" and is ashamed of his false position. What we have here is the symptom, the leading edge, of a dilemma on which Lawrence sat for two years—and not the simple hypocrisy that some see in it. The problem goes much deeper: As Albert Memmi says of the position of the colonized, "a man straddling two cultures is rarely well seated."[9] One part of Lawrence, particularly the romantic part of motive (iii), sees the Arab struggle as truly heroic; another part, the British agent, is able to view that heroism as nothing more than a tool for winning the war for the British. Lawrence penetrates Arab culture to the extent that he can criticize the British with Arab eyes, but he never loses his sense of patriotism either and can criticize the Arabs, including their fickleness as allies, as an Englishman: thus "negative capability."

The Problem's Literary Results

The very openness of Lawrence's internal conflict, the crude juxtaposition of British-Arab contradictions, demonstrates not hypocrisy but Lawrence's very real dilemma. If he had wanted to hide the truth completely, he could have done a much better job of smoothing out the clash that runs all through the book: He surely was intelligent enough to accomplish that, to choose either the British or the Arab side for glorification and to completely suppress any contradictory evidence. But what he gives us in *Seven Pillars* is the actual internal battle he fought during the revolt, a process of mind. Life is seldom as smooth as fiction, and the autobiographical *Seven Pillars* is looser, less tightly shaped, than a novel. In life it is possible for one to be a patriotic British agent and also to sympathize deeply with an alien nationality without fully understanding all the dynamics of this conflict. As Dennis Porter writes, "*Seven Pillars of Wisdom* . . . is an extreme case, a work apparently written from a position of power and privilege . . . within the Western imperial system. Yet, it is soon evident that Lawrence's book is also the site of a struggle in which other, counterhegemonic voices struggle to be heard for a complex set of psychological and social reasons. Whether or not one attributes such resistances in the text to factors such as Lawrence's illegitimacy or homophilia, his own sense of his marginality to mainstream English culture and his determined pursuit of alternative forms of existence among alien peoples are evident."[10] In Lawrence's wild fluctuations from veil to veil, we have a drama at least as interesting as the more consistent products of fiction and well presented enough to be called artistic. As Lawrence writes to Ede about this problem of all autobiographers, "the interests of truth and form differ."[11]

The political contradictions Lawrence experienced during the revolt were not reconciled at the time of the writing of *Seven Pillars;* one reason he could offer no smoothly consistent view is that the results of his military and diplomatic work still hung in the balance of the Peace Conference of 1919 and its aftermath, as he explained to Frederick Manning in 1930:

Your remarks hit off very closely the obstacles that attended the delivery of *The Seven Pillars*. I was a rather clumsy novice at writing, facing what I felt to be a huge subject with hanging over me the political uncertainty of the future of the Arab Movement. We had promised them so much, and at the end wanted to give them so little. So for two years there was a dog fight, up and down the dirty passages of Downing St., and then all came out right—only the book was finished. It might have been happier, had I foreseen the clean ending. I wrote it in some stress and misery of mind.

The second complicity was my own moral standing. I had been so much of a free agent, repeatedly deciding what I (and the others) should do: and I wasn't sure if my opportunity (or reality, as I called it) was really justified. Not morally justifiable. I could see it wasn't: but justified by the standard of Lombard St. and Pall Mall. By putting all the troubles and dilemmas on paper, I hoped to work out my path again, and satisfy myself how wrong, or how right I had been. (*L*, 691–92)

When he writes of a "clean ending," Lawrence means that Feisal, after having been evicted from Syria by the French in 1920, was placed in 1921 upon the throne of Iraq by the British, while his brother Abdullah was given the throne of Transjordan.[12] Lawrence's retrospective footnote in the final edition declaring that England "was quit of the war-time adventure, with clean hands" (*S*, 276) refers to these facts. As an adviser to Winston Churchill in the Colonial Office, Lawrence had been instrumental in these decisions taken at the Cairo Conference of 1921. But as he wrote the early drafts of *Seven Pillars,* he was not sure how everything would turn out, and this uncertainty, despite the retrospective footnote, appears in various ways in the final edition. For instance, in the synopsis of the "Strangeness and Pain" chapter, he calls attention to "The strained mentality of rebellion which infects me and still, a year afterwards, prevents my judgement" (*S*, 7). Lawrence's phrase "The strained mentality of rebellion" implies cultural and literary as well as political strain.

Despite Lawrence's comment that the following quotation applies only to *The Mint,* the wide fluctuations of feeling in *Seven Pillars* indicate that it applies equally to that book: "I tie myself into knots trying to re-act everything, as I try to write it out. It's like writing in front of a looking-glass, and never looking at the paper, but always at an imaginary scene" (*L*, 624). He wrote under the immediate impact of the story as he re-created it from memory on paper: "I feel the transition from the winter war to the expedition against Damascus to be rather abrupt: but that's because of the strain we went through in the intermediate period which seemed interminable to me, and some of whose longueurs I successfully passed into print" (*L,* 383). We recall that he attributed an "indirection" to the Oxford text because it was based on the indirection of a chronicle diary. In the chronicle of *Seven Pillars,* we see Lawrence's feelings change from one moment to the next. Nowhere is this wandering more obvious than in his dealings with the Arabs, which change from moment to moment according to his mood. Lawrence gives us on paper the very process of his absorption into the Arab culture and way of thinking. This process moves in the direction of progressive Arabization through the revelation of Deraa and the massacre at Tafas, until the alienation of the last book, but it proceeds by "two steps forward and one back," depending again on the events of the moment; the connection between events and Lawrence's feelings, however, is not always clear.

When such a process is described in fiction, authors usually resort to first-person narration. Thus, in Nathanael West's *Day of the Locust,* Tod's pilgrimage from the Eastern establishment (symbolized by the Yale School of Art) to his spiritual rape by the city of Los Angeles and his becoming one of the crowd of "Angelinos" is told by a third-person narrator. In *The Rock Pool,* Cyril Connolly uses a third-person narrator to describe Naylor's journey from Oxford snobbishness to the washed-out viciousness of the émigré in a seedy French subculture. In a novel like Dickens's *Great Expectations,* only a distancing in time permits the first-person narrator, Pip, to describe with objectivity his journey from innocence to experience. When Henry Adams (in his *Education*) or Norman Mailer (in the first section of *Armies of the Night*) seek to reveal their personalities in the context of large historical events, they choose to write oratorical autobiography, using third-person narration to distance themselves from themselves as characters and calling themselves by their own names rather than "I." In a letter to Shaw, Lawrence himself asks about *Seven Pillars:* "Isn't it treated wrongly? I mean, shouldn't it be objective, without the first-person singular?" (*L,* 390).

Lawrence, on the other hand, was temperamentally unsuited to the oratorical autobiography and could never achieve such an objective, distanced view of himself. In *Seven Pillars,* he attempts to describe his own process of absorption in the other culture himself, in the first person, without the necessary distancing in time. It is as if he tries to lift himself by his own bootstraps or as if Kurtz himself were to try to describe his own descent into savagery without the benefit of an objective, intermediary narrator like Marlow. To a large extent, it is impossible for anyone without great distancing in time to understand the gradations by which one slips into such a process. As a difficult, poetic personality, Lawrence cannot in any case grasp his own self in its entirety—and perhaps no one can, even a person less deep and involuted than Lawrence. His chapter "Myself" is an attempt at self-analysis deliberately written in "cypher" as he wrote to Edward Garnett and so not wholly understandable. But even if not aiming at romantic and symbolic ambiguity, Lawrence could not have analyzed himself satisfactorily.

Lawrence thus gives us the record of his day-to-day process of Arabization and involvement in the revolt but in his role as narrator cannot fully understand it or explain how it happened. As he wrote to Vyvyan Richards, "it was and is hard to write about oneself in action."[13] This Homer presents us with the raw material of what happened to him as Achilles but cannot interpret it for us. Lawrence could not explain to us what happened to him or make his book objective by referring to analogous processes and situations, as R. P. Blackmur points out:

> One barrier to satisfaction—perhaps the only barrier— was in the limiting factor of subjectivity. Lawrence wrote always about himself, the individual who, ultimately, could not cope—with nothing, no plan or frame or conception, to fit himself into to make his tale objective in immediate import. His plain ambition is, as it were, untested; he could not steer for it, whether instinctively or deliberately; which is the difference in value between his books, and his life, and the books of the "Titans" he desired so to emulate.[14]

Because he does not understand the genre of poetic autobiography in which Lawrence is writing, Blackmur is right about the problem but wrong in his literary estimate of Lawrence. Poetic autobiography *should* be subjective, with the autobiographer's personality dominating the story. As Lawrence wrote to H. S. Ede, "the latter third of *Seven Pillars* is a narrative of my personal activity"[15] and even before that he is the one and only star of the show, as he wrote Richards: "*The making of a great tragedy in its being not really my triumph. I tried to bring this out, just this side egotism, as a second note running through the book after chapter 5, and increasing slowly towards the close, but it would be a fault in scale to present the Arab Revolt mainly as a personal tragedy to me.*"[16] Yet this is exactly what he has done, and rightly, too, for *Seven Pillars* is an "introspection epic," a poetic autobiography growing out of the "autobiography of travel" tradition and utilizes all the mysterious and symbolic tools possible for romantically veiling the personality of the one and only major character. As Lawrence writes to Lionel Curtis in 1923, "Isn't it just faintly possible that part of the virtue apparent in the book lies in its secrecy, its novelty, and its contestability?" (*L,* 417). Lawrence leaves it to us to create the exact outlines of his self-portrait, and the best way to begin is by taking a look at the self-portrait of the kind of man he was not and knew he was not: Charles Doughty.

Lawrence and Doughty Revisited

In his introduction to *Arabia Deserta,* Lawrence writes at his own modern expense and in favor of the Victorian Doughty:

> We export two chief kinds of Englishmen, who in foreign parts divide themselves into two opposed classes. Some feel deeply the influence of the native people, and try to adjust themselves to its atmosphere and spirit. . . . They imitate the native as far as possible, and so avoid friction in their daily life. However, they cannot avoid the consequences of imitation, a hollow, worthless thing. . . . The other class of Englishmen is the larger class. In the same circumstances of exile they reinforce their character by memories of the life they have left. In reaction against their foreign surroundings they take refuge in the England that was theirs. They assert their aloofness, their immunity, the more vividly for their loneliness and weakness. They impress the peoples among whom they live by reaction, by giving them an example of the complete Englishman, the foreigner intact.
>
> Doughty is a great member of the second, the cleaner class.[17]

Lawrence, a man of the first, in his opinion the dirtier class, ultimately neither an Arab nor a complete Englishman, here looks with envy on the kind of traveler he could never be. But in letters he wrote to Mrs. Shaw in 1927, Lawrence reveals what he really thought of the "second, the cleaner class" of Englishmen abroad:

> Doughty really believed in his superiority to the Arabs. It was this pride that made him meek in oppression. He really believed that he held a knowledge of the truth, and that they were ignorant. He really believed that the English were better than the Arabs: that this thing was better than that thing: in fact, he really did believe in something. That's what I call an absolute. Doughty, somewhere, if only in the supremacy of Spenser, had a fixed point in his universe, and from one fixed point a moralist will,

like a paleontologist, build up the whole scheme of creation. Consequently, Doughty's whole book is rooted; definitive; assured. . . . Doughty sees through his eyes, and not through the eyes of his companions. He was devoid of sympathy. . . . Such love and hatred ought not to be.[18]

In a letter written to Mrs. Shaw one month later, Lawrence again compares his relativistic viewpoint with Doughty's fixed point:

> Search my book through, and you will hardly find an assertion which is not immediately qualified; and certainly not an assertion which is not . . . eventually qualified. It's due to an absence of the fixed point from which Doughty radiated. My views are like my photographs of Jidda: the edges, even of the sharpest, are just modulated off, so that you can't put a pin point on them. Drawn, not in line, but in tone. Atmospheric. It's the difference between impressionism and the classical.[19]

In the same letter, Lawrence sums up his criticism of Doughty as Victorian judge of the Arabs: "Who are we to judge? I don't believe even God can." In 1923 he writes about Doughty that "A bigger man would not read the *Morning Post*" (*L,* 438). David Garnett clarifies this comment with a footnote: "The simplicity of Doughty's patriotism, which was without reservations, was not possible to Lawrence after the Peace Conference." To this we might add that Lawrence shows no sign of this simple patriotism before the conference, either. Because Lawrence lacks the fixed point of Victorian pride, *Seven Pillars* becomes contradictory, "atmospheric," and contains a more subtle drama than that involved in the works of Doughty[20] and Kinglake: He traces the absorption of himself into Arab culture and his subsequent realization that he has become neither English nor Arab, that he sees the West with new eyes "which destroyed it all for me." This is not to say, however, that Lawrence becomes fully like Conrad's Kurtz and ever abandons entirely his Western identity. E. M. Forster, who knew him very well, makes this point clearly in *Abinger Harvest*:

> He was, of course, devoted to the Arab cause. Yet when it triumphed he felt he had let down both his own countrymen and the foreigner by aping foreign ways, and became more English than ever. To regard him as "gone native" is wrong. He belonged body and soul to our islands. And he should have been happier in olden days, when a man could feel surer that he was fighting for his own hearth, and this terrible modern mix-up had not begun. (170)

To trace how far "this terrible modern mix-up" of cultures—also ex-emplified, in the case of Englishmen and Italians, in the Forster novels *Where Angels Fear to Tread* and *A Room with a View*—and the lack of a fixed point of cultural pride took its toll on Lawrence, we have only to compare his view of the Arabs with Doughty's, note his attraction to them, and then examine the drama resulting from this attraction.

In the chapter on Semitic religiosity, the Arabs appear to think and see like Doughty, according to Lawrence's view of him, although Lawrence does not make the direct connection:

> Semites had no half-tones in their register of vision. They were a people of primary colours, or rather of black and white, who saw the world always in contour. They were a dogmatic people, despising doubt, our modern crown of thorns. They did not understand our metaphysical dif-ficulties, our introspective questionings. They knew only truth and untruth, belief and unbelief, without our hesitating retinue of finer shades. (*S,* 38)

Like Doughty, the Arabs see in sharp photographs according to Law-rence, whereas Lawrence himself, wearing the "modern crown of thorns," sees the fine gradations of color of the impressionistic late Victorians. This passage comes almost wholly into *Seven Pillars* from Lawrence's introduction to Doughty's book (or from *Seven Pillars* into Lawrence's introduction), revealing that the connection between Doughty and the nomads may not have been far from his mind. The Arabs are the "least morbid of peoples, they had accepted the gift of life unquestioningly, as axiomatic" (*S,* 38). In Lawrence's preface, Doughty is "never morbid, never introspective." Now we understand Lawrence's dislike of Dickens (*L,* 735), who tends to see moral issues in terms of black and white, like Doughty.

But, as much as Lawrence is unlike his description of the Arabs, he feels a powerful attraction to what he sees as their habits of renunciation and austerity: "But at last Dahoum drew me: 'Come and smell the very sweetest scent of all,' and we went into the main lodging, to the gaping window sockets of its eastern face, and there drank with open mouths of the effortless, empty, eddyless wind of the desert, throbbing past. . . . 'This,' they told me, 'is the best: it has no taste' " (*S,* 40). Lawrence's identification of himself with this passage is evident from its highly col-ored aesthetic style and the mention of Dahoum, whom he names openly nowhere else in the book.

In Lawrence's presentation, the God of the Bedouin seems to be
superior to the distant God of Christianity because He is more familiar:

> The Beduin could not look for God within him: he was too sure that
> he was within God. He could not conceive anything which was or was
> not God, Who alone was great; yet there was a homeliness, an everyday-
> ness of this climatic Arab God, who was their eating and their fighting
> and their lusting, the commonest of their thoughts, their familiar
> resource and companion, in a way impossible to those whose God is so
> wistfully veiled from them by despair of their carnal unworthiness of
> Him and by the decorum of formal worship. (S, 40–41)

Further, according to Lawrence, a Bedouin tribesman's

> sterile experience robbed him of compassion and perverted his human
> kindness to the image of the waste in which he hid. Accordingly he hurt
> himself, not merely to be free, but to please himself. There followed a
> delight in pain, a cruelty which was more to him than goods. The desert
> Arab found no joy like the joy of voluntarily holding back. He found lux-
> ury in abnegation, renunciation, self-restraint. (S, 41)

Lawrence, swinging such a people "on an idea as on a cord," brought up
a great wave "till it reached its crest, and toppled over and fell at Damascus" (S, 42–43). He expresses the hope that "The wash of that wave,
thrown back by the resistance of vested things [read the French] will
provide the matter of the following wave, when in fullness of time the
sea shall be raised once more" (S, 43). The heightened style, comprising
rich metaphors and crests of waves of excitement, indicates Lawrence's
pleasure in these features of the Arab "veil." Later he expands the idea of
renunciation to include servitude, which, like pain, was another of his
own predilections: "Servitude, like other conduct, was profoundly modified to Eastern minds by their obsession with the antithesis between
flesh and spirit. These lads took pleasure in subordination; in degrading
the body; so as to throw into greater relief their freedom in equality of
mind: almost they preferred servitude as richer in experience than
authority, and less binding in daily care" (S, 466). Lawrence, attracted to
the Bedouin—as opposed to the town Arabs—in some ways but still
unable to see in terms of black and white as he says they do, paints a
largely favorable picture of them.

Doughty, who does see in those terms, also prefers the Bedouin to the
town Arabs but paints a more unfavorable picture of the Bedouin: He col-

lides head-on with those who think like himself in most respects but hold different religious views. Unlike Lawrence, he could never praise Allah at the expense of his God. In Arabia, although liking many things about the Bedouin way of life, he sees "the bitterness and blight of a fanatical religion, in every place."[21] Christianity "were fain to cast her arms about the human world, sealing all men one brotherhood with a virginal kiss of meekness and charity," but "the Mohammedan chain-of-credulities is an elation of the soul, breathing of God's favour only to the Moslemin: and shrewdness out of her cankered bowels to all the world besides."[22] Like Kinglake, Doughty may criticize individual Christians, but he never admits Islam to a spiritual equality with Christianity nor understands that in his attitude toward Islam he is as dogmatic as he claims the Moslems are in their attitude toward Christianity. Instead of engendering in Doughty an attraction to or understanding of the Bedouin, their fatalism and renunciation offend his Victorian ideal of progress: "[The] nomads lie every day of their lives upon their hungry maws, waiting for the mercy of Ullah: this is the incurious misery of human minds faint with the hunger of generations grown barren in the desert."[23] It is no wonder that Doughty's surprisingly liberal contemporary, Sir Richard Francis Burton, a greater Arabist than either Doughty or Lawrence, decided that Doughty's book taught, if nothing else, "the need for a certain pliancy in opinion, religious and political, in a traveller."[24]

Unlike Doughty, Lawrence was a post-Christian, and he was divided over the value of technology, using new devices to destroy the railroad that was bringing progress into Hejaz (and that had been envisioned by Doughty in *Arabia Deserta*). In replying to Herbert Read's criticism of *Seven Pillars,* Lawrence writes: "I entirely repudiate his suggestion that one race is better than another. That is the purest jingoism and Morning Postliness" (*L,* 550). This remark applies equally to the difference between Lawrence and Doughty. Rather than a sweeping condemnation of Doughty, a victim of his time and of a certain conditioned mentality (but who was also influenced by the Arabs far more than he admitted),[25] Lawrence's criticism shows his own modernistic relativity, a vision that cost him dearly.

The Colonizer Who Refused

In a telling passage that was eliminated from the final edition, Lawrence compares himself to Vickery, another Englishman of "The second, the cleaner class," like Doughty. Lawrence says that he keeps apart from the

Arabs in spirit, though not in manner, because he fears that they would see through the "legend of our greatness." Vickery, on the other hand, feels condescension toward the "natives" rather than self-deprecation before them:

> Vickery tended to be a regal boon companion, and risked earning their contempt by showing an unconscious condescension. To this society of Sheiks and Sherifs with their sense of personal dignity, he came fresh from years in Government circles, where he had experienced servility and rebellious insolence, but never friendship. His examples of native authority had been clerks or officials, not men born to power, and the veil of office as subtle and impermeable as our veil of flesh, lay between him and the people. For this difficulty the East preferred stupid Englishmen as governors. The brilliant sometimes guessed, and then were dangerous, but it salved a little the hurt native self-respect to fool the others. The first meeting in native dress with an Englishman, witnessing that awful blankness in his eye, which saw, not a fellow man, but a landscape or local colour, had illuminated my dark places. Use would either impress his opinion to the ruin of my self-respect, or it would have brought resentful violence in assertion of a common humanity. It led me to a constant reading of the Houhynyms [sic], whether I was dressed Arab or English fashion, but that grace was because I inhabited the same body under another envelope, and could always laugh. (Oxford text, 55)

Albert Memmi points out that "another sign of the colonizer's depersonalization is what one might call the mark of the plural. The colonized is never characterized in an individual manner; he is entitled only to drown in an anonymous collectivity."[26] Like John Howard Griffin, the author of *Black Like Me,* who had his skin dyed black in order to experience the feelings of an African-American in the South, Lawrence had direct personal experience of what it felt like to be condescended to by other Englishmen who thought he was an Arab, as this passage shows. How well he understands the feeling of an Arab in this position, who is regarded as a "landscape or local colour," is apparent. In Vickery, Lawrence has described the Anglo-Indian social club members who Fielding confronts in *A Passage to India.* Like Fielding, he sees too deeply to practice their prejudices at this early stage; later, like Fielding, he is to find himself alienated from the other culture and becomes more English than ever, as Forster points out. Here Lawrence can laugh at the comic situation by which one nation can regard itself as Houyhnhnms and everyone else as Yahoos. But later Lawrence will say that he has prostituted himself to Yahoos in the form of the Arabs.

After noting the incongruity of the Australian Lewis, who feels superior to all brown men although "he was browner by far than my new followers," Lawrence launches into a precise description of Rahail ("a freebuilt, sturdy fellow, too fleshy for the life we were to lead, but for that the more tolerant of pains. His face was high-coloured; his cheeks a little full and low-pouched, almost pendent" [*S*, 346]), proving that he does not see the Arabs as "local colour" but as individuals. All of his Arab portraits reveal this same particularity, especially in physical features. The fact that Lawrence does not portray anyone—Arab or British, including himself—in the book as a fully rounded character has more to do with his artistic aims and abilities than with his spiritual outlook on the Arabs. He notices clearly physical differences but never enters fully into the mind of anyone but himself—and fails there as well.

Like Fielding, Lawrence sees past the barriers between colonizer and colonized and finds the situation humiliating when not openly humorous: "It was humiliating to find that our book-experience of all countries and ages still left us prejudiced like washerwomen, but without their verbal ability to get on terms with strangers" (*S*, 346). We should remember that Lawrence is of Irish ancestry and naturally feels more sympathy with the colonized than do Forster's Turtons, for example, although not more than Fielding. Dennis Porter is right that sometimes "Lawrence shows no critical awareness of that nineteenth-century European discourse on race in general that he reproduces, a discourse that transmitted the doctrine of national characteristics, fixed ethnic identities, and transported essences that were enabling or disabling for individual members of a given group."[27] But the important point is that although Lawrence sometimes generalizes about the British, the French, the Arabs, and others in the unfortunate manner typical of his and earlier periods, few other people of that era could have written a passage like the following:

> Arab processes were clear, Arab minds moved as logically as our own,
> with nothing radically incomprehensible or different, except the premiss:
> there was no excuse or reason, except our laziness or ignorance, whereby
> we could call them inscrutable or Oriental, or leave them misunderstood.
> (*S*, 220)

Lawrence thus represents a considerable advance, if a partial one, from the stereotypical cultural generalizations of the past in the direction of genuine cultural relativity.

Lawrence's dilemma is indeed strange. He leads an anticolonial movement against the Turks, who have colonized the Arabs for centuries, and comes to sympathize more and more with the Arab antipathy to Turkish oppression; yet, as the agent of a British movement that will culminate in European domination of the Arabs, he must act out the role of colonialist. Seen in this light, Lawrence winds up in what Memmi describes as the position of the "colonizer who refuses":

> A colonizer who rejects colonialism does not find a solution for his anguish in revolt. If he does not eliminate himself as a colonizer, he resigns himself to a position of ambiguity. If he spurns that extreme measure, he contributes to the establishment and confirmation of the colonial relationship. It is understandable that it is more convenient to accept colonization and to travel the whole length of the road from colonial to colonialist.
>
> A colonialist is, after all, only a colonizer who agrees to be a colonizer. By making his position explicit, he seeks to legitimize colonialization. This is a more logical attitude, materially more coherent than the tormented dance of the colonizer who refuses and continues to live in a colony.[28]

We cannot dismiss Lawrence's worries over this situation as the superficial and hypocritical complaints of one who has deeper psychological problems, or *Seven Pillars* reduces to a casebook of abnormal psychology when in fact it is a very brilliant and valuable document of the many problems of the spirit attendant on World War I. Lawrence, after all, is in Arabia because of the war, not because he wanted to settle there himself. The best compromise he could work out is that of the "colonizer who refuses." Such a person is in the position of seeing through two veils at once, and Lawrence knows that he is in this position:

> You guessed rightly that the Arab appealed to my imagination. It is the old, old civilisation, which has refined itself clear of household gods, and half the trappings which ours hastens to assume. The gospel of bareness in materials is a good one, and it involves apparently a sort of moral bareness too. They think for the moment, and endeavour to slip through life without turning corners or climbing hills. In part it is a mental and moral fatigue, a race trained out, and to avoid difficulties they have to jettison so much that we think honourable and grave: and yet without in any way sharing their point of view, I think I can understand it enough to look at myself and other foreigners from their direction, and without condemning it. I know I'm a stranger to them, and always will be; but I

cannot believe them worse, any more than I could change their ways. (*L*, 244)

Lawrence was fully capable of seeing the British, including himself, with Arab eyes; his position forced him to do so. He must himself seek out Gasim, his lost servant, for

> My shirking the duty would be understood, because I was a foreigner: but that was precisely the plea I did not dare set up, while I yet presumed to help these Arabs in their own revolt. It was hard, anyway, for a stranger to influence another people's national movement, and doubly hard for a Christian and a sedentary person to sway Moslem nomads. I should make it impossible for myself if I claimed, simultaneously, the privileges of both societies. (*S*, 254)

Lawrence is like a white man who is somehow placed in the position of aiding a "black power" movement; he constantly charts his forced immersion into Arab mores and the effect this had on him, without totally understanding it.

Knightley and Simpson quote Lawrence's *Twenty-Seven Articles*, a cultural primer on the Arabs that he wrote for the benefit of British servicemen in the Near East as evidence of his manipulation of Arab customs for his own ends, in order to demonstrate that he cared only for these "sinister" ends ("biffing the French out of Syria") and not for the Arab movement at all. Yet they ignore the implications of the clear warning he gives at the end of Article 20:

> If you wear Arab things at all, go the whole way. Leave your English friends and customs on the coast, and fall back on Arab habits entirely. It is possible, starting thus level with them, for the European to beat the Arabs at their own game, for we have stronger motives for our action, and put more heart into it than they. If you can surpass them, you have taken an immense stride toward complete success, but the strain of living and thinking in a foreign language, the savage food, strange clothes, and still stranger ways, with the complete loss of privacy and quiet, and the impossibility of ever relaxing your watchful imitation of the others for months on end, provide such an added stress to the ordinary difficulties of dealing with the Bedu, the climate, and the Turks, that this road should not be chosen without serious thought.[29]

In the end, Lawrence is as much manipulated by Arab society as he manipulates individual Arabs: hence his feeling of having "prostituted" himself. Especially (but not only) because they are operating within a colonial system, neither Fielding nor Lawrence ultimately succeeds in bridging the cultures.

Foundations of Cultural Clash: Chapters 1–7

The very title, *Seven Pillars of Wisdom,* of Lawrence's book reveals the complex mixture of East and West that makes up its contents. The Bible is both an Eastern book (in its origins) and a Western book (in its translations and immense influence), and the phrase that supplies Lawrence's title comes directly from Prov. 9:1, "Wisdom hath builded her house, she hath hewn out her seven pillars." There are other biblical resonances as well, for in Deut. 1:13 and Exod. 18:21 leaders of the people of Israel are said to have *seven* qualities: wisdom, understanding, experience, ability, fear of God, trustworthiness, and incorruptibility. And we must not forget the "Five Pillars of Faith" of Islam either. Further, as Lawrence points out (*L,* 514), the phrase implies "a complete edifice of knowledge" because "The figure 'seven' implies completeness in the Semitic languages." Lawrence is certainly right about this, for in Hebrew *seven* is *sheva,* and *full, save'ah,* derives from the same root. On the other hand, just as the title indicates a full, or completed, building, it also implies a ruin lying in the desert along the lines of Percy Bysshe Shelley's poem "Ozymandias." The degree to which Lawrence felt he failed in building this edifice according to the seven desirable qualities is also indicated in the subtitle, "A Triumph," which is certainly ironic if one considers the bitter personal as opposed to triumphant military events.

Similarly, the motto "the sword also means cleanness and death" is a multilingual pun, for *Feisal* in Arabic means *sword.* The introductory poem shares the same exotic, un-English fullness of phrase and aspiration, and in it the revolt is compared to "an inviolate house" based on seven pillars of freedom, which is however shattered "unfinished" in this case by Lawrence's own Western, assertive will as a monument to his unfulfilled love of the dead S. A. (However, in the epilogue to the book, which is couched in the same high romantic tone as the title, motto, and introductory poem, Lawrence contradictorily claims that the revolt was not completed because of "the exhaustion of my springs of action" rather than by his willed choice.) The chapter on "Strangeness and Pain" echoes this high romantic tone that on the one hand glorifies exotic Eastern adventures and on the other is undercut by its content: the toll his adventures took on the Western Lawrence. The feeling throughout this introductory matter is of an attraction to the East but also a negative realization that the revolt did not end for Lawrence as it should have, that his Western self has brought him back down to earth even as he writes in as highly colored a style as possible.

The mixed tone of this preliminary but retrospective material appears most clearly in the introductory chapter of the Oxford text:

> I meant to make a new nation, to restore a lost influence, to give twenty millions of Semites the foundation on which to build an inspired dream-palace of their national thoughts. . . .
>
> . . . All the subject provinces of our Empire to me were not worth one dead English boy. If I have restored to the East some self-respect, a goal, ideals: if I have made the standard rule of white over red more exigent, I have fitted those peoples in a degree for the new commonwealth in which the dominant races will forget their brute achievements, and white and red and yellow and brown and black will stand up together without side-glances in the service of the world. (Oxford text, 1)

When Lawrence speaks of making "a new nation" and "an inspired dream-palace," his prose becomes high romantic, revealing the Lawrence who is the "music-maker, maker of dreams" of the O'Shaughnessy "Ode" that he read in his *Oxford Book of English Verse* during the campaign; when he speaks of "self-respect," the "service of the world," and "one dead English boy," he reveals the Kiplingesque British schoolmaster in him: We have both Arab and British patriotism side by side here, the romantic Arab tone somewhat higher pitched and more exotic, the British flatter and more clichéd but still powerfully felt and expressed.

In this introductory chapter,[30] Lawrence's retrospective balance between his cultural and political loyalties is more evenly stated than in the rest of the opening book of *Seven Pillars,* in which he describes Arab mores and religion and the political history of the revolt in the most sympathetic terms. In the opening book, he takes the position of the colonized people, understands their psychological defenses against their traditional colonizer, the Turks, and almost projects himself into Arab shoes: "The Arabs would not give up their rich and flexible tongue for crude Turkish. . . . The knowledge that his religion was his own, and that only he was perfectly qualified to understand and practice it, gave every Arab a standard by which to judge the banal achievements of the Turk" (*S,* 45). The Turks even appear corrupt from within, in Lawrence's presentation: "Medical examination of some batches of Turkish prisoners found nearly half of them with unnaturally acquired venereal disease. . . . The Turkish peasantry of Anatolia were dying of their military service" (*S*, 56). In contrast, Arab youths "slake one another's few needs in their own clean bodies" (*S*, 30). Turkish venereal disease (and not homosexuality, except when it amounts to rape) becomes an emblem of corrupt rule. The idea is that Feisal's movement (which represents cleanness and romantic death, according to the motto) and Lawrence's love for S. A. are essentially pure-hearted, idealistic phenomena, whereas Turkish colonial rule is corrupt in practice and conception.

By contrast with Arab cleanness, the English themselves appear corrupt in Lawrence's opening portraits of the men with whom he worked in Cairo, especially in the Oxford text (as Meyers and O'Donnell correctly point out), but the final edition's characterizations are critical enough. Ronald Storrs appears in the final edition as one who could have achieved more brilliantly "had he been able to deny himself the world, and to prepare his mind and body with the sternness of an athlete for a great fight" (*S*, 57). The portraits of all the "Intrusives" of the Arab Bureau except Hogarth, Lawrence's mentor and the first in a series of father figures, are carefully balanced between praise and criticism. Lawrence brings up the specters of the devastating British failures at Gallipoli and Kut and (until the arrival of Allenby) scarcely sings an epic of British arms. Sir Archibald Murray and his chief of staff, Lynden Bell, come off as badly as the slow-witted and blundering Turkish commanders Lawrence later derides.

He closes this introductory book with a clear statement of his spiritual—rather than coldly political or military—involvement in the Arabs' revolt against Turkey:

> . . . I justified myself by my confidence in the success of the Arab Revolt if properly advised. I had been a mover in its beginning; my hopes lay in it. The fatalistic subordination of a professional soldier (intrigue being unknown in the British army) would have made a proper officer sit down and watch his plan of campaign wrecked by men who thought nothing of it, and to whose spirit it made no appeal. *Non nobis, domine.* (*S*, 63)

To Akaba: Books 1–4 (Chapters 8–54)

In the beginning of book 1, which details Lawrence's initiation into the adventure, "the heat of Arabia came out like a drawn sword and struck us speechless" (*S*, 65). This unfamiliar heat signals the beginning of the conflict between the Westerner and the new environment. Like the fever that Marlow experiences in his descent into the "heart of darkness," the heat of Arabia is "the playful paw-strokes of the wilderness, the preliminary trifling before the more serious onslaught which came in due course";[31] although Jidda was "a remarkable town," its "atmosphere was oppressive, deadly" (*S,* 72–73). In a symbolic touch worthy of Conrad, Lawrence uses the captured Turkish band's rendition of the German "Hymn of Hate" to introduce the theme of the jumble of cultures: "[N]o one could recognize a European progression in it at all" (*S,* 75). But Lawrence, at least in the Oxford text, enjoys the music nonetheless: "There was a satisfying ring in that tune played in Jidda to the leaders of the new revolt in Islam by the captured band of the Turkish governor of the holy places" (Oxford text, 17).

Lawrence wrote Edward Garnett that his best writing is to be found in the long ride up to Feisal that follows (*L,* 513), and in fact that section of the book contains outstanding travel writing. Romantic hope and diction infuse the whole account; the new scenery, language, and customs become delightful toys for Lawrence, despite the hint of unknown danger beneath the surface. He mounts Sherif Ali's "own splendid riding camel," whose every detail of embroidery he notes with admiration and pleasure. He travels the Mecca pilgrimage road "down which, for uncounted generations, the people of the north had come to visit the Holy City . . . and it seemed that the Arab Revolt might be in a sense a return pilgrimage, to take back to the north, to Syria, an ideal for an ideal, a belief in liberty for the past belief in revelation" (*S,* 78). In the manner of Doughty, Lawrence transposes contemporary Arabic into archaic English, as in his conversation with Tafas. But always under the beauty and interest lurks a sinister note: "The particles of sand were clean and polished, and caught the blaze of sun like little diamonds in a reflection so fierce, that after a while I could not endure it" (*S,* 83).

At this point, Lawrence still "had no sense of how to ride" and feels the strangeness of his surroundings at every step, for "The last two years I had spent in Cairo, at a desk all day or thinking hard in a little over-crowded office full of distracting noises. . . . In consequence the novelty of the change was severe, since time had not been given me to gradually accustom myself to the pestilent beating of the Arabian sun, and the long monotony of camel pacing" (*S,* 84). He "was always falling asleep in the saddle, to wake a few seconds later suddenly and sickeningly, as I clutched by instinct at the saddle post to recover my balance. . . . It was too dark, and the forms of the country were too neutral, to hold my heavy-lashed, peering eyes" (*S,* 85). He can eat only a little of the Arabs' unleavened dough cake "on this, my first attempt." Yet he is interested "to find myself in a new country" in which the colors are "joyously blended" (S, 86).

Lawrence comes on Feisal suddenly: "I felt at first glance that this was the man I had come to Arabia to seek—the leader who would bring the Arab Revolt to full glory" (S, 91). There follows an exotic and embroidered description of Feisal. In the best colored tones of Anglo-Arabian writing, Lawrence has built suspense about this meeting by means of rich metaphors and detail and thus justifies it artistically. His attraction to the adventure comes through plainly on these pages.

Lawrence now gives an account of the "bitter taste of the Turkish mode of war" as he creates sympathy for the Arabs as an oppressed people. He makes no attempt to hide Feisal's unreasonable qualities, but in sum, "if he had the strength to realize his dreams he would go very far, for he was wrapped up in his work and lived for nothing else" (S, 97). To the tribes, Feisal like his father is "heroic" (S, 98). But Feisal suspects British intentions:

> "You see," he explained, "we are now of necessity tied to the British. We are delighted to be their friends, grateful for their help, expectant of our future profit. But we are not British subjects. We would be more at ease if they were not such disproportionate allies. . . . I am not a Hejazi by upbringing; and yet, by God, I am jealous for it. And though I know the British do not want it, yet what can I say, when they took the Sudan, also not wanting it? They hunger for desolate lands, to build them up; and so, perhaps, one day Arabia will seem to them precious. Your good and my good, perhaps they are different, and either forced good or forced evil will make a people cry with pain. Does the ore admire the flame which transforms it?" (S, 99–100)

After this eloquent presentation of the Arab case against colonialism through the mouth of Feisal, Lawrence's British veil suddenly swings into place. He comments favorably on the weakness of the Arabs and their natural antipathy to the centralized state: "Were it otherwise, we should have had to pause before evoking in the strategic centre of the Middle East new national movements of such abounding vigour" (S, 101). Negative capability: Lawrence himself writes up an attack on British imperialism and then in the next breath speaks as a British agent. Here we refers to the British; later, as he becomes more involved in the revolt, we will signify the Arabs. The story of Seven Pillars is largely that of this shift in the meaning of we, of the transformation of "Lawrence" to "Aurens" and back again, and finally in The Mint to Ross and then Shaw. Whenever the British side of Lawrence's dual role appears, his upper lip stiffens and his prose shows it by becoming flatter, less exalted, less personal. He must switch his eyes "straight to my brain" in his British capacity "that I might note a thing or two the more clearly by contrast with the former mistiness" (*S*, 102). His romantic self is impressionistic. In his British mood, he sees clearly and stands apart from "romantics": "I believed in the Arab movement, and was confident, before ever I came, that in it was the idea to tear Turkey to pieces. . . . By noting down something of these romantics in the hills about the Holy Cities I might gain the sympathy of Cairo" (*S*, 102). Yet a fight for freedom appeals to him even in his cooler British mood: "There was among the tribes in the fighting zone a nervous enthusiasm common, I suppose, to all national risings, but strangely disquieting to one from a land so long delivered that national freedom had become like water in our mouths, tasteless" (*S*, 105–6).

Lawrence leaves Feisal, having been attracted to the movement with one side of his personality but having finally assessed it in purely British terms. But when he returns to "civilization" in the form of the ship *Suva*, captained by Boyle, a strange thing happens: He already finds himself identified as less than British by an Anglo-Arabian:

He had done much in the beginning of the revolt, and was to do much more for the future: but I failed to make a good return impression. I was travel-stained and had no baggage with me. Worst of all I wore a native head-cloth, put on as a compliment to the Arabs. Boyle disapproved.

Our persistence in the hat (due to a misunderstanding of the ways of heat-stroke) had led the East to see significance in it, and after long thought their wisest brains concluded that Christians wore the hideous thing that its broad brim might interpose between their weak eyes and the uncongenial sight of God. So it reminded Islam continually that God was miscalled and misliked by Christians. The British thought this prejudice reprehensible (quite unlike our hatred of a head-cloth) one to be corrected at any price. If the people would not have us hatted, they should not have us any way. Now as it happened I had been educated in Syria before the war to wear the entire Arab outfit when necessary without strangeness, or sense of being socially compromised. The skirts were a nuisance in running up stairs, but the head-cloth was even convenient in such a climate. (*S*, 109)

Lawrence's desire to wear Arab clothing goes beyond mere playing to the Arab gallery, as the photographs he posed for Lowell Thomas's photographer Harry Chase reveal: Like the liberal anti-imperialist Blunt, he enjoyed the romance of Arab gear and found it useful. Because of this liberality, he begins his adventures at some distance from the overt colonizers of "the second class," like Boyle.

In the following books, Lawrence charts his forced immersion into Arab mores and even thought processes, abetted by his own romantic desire for strangeness. Thus, he agrees "very gladly" when Feisal asks him to wear Arab robes while in camp (S, 126). In the description of the march on Owais, it is "we" who "filled the valley to its banks with our flashing stream" (S, 141), referring to himself and the Arabs. Sir Mark Sykes realized the strong strain of Arab sympathy in Lawrence. As early as 22 July 1917 he speaks of eventual Arab independence under Entente tutelage and adds about Lawrence: "Let him consider this as he hopes for the people he is fighting for."[32]

During the march on Wejh, Lawrence feels gloriously happy: "[T]he freshness of the day and the life and happiness of the Army gave inspiration to the march and brought the future bubbling out of us without pain" (S, 149). In the Oxford text, he speaks at this point of the "moral greatness of the march up-country" (Oxford text, 53), with Xenophon's *Anabasis* clearly in mind. He even sacrifices his beloved privacy for the revolt because "the work suffered by the creation of such a bar between the leaders and the men" (S, 157). His characterization of Sherif Nasir has the ring of chivalric title: "He was the opener of roads, the forerunner of Feisal's movement . . . and from the beginning to end all that could be told of him was good" (S, 160). At the same time he can speak with pleasure of "Englishmen and Arabs" dining and discussing together (S, 144).

When he discusses the blacks in Feisal's camp, we get a passage that Aldington cites as an example of what he terms Lawrence's "feeling of racial superiority": "It was as with the negroes, tom-tom playing themselves to red madness each night under the ridge. Their faces, being clearly different from our own, were tolerable; but it hurt that they should possess exact counterparts of all our bodies" (S, 171). This passage undoubtedly contains a negative, stereotypical element, and Lawrence would probably not have expressed himself this way were he writing today instead of 70 years ago. But instead of blind racism, this passage actually indicates very clearly Lawrence's shock of immersion into a foreign culture. Compare Marlow's statement on the tribesmen in Africa: "It was unearthly and the men were . . . No, they were not inhuman . . . that was the worst of it—this suspicion of their not being inhuman."[33] Alan Sandison writes this about the Conrad passage above:

> Confrontation with the primitive, unorganized native discloses a horrible and unsuspected affinity between him and the sophisticated alien which makes clear just how much of an assumption, how much of a carefully erected, entirely superficial thing, individual identity is. One's own moral organization depends on the degree of social organization experienced environmentally. And when this is exposed as brutally as it is by these primitive people the whole basis of integrity is undermined.[34]

What Lawrence experiences here is not unusual to his own psyche, though, characteristically, he thinks it is: The tom-tom players call up "something hateful to my pride." According to Sandison, this experience is common to all those Englishmen who venture into unknown and more primitive environments in British imperial literature; the result, as Sandison notes, is a threat to their identities. They recognize themselves in the tribesmen rather than feeling "above" them. As the book progresses, Lawrence the Oxford aesthete experiences more and more frequently this journey into the heart of his own savage darkness and becomes more and more capable of unquestioning brutality, as we see especially in the massacre of the Turks at Tafas in the last book of *Seven Pillars*. He increasingly identifies himself with the warlike values of the Bedouin and outlaw town Arabs and pays the price for this affinity. He begins to wonder just who he is and what, if anything, in his beliefs separates him from the Bedouin, who in Lawrence's time were still living by a warrior code. It is the same journey Kurtz makes; if Kurtz goes farther, it is because he has no Allenby—and no conscience—to lean on. This is one source of Lawrence's final feeling that he has prostituted himself to Yahoos, when he frees himself from the movement and steps back to take a good look at it and himself in it, while still however under its influence. In *Lord Jim*, Conrad—in the voice of Marlow—concludes that without firm faith in the idea of a mission, giving one's life to men of brown, yellow, or black skins "was like selling your soul to a brute" (338–39), the very phrase Lawrence uses, and Lawrence corresponded with Conrad and read most of his books. Because Lawrence lacks the colonialist's faith and sense of mission and is also unable to believe in Western superiority (terming, for instance, the battles on the European front "murder war"), he ultimately becomes a nihilist.

The execution of Hamed (also discussed in chapter 3 of this book), which he calls "Another Murder" (*S*, 182), is a way station on Lawrence's pilgrimage into mindless violence. A more subtle force operating on him in the same way is the key to the Arab war, preaching, which he terms

the "diathetic" element. Instead of merely advising Feisal or leading mil-
itarily, Lawrence must continually project himself into the minds of people fighting for their own national liberation: "[T]he diathetic for us
would be more than half the command" (S, 195). The nature of this war
itself pushes Lawrence more and more into his Arab role, and by chapter
36 he speaks of "the mental tug of war" between honesty to the Arabs
and loyalty to "my English masters" (S, 213), a phrase that indicates the
depth of Lawrence's estrangement from his own people even by this relatively early point in the narrative.

As Lawrence slides more deeply into involvement in the Arab movement, his character sketches become fuller and more subtle; in chapter
36, he amplifies his view of Abdullah, Feisal's brother. But as Blackmur
correctly comments, all of Lawrence's characters, British, Arab, Turkish,
and French, remain "asserted," external rather than internal, outlined
rather than portrayed in depth. Either they are obtuse like Lynden Bell,
heroic like Auda, corrupt like the Bey at Deraa, or noble like Nasir. But
this is because Lawrence wanted to write a broad background for his epic,
in which the spotlight shines fully only on his autobiographical self. His
characters remain the one or two dimensional creations of a William
Morris romance rather than the deeply realized studies of a modern
novel. Auda, for instance, in contrast to Feisal and Abdullah, appears in
Shaw's words as a "Verdi baritone," strong in war and comic in peace.
Instead of a fault, this is a natural result of Lawrence's literary aims and
his genre of poetic autobiography. But another, more practical, reason is
responsible for the lack of depth of some of Lawrence's characters: his
uncertain grasp of Arabic, which keeps him from appreciating all the
nuances of his Arab characters. Furthermore, his imperfect discourse prevents his full absorption into the other culture: "The fluency had a lack of
grammar, which made my talk a perpetual adventure for my hearers.
Newcomers imagined I must be the native of some unknown illiterate
district; a shot-rubbish ground of disjected Arabic parts of speech" (S,
233). Despite this, "The long ride to Akaba had made companions of our
minds and bodies. The hazardous goal was in our thoughts, day and
night; consciously and unconsciously we were training ourselves; reduc-
ing our wills to the single purpose which oftenest engrossed these odd
moments of talk about an evening fire" (S, 260). Where he once could
not eat simple dough cake, he now has no trouble in downing "the
boiled, upturned heads, propped on their severed stumps of neck, so that
the ears, brown like old leaves, flapped out in the rich surface" (S, 266),
parts of the flayed lamb offered him during a tribal feast.

This acclimatization is only the symptom of a deeper absorption in the Arab world that Lawrence suspects when he comments, looking ahead, that "After a successful capture of Akaba I would never again possess myself freely" (*S*, 276). Despite this prediction, Lawrence at this point still remains happy, hopeful, able to mock Auda's heroic style, even blow out his own camel's brains and laugh, but increasingly after Akaba he can hold less apart from the Arabs, and his Western identity becomes more uncertain. He becomes more than a mere adviser, commenting "Suffice it to say that since the march to Akaba I bitterly repented my entanglement in the movement, with a bitterness sufficient to corrode my inactive hours, but insufficient to make me cut myself clear of it. Hence the wobbling of my will, and endless, vapid complainings" (*S*, 552). Even at this point, before the taking of Akaba, Lawrence in the Oxford text wishes for a drastic way out of his confusion of loyalties and cultures: "A bodily wound would have been a grateful vent for my internal perplexities, a mouth through which my troubles might have found relief" (Oxford text, 100). Later he will hope for death in an air crash (*S*, 545). Typically, Lawrence does not explain exactly what his "internal perplexities" were or the full reasons for his intense despair. Joseph Conrad may understand Lawrence's dilemma with respect to the other culture better than Lawrence himself does. In his short story "Outpost of Progress" Conrad writes

> But the contact with pure, unmitigated savagery, with primitive nature and primitive man, brings sudden and profound trouble into the heart. To the sentiment of being alone of one's kind, to the clear perception of the loneliness of one's thoughts, one's sensations—to the negation of the habitual, which is safe, there is added the affirmation of the unusual, which is dangerous; a suggestion of things vague, uncontrollable, and repulsive, whose discomposing intrusion excites the imagination and tries the civilised nerves of the foolish and wise alike.[35]

In the clash between the epic quality of the revolt, which constitutes the Arab veil of Lawrence's personality, and the political and cultural reality of his alienation from it, Lawrence resorts to the same tool that Kinglake did for protection against unpleasantness: irony, directed against himself as well as others. In a conversation about astronomy, Lawrence tells Auda that Westerners "want the world's end" (*S*, 282). Auda, in an unusual display of wit, comments that "if the end of wisdom is to add star to star, our foolishness is pleasing." He undercuts Lawrence's strained desire for the absolute, and Lawrence allows him the last word. It is entirely characteristic of Lawrence that the conclusion of the Akaba campaign be undercut by the irony of his self-induced fall from his camel. As he recites a fin de siècle Ernest Dowson poem while waiting to be crushed by the charge of his companions' camels, after having sailed "grandly through the air" as the Kennington portrait shows (*S*, 302–3), we get a picture of the aesthete and intellectual totally out of place in his position and environment. Lawrence rarely allows himself to move into the heroic vein without qualification, and his irony helps him to keep a sense of who he is and what his position amounts to, if less successfully than Kinglake's.

In the capture of Aba el Lissan, "we were subject for the moment to the physical shame of success, a reaction of victory, when it became clear that nothing was worth doing, and that nothing worthy had been done" (*S*, 307). Similarly, the capture of Akaba results for the romantic, absolutist Lawrence who must always strive and never reach, in a feeling of meaninglessness: "In the blank light of victory we could scarcely identify ourselves. We spoke with surprise, sat emptily, fingered upon our white skirts; doubtful if we could understand or learn whom we were. Others' noise was a dreamlike unreality, a singing in ears drowned deep in water. . . . to-day each man owned his desire so utterly that he was fulfilled in it, and became meaningless" (*S*, 314). Now Lawrence eats the dust of discontent after having achieved his goal; later he will seek relief from "the almost insane tension of too-constant striving after an ideal" (Oxford text, 176). In Cairo he demands from Clayton not less but more free will: "There was much more I felt inclined to do, and capable of doing:—if he thought I had earned the right to be my own master" (*S*, 323). Later he will be "tired to death of free-will" (*S*, 502) and desire the subservient role of his Arab bodyguard. With the capture of Akaba, Lawrence's troubles are about to begin.

Beyond Akaba: Books 5–10 (Chapters 55–122)

As Lawrence advances deeper into his contact with the Bedouin, he realizes that there is more to their culture than bare renunciation. In the Wadi Rumm, he hears an old man who appears out of nowhere like Wordsworth's leech gatherer say that "The love is from God; and of God; and towards God." This one sentence "seemed to overturn my theories of the Arab nature" (*S*, 357). In contrast with the barren infertility of Lawrence's nihilism, here is another way out. This is Lawrence's Marabar Caves experience, but where Forster's Mrs. Moore learns in the caves that nihilism is the truth of the universe instead of Christianity's doctrine of all-embracing order, Lawrence here glimpses love and fertility amid the meaninglessness and confusion of politics, cultural clash, and war. In a telling comment that points to possible mutual influence, E. M. Forster finds in the Wadi Rumm passage a "lodestar" of compassion that "may lead us through the psychology of *Seven Pillars* as surely as Damascus led us northward through the geography."[36] But instead of Lawrence's conclusion, this incident represents only a momentary stage in his relations with the Arabs. As we will find later, the message of *Seven Pillars* in the end is not "God is love" but "God si love," the same message of jumbled meaninglessness that Mrs. Moore learns. Rather than a realization of the ideal of love between peoples, *Seven Pillars* speaks of the abortive attempt at that ideal. Unlike Forster and his character Fielding, who recognize the impasse but can be satisfied with something less than an absolute and do not despair, Lawrence becomes a nihilist.

However, on the way to the bridges over the Yarmuk River, Lawrence is happy: "I felt only that it was very gentle, very comfortable, that the air was happy, and my friends content. . . . There was no thought or care at all. My mind was as near stilled those days as ever in my life" (*S*, 402). Alone with the Arabs on a mission, Lawrence feels content. Lawrence was "admiring ourselves," referring to himself and the Arabs. Yet, *Seven Pillars* moves according to emotional wave crests and troughs, and Lawrence immediately notes that "to have generalized and called the Arabs pro-English, would have been a folly. Each stranger made his own poor bed among them" (*S*, 408).

In preaching to the Serahin, Lawrence strikes exactly the right note for the nomads: "[T]o be of the desert was, as they knew, a doom to wage unending battle with an enemy who was not of the world, nor life, nor anything, but hope itself; and failure seemed God's freedom to mankind. . . . Omnipotence and the Infinite were our two worthiest foemen" (*S*, 412). This is just one example of the kind of Faustian thinking that Lawrence learned from his reading of Herman Melville's *Moby Dick:* This might be Ahab speaking. Lawrence projects himself into Bedouin minds by fusing his Western striving for an impossible ideal with what he sees as the Eastern urge toward renunciation, and he loses himself in the speech: "[F]or once my picture-taking memory forgot its trade and only felt the slow humbling of the Serahin . . . and at last their flashing eagerness to ride with us, whatever the bourne." Despite Lawrence's dictum that "to the clear-sighted failure was the only goal," he feels "sick with failure" (*S*, 424) when the raid collapses owing to chance clumsiness. Although Lawrence does not always practice what he preaches, he has the ability to at least momentarily merge himself completely with the Arab movement.

As explained in my chapter 4, we are not sure what really happened at Deraa, but Lawrence's presentation of this incident connects directly to the theme of cultural clash as it appears in the rest of *Seven Pillars* as well. Lawrence tries to "avoid measuring myself against the pitiless Arab standard" but feels that at Deraa he has failed to measure up to that standard and that he is more deeply akin to the Arabs than he previously thought.

Lawrence's torture becomes "the earned wages of rebellion" (*S*, 13) against his Western self. In order to survive, he must suppress his British identity completely, crying out only in Arabic until he faints (*S*, 444), thus entering completely into his Arab role. Although according to the account in *Seven Pillars*, he successfully hid his true British identity, he feels "completely broken" by the torture and that "in Deraa that night the citadel of my integrity had been irrevocably lost" (*S*, 447). In a letter to Mrs. Charlotte Shaw, Lawrence confessed that he allowed himself to be raped when he could no longer stand the beating.[37] He refers to this when he writes, "I was being dragged about by two men, each disputing over a leg as though to split me apart: while a third man rode me astride. It was momentarily better than more flogging" (*S*, 445). Five months after Deraa, two members of Lawrence's bodyguard are whipped. One member of the guard, Awad, stands up to the beating, and Lawrence calls it off because "the Zaagi's shrill whip-strokes were too cruel for my taught imagination" (*S*, 486). But the other member, Mahmas, breaks down and cries. Lawrence comments,

> Arabs did not dissect endurance, their crown of manhood, into material and moral, making allowances for nerves. So Mahmas' crying was called fear, and when loosed, he crept out disgraced into the night to hide.
>   I was sorry for Awad: his hardness put me to shame. (*S*, 486)

The phrase "crown of manhood" is curiously similar to "citadel of my integrity." What probably happened to Lawrence at Deraa is that he submitted to, or felt that he had submitted to, a personal indignity like rape (as he wrote to Mrs. Shaw), probably thinking that this was the only way to protect his British identity, when he found that he could no longer bear the beating.[38] Thus, the Arab Revolt required him to sell or prostitute his physical as well as political integrity in its service. This is the dark underside of victory, the price that had to be paid. Lawrence feels that he was not as tough as he should have been in resisting the beating. Awad's hardness puts Lawrence to shame in comparison with his own performance at Deraa, and so in his own eyes he fails the test of the Bedouin standard for bearing pain.

Although Lawrence feels that he did not meet that standard, he accepts it, showing how much like a Bedouin (or like his image of a Bedouin) he has become. In speaking of his bodyguards, he stresses their attraction to pain: "Pain was to them a solvent, a cathartic, almost a decoration, to be fairly worn when they survived it" (*S, 466*). In both the Oxford and final texts, Lawrence admits his own masochistic pleasure in pain. In the Oxford text, Lawrence also writes that a part of him has "gone dead" as a result of this beating: His Western self has gone dead for the moment. However, we should note that 20 days later he is standing at Allenby's side in captured Jerusalem, enjoying "the supreme moment of the war" (*S, 453*) and comments on this in his synopsis, "I find healing in Jerusalem" (*S, 13*). Book 6, which contains the military failure at the Yarmuk bridge and Lawrence's parallel felt personal failure at Deraa, ends ironically with supreme British victory. Lawrence had to suppress his Western identity in order to help achieve a British victory, yet is revolted by his feeling that he has become too much like his bodyguards, who according to him, enjoy pain. He finds healing in assuming his Western identity as an officer in the British army again. The Deraa incident is therefore the peak, the climax of the drama of the two veils in which Lawrence is at once fully absorbed into the "strangeness and pain" that he sees as major components of the Arab veil and, as a puritanical Westerner, most repelled by that fact. In that incident, he is forced physically, spiritually, and symbolically to see through the two veils at once. As autobiographer, Lawrence has given us the chaotic, raw material of his feelings about this incident, but readers must try to assemble it into a coherent picture for themselves. As I have shown, I believe that one of the best ways of understanding it is in the context of Lawrence's perceived division between what he seems to present as the Eastern and Western components of his personality.

Although he does not overtly connect the Deraa incident and the theme of cultural clash, Lawrence in the very next chapter gives us the necessary clue to do so:

> Now I found myself dividing into parts. There was one which went on riding wisely, sparing or helping every pace of the wearied camel.

Another hovering above and to the right bent down curiously, and asked what the flesh was doing. The flesh gave no answer, for, indeed, it was conscious only of a ruling impulse to keep on and on; but a third garrulous one talked and wondered, critical of the body's self-inflicted labour, and contemptuous of the reason for effort. (*S, 452*)

This is exactly the same wording and the same effect that Lawrence in the first chapter described as the result of seeing through "the veils at once of two customs, two educations, two environments" (*S*, 32). But Lawrence does not spell this out, leaving us to find the connection. What Lawrence learned at Deraa is exactly what the alien environment teaches Kurtz. Having been forced to experience brutal actions that would normally have been morally impossible for him as a puritan and an Englishman to encounter in his usual Oxford environment, Lawrence discovers that he likes them to some degree. Like Kurtz, Lawrence learns that he

> lacked restraint in the gratification of his various lusts, and there was something wanting in him—some small matter which, when the pressing need arose, could not be found under his magnificent eloquence. . . . the wilderness found him out early, and had taken on him a terrible vengeance for the fantastic invasion. I think it whispered to him things about himself which he did not know, things of which he had no conception until he took counsel with the great solitude—and the whisper had proved irresistibly fascinating. It echoed loudly with him because he was hollow at the core.[39]

Is it not this same central hollowness that Lawrence tells us about in the chapter on himself?

> There was a special attraction in beginnings, which drove me into everlasting endeavour to free my personality from accretions and project it on a fresh medium, that my curiosity to see its naked shadow might be fed. The invisible self appeared to be reflected clearest in the still water of another man's yet incurious mind. . . . Much of my doing was from this egoistic curiosity. (*S, 566*)

Lawrence is a man who defines himself against the outside world. Consequently, when he is with the Arabs, he becomes an Arab; when sipping tea with Dawnay, British—or, to serve his special purposes, he plays an Arab before the British, or an Englishman before the Arabs. The actor gets lost among his roles.

Most of all, he wants to be told what to do and what to be. Hence his attraction to Allenby and earlier, Hogarth:

> Always in working I had tried to serve, for the scrutiny of leading was too prominent. Subjection to order achieved economy of thought, the painful, and was a cold-storage for character and Will, leading painlessly to the oblivion of activity. It was part of my failure never to have found a chief to use me. All of them, through incapacity or timidity or liking, allowed me too free a hand; as if they could not see that voluntary slavery was the deep pride of a morbid spirit, and vicarious pain its gladdest decoration. . . .
>
> Feisal was a brave, weak, ignorant spirit, trying to do work for which only a genius, a prophet or a great criminal, was fitted. I served him out of pity, a motive which degraded us both. Allenby came nearest to my longings for a master, but I had to avoid him, not daring to bow down for fear lest he show feet of clay with that friendly word which must shatter my allegiance. Yet, what an idol the man was to us. (S, 565)

The Oxford text makes this desire for outside control even more clear. In sum, "the truth was I did not like the 'myself' I could see and hear" (S, 566). Colin Wilson (in *The Outsider*) characterizes this type of man and particularly Lawrence as "the Outsider," one who cannot find his real self and can only desire control from the outside as a substitute for a real identity. Lawrence's ease in changing names and dropping identities, especially in connection with his surrendering to the drudgery of the ranks in *The Mint,* corroborates this view of him.

Much like Kurtz, who "could get himself to believe anything—anything" (*Heart of Darkness,* 65) and ends by believing in nothing, Lawrence finds that "the practice of our revolt fortified the nihilist attitude in me" (S, 468). Like a piece of pliable metal, Lawrence is bent back and forth between the two cultures until he snaps. He has no clear-cut self to oppose to this fluctuating motion. After Deraa, Lawrence does not care a "hoot" (S, 447) about the Arab movement, he says, and after Zeid foolishly spends the all-important British gold used to pay the Arab army, Lawrence decides to follow through in the hollow spirit of a games-player: "It might be fraud or it might be farce: no one should say that I could not play it" (S, 503). Also, "My will had gone and I feared to be alone, lest the winds of circumstance, or power, or lust, blow my empty soul away" (S, 502). Lawrence has in his own eyes failed the test of will at Deraa and has learned unpleasant things about himself, but his saving grace, the thing that prevents total abandonment à la Kurtz, is this sense of puritanical conscience, the fear of his soul being "blown away."

In the two last two books of *Seven Pillars,* the drama of the two veils reaches its culmination: Due to the combined participation of English and Arab troops, Lawrence sees the two cultures side by side. The fluctuations build to a crescendo: "In my English capacity I shared this view, but on my Arab side both agitation and battle seemed equally important, the one to serve the joint success, the other to establish Arab self-respect, without which victory would not be wholesome" (*S,* 539). Even his aesthetic perceptions have changed because of his immersion in the Arabs' culture: "For the rest they were a broad-faced, low-browed people, blunt-featured beside the fine-drawn Arabs whom generations of in-breeding had sharpened to a radiance ages older than the primitive, blotched, honest Englishmen. Continental soldiers seemed lumpish beside our lean-bred fellows: but against my supple Nejdis the British in their turn looked lumpish" (*S,* 544). The Continentals come out lowest in this scale, but "*my* [emphasis mine] supple Nejdis" top the British in beauty. At the same moment that he calls the Arabs "my," he refers to the British soldiers as "*our* [emphasis mine] lean-bred fellows," a small symptom of the cultural dichotomy in Lawrence's mind. Immediately after he states that the Arabs are more handsome than the British, without warning "a home-sickness came over me, stressing vividly my outcast life among these Arabs" (*S,* 544).

Now he tries to identify with England, the power for which he has traded "the citadel of my integrity": "We English, who lived years abroad among strangers, went always dressed in the pride of our remembered country, that strange entity which had no part with the inhabitants, for those who loved England most, often liked Englishmen least" (*S,* 544). Memmi notices a common characteristic of colonialists: "Having assigned to his homeland the burden of his own decaying grandeur, he expects it to respond to his hopes. He wants it to merit his confidence, to reflect on him the image of itself which he desires. . . . Often, by dint of hoping he ends up beginning to believe it."[40] Lawrence lacks even this consolation. In the Oxford text, he comments at this point that "We idealised our country so highly, that when we returned sometimes the reality fell too short of our dreams to be tolerable" (Oxford text, 228).

The fluctuations between the two veils become more rapid and disordered as the campaign reaches its climax:

[O]n this march to Damascus (and such it was already in my imagination) my normal balance had changed. I could feel the taut power of
Arab excitement behind me. The climax of the preaching of years had
come, and a united country was straining toward its historic capital. In
confidence that this weapon, tempered by myself, was enough for the
utmost of my purpose, I seemed to forget the English companions who
stood outside my idea in the shadow of ordinary war. I failed to make
them partners of my certainty. (*S,* 583)

In the midst of this completeness of the Arab veil, Lawrence's British
self slips back into place unexpectedly when he sees the two armies side
by side at Azrak:

[T]he wind in the dusty green branches played with such sounds as it
made in English trees. It told me I was tired to death of these Arabs;
petty incarnate Semites who attained heights and depths beyond our
reach, though not beyond our sight. They realized our absolute in their
unrestrained capacity for good and evil; and for two years I had prof-
itably shammed to be their companion. (*S,* 586)

Rather than a hypocritical glorification of or attack on one side or the
other, Lawrence gives us here the tortured confusion through which he
lived in the form of contradictory passages not more than three pages
apart. Sometimes he stands apart from both sides and views them from
a distance: "It was a thing typical, as instinct with our national character
as the babbling laughing turmoil over there was Arab. In their crises
one race drew in, the other spread" (*S,* 589). Here "our" is British,
although Lawrence clinically dissects both British and Arabs. In the
Oxford text at this point, "ourselves" sets Lawrence against the British:
"I was accustomed, callous now, to the Arab courage, for they were
fighting for their freedom, a very urgent end, but these English were
men as good as ourselves, but moved only by duty, or the mass-instinct
of industry" (Oxford text, 262). Later Lawrence is "jealous for the Arab
honour, in whose service I would go forward at all costs" (*S,* 624).

A peak of involvement in his Arab veil comes for Lawrence at the vil-
lage of Tafas in chapter 118. Back near Deraa 10 months after his own
torture there, Lawrence catalogs the Turkish atrocities against the villagers
of Tafas as a doubling of his own sufferings: "I looked close and saw the
body of a woman folded across it, bottom upwards, nailed there by a saw
bayonet whose haft stuck hideously into the air from between her naked

legs. She had been pregnant, and about her lay others, perhaps twenty in all, variously killed, but set out in accord with an obscene taste" (*S*, 631). Lawrence's recounting of atrocities is meant to justify the fact that "By my order we took no prisoners, for the only time in our war" (*S*, 632), for "In a madness born of the horror of Tafas we killed and killed, even blowing in the heads of the fallen and of the animals; as though their death and running blood could slake our agony" (*S*, 633). Although couched in a Homeric tone of justified revenge, including Tallal's brave charge, it is clear that here as in the killing of Hamed and the massacre at Wadi Hesa "there was no glory left, but the terror of the broken flesh" (*S*, 482). In these events, full of the unthinking barbarism of tribal war, Lawrence's imitation of the participants has gone beyond an act, and like Kurtz, he has realized an "unrestrained capacity" for evil in himself.

Lawrence begins to waken fully from the dream (or nightmare) of the last two years as he nears Damascus and finds himself "strangely alone" (*S*, 641). In a passage of deep sensual perception, he realizes his alienation from both sides:

> About the soldiers hung the Arabs: gravely gazing men from another sphere. My crooked duty had banished me among them for two years. Tonight I was nearer to them than to the troops, and I resented it, as shameful. The intruding contrast mixed with longing for home, to sharpen my faculties and make fertile my distaste, till not merely did I see the unlikeness of race, and hear the unlikeness of language, but I learned to pick between their smells: the heavy, standing, curdled sourness of dried sweat in cotton, over the Arab crowds; and the feral smell of English soldiers: that hot pissy aura of thronged men in woollen clothes: a tart pungency, breathcatching, ammoniacal; a fervent fermenting naphtha smell. (*S*, 642)

His duty completed at great physical and mental cost to himself, his absolute of complete freedom, belief, and wholeness still unrealized, his position between colonizer and colonized more sharply defined than ever, Lawrence finds that his new loneliness makes final victory "sorrowful" and the phrase of freedom "meaningless" (*S*, 652). Wading through the filth of the Turkish hospital in his white robes, Lawrence feels that "anyone who pushed through to success a rebellion of the weak against their masters must come out of it so stained in estimation that nothing in the world would make him feel clean" (*S*, 659). Lawrence's best efforts, carried through at so much cost to himself, as in cleaning out the Turkish hospital, earn him only a slap in the face. And when he was writing and revising his book, he knew that in 1920 Feisal had been forced out of Syria by the French, so *Seven Pillars* was a monument to a political endeavor that had failed only two years after its military goal had been achieved. In the Syrian settlement, the French government, not the British or the Arabs, triumphed. The reader is left pondering the question of whether all of the mental and physical sacrifice of Lawrence and his British and Arab colleagues was worth this scanty achievement, although the defeat of the Turks certainly helped end World War I. So Lawrence was not fulfilled in either his Arab or his British sympathies. Rarely has an idealistic dreamer been forced down to earth so harshly.

It is not hard to see why a reading of Lawrence's book helped Forster finish his own *Passage to India*, as he wrote to Lawrence in February 1924: "By the way your book helped me to finish a book of my own. Seemed to pull me together."[41] It is also not surprising that Lawrence saw his own situation mirrored in the pages of Forster's book:

> If excellence of materials means anything, my book would be as good as yours: but it stinks of me: whereas yours is universal: the bitter terrible hopeless picture a cloud might have painted, of man in India. You surpass the Englishman and surpass the Indian, and are neither: and yet there is nothing inhuman (like Moby Dick) in your picture. . . .
>
> If the flea may assert a kindred feeling with the lion . . . then let me suggest how my experience (and abandonment) of work in Arabia repeats your history of a situation-with-no-honest-way-out-of-it. You on the large thinking plane, me on the cluttered plane of action . . . and both lost. (*L,* 462)

What Lawrence learned in Arabia is exactly what Mrs. Moore learned in India: "Pathos, piety, courage—they exist, but are identical, and so is filth. Everything exists, nothing has value."[42] His experience in Arabia results in "a muddle (as we call it), a frustration of reason and form."[43]

Lawrence states this as eloquently as any other writer of his period when he writes that

> In my case, the effort for these years to live in the dress of Arabs, and to imitate their mental foundation, quitted me of my English self, and let me look at the West and its conventions with new eyes: they destroyed it all for me. At the same time I could not sincerely take on the Arab skin: it was an affectation only. Easily was a man made an infidel, but hardly might he be converted to another faith. I had dropped one form and not taken on the other . . . with a resultant feeling of intense loneliness in life, and a contempt, not for other men, but for all they do. (*S,* 31–32)

Like all the colonial—and war—protagonists of early twentieth century British literature who learned too much about the world and about themselves, Lawrence returns home unable to "focus anything," in the words of Kipling's Mrs. Mallowe. He has learned that true friendship between alien peoples (especially but not only those with unequal control of technology and power) is difficult to achieve; in Forster's words, "alas, the two nations cannot be friends."[44] He has learned unpleasant truths about himself and his own dark corners of savagery and masochism. He has learned that political goals are elusive. If there is any fitting message of *Seven Pillars,* it is Kurtz's "The horror! The horror!"

Chapter Six
Seven Pillars of Wisdom: Literary Evaluation

Is *Seven Pillars of Wisdom* a literary success? Certainly Lawrence had to contend with many negative factors when he was writing it: He was divided between his British and Arab loyalties, he was too close in time to the events narrated in *Seven Pillars*, and he was unwilling or unable to fully discuss some secret military and embarrassing personal events. But over 60 years of unbroken publication and readership prove that despite these obstacles he produced a classic literary work. For Lawrence succeeded in the most important goal of any autobiographer: projecting his personality and making it interesting. Despite the mysteries and ambiguities in *Seven Pillars of Wisdom,* several generations of readers have felt that they know Lawrence intimately. He convinces us that we are privy to what it was like to be T. E. Lawrence during the Arab Revolt. He creates this impression by means of his intriguing self-characterization, his brilliant styles of writing, his skillfully shaped military plot line, and his occasional counterpointing of that plot with the less structured, personal, introspective plot.

Plot Lines

Although to his critics the military plot takes a subordinate place to the story of personal doubt and failure—as well it might—this basic plot remains interesting, exciting, and well organized. The title "Seven Pillars of Wisdom" can be explicated in so many ways, either as in chapter 5 or as a reference to Ruskin's "Seven Lamps of Architecture"[1] or to the seven biblical lands that must be governed morally.[2] But it refers first and foremost to the military architecture of the revolt. A manuscript notebook in the Houghton Library[3] makes this clear and demonstrates the fundamental importance of the military plot to Lawrence's conception of the book's structure. In that notebook, we learn that Lawrence first envisioned *Seven Pillars* as comprising eight books, each of which has a label such as "Materials," "Foundations," "First Courses," and so on until the final book, "House is Perfected." These stages refer to the military building of the revolt rather than to Lawrence's personal struggle, which can scarcely be so neatly schematized.

A clear reference to this meaning of the title and to the basically military conception of the book remains embedded in the final text:

> When it grew too hot for dreamless dozing, I picked up my tangle again, and went on ravelling it out, considering now the whole house of war in its structural aspect, which was strategy, in its arrangements, which were tactics, and in the sentiment of its inhabitants, which was psychology; for my personal duty was command, and the commander, like the master architect, was responsible for all. (*S*, 191–92)

Lawrence, attempting to be a master architect of war and literature, strives for the kind of comprehensive literary framework that Doughty, for instance, was unable to attain.

In shaping the military plot line, Lawrence is successful in conveying the external drama of the adventure in a consistently engrossing manner far surpassing the interest of the usual memoir. In the chapter on "Strangeness and Pain," Lawrence writes that "We lived always in the stretch or sag of nerves, either on the crest or in the trough of waves of feeling" (*S*, 29). The military plot is organized in terms of wave crests and troughs. In the military campaign, initial difficulties are followed by incredible success at Akaba, failure at the Yarmuk bridge, a period of regrouping of energies, and a final victorious sweep. The drama here is that of the novice at war who gradually perfects his abilities as a commander through trial and error and leads a national movement to overcome its oppressors. We watch Lawrence's experiments as he gains a confident control of the materials of command. "War was made up of crises of intense effort," (*S*, 511) and we move from peaks of excitement to troughs of inactivity. Lawrence's letters demonstrate his concern over structuring this movement of the book from trial to action to meditation and rest to renewed action, the wave that finally breaks over Damascus. To Forster he writes that he "let the activity of the book fall into a trough for twenty pages, to give my imaginary reader a rest before piling up the agony of the last advance on Damascus" (*L*, 457). To Garnett he expresses the fear that the last 50 pages are "flatter than the VIth and VIIth parts (the failure of the bridge and the winter war) and formed an anticlimax—a weak ending" (*L*, 368).

In structuring the war narrative, Lawrence accomplishes his goal of presenting architecturally the difficulty of consolidating the house of military wisdom and action. He conveys the feeling of retrogression and advance that he experienced as commander of the revolt. Within each book we have the effect of traveling from peak to trough to peak that we see in the larger military structure of *Seven Pillars*. For instance, within book 7 itself, Lawrence's exhilaration during the battle of Tafileh gives way to despair when he learns that Zeid has squandered the gold with which Lawrence was to pay the Arabs. On the larger level, the failure at the Yarmuk bridge in book 6 follows the "flat" period of minor raids of book 5, which in its turn comes after the high peak of the capture of Akaba in book 4. Here are two long marches that produce opposite results, separated by a "flat": two wave crests of emotion, one positive and one negative, with a trough in between.

Although Lawrence's book follows a chronological diary sequence, some days take pages to recount, whereas others are passed over in silence or in a few paragraphs, as Robert Payne points out.[4] By means of these selective stresses, Lawrence shapes the drama. Events that are too flat, like the abortive reconnaissance raid (Oxford text) that disappears from book 8 of the final edition are eliminated. Lawrence keeps us balancing between the peaks and troughs of dramatic emotion by making rigorous use of the autobiographer's technique of dwelling on the most interesting events.

The military plot contains—in addition to antiromantic and antiheroic tales of failures, ignobility, and massacres—Lawrence's grab at glorious adventures properly belonging to centuries previous to his— and ours. But Lawrence's reactions to these adventures—which we might term the personal or introspective plot of the book—are less organized, more fragmented, and more difficult to understand because they often do not follow logically from the adventures themselves. In chapter 5, we saw how he fluctuates wildly between the two veils, changing his allegiance between the cultures without notice or explanation. His reaction to military events is no less arbitrary than his cultural shifts. For instance, the capture of Akaba, glorious as it is, results primarily in a sense of personal worthlessness and worry for Lawrence. The triumph at Damascus results in his feeling of alienation from both sides. Another person might have felt much differently about these events. His desire to die in a plane crash seems disproportionate to his military and political troubles. Since Lawrence does not tell us the "S. A." or Dahoum story in *Seven Pillars,* we do not know that his moodiness and disappointment are partly the result of Dahoum's death. The lack of order and explanation in the personal plot line may give some readers the feeling that there is a failure of artistic control here. On the other hand, Keith Hull has argued that it is precisely Lawrence's lack of explanation and air of mystery and contestability that make the book appealing to readers.[5]

Critics may differ on this issue, but what is clear is that Lawrence sometimes counterpoints the military and the introspective plots with great effect. When that happens, Lawrence fits a modern mentality of fragmentation and dislocation into a narrative of adventure by contrasting military ups with personal downs and thus creates the mixed mood that prevails throughout the volume, especially after Akaba. By grouping them together in book 6, Lawrence deliberately parallels the defeat at the Yarmuk bridge with his felt personal failure at Deraa and then contrasts these disasters with his triumphal entrance into Jerusalem at Allenby's side, which allows book 6 to end on a positive note. Conversely, the final victory and triumphal entry into Damascus is deliberately contrasted with the unhygienic Turkish hospital, in which Lawrence's white robes get soiled, and the final book ends with Lawrence's feeling of alienation and displacement. Sometimes we may not understand just why Lawrence feels so worthless, but when this counterpoint works, as it does in book 6 and at the end of *Seven Pillars,* the effect is grating and powerful, a statement of the death-in-life caused by World War I. Thus, Lawrence's book leaves the contradictory impression of having given us something—a completed house of the Arab Revolt—and, in his story of personal undoing (to which can be added his knowledge that the French evicted Feisal from Syria in 1920, transforming the victory into a defeat), of having taken it away again. *Seven Pillars* itself can be seen simultaneously as a completed, triumphant monument and as a ruin lying in the desert. This mixed quality of *Seven Pillars* offers a unique and powerful reading experience.

Self-Characterization

Lawrence's character as he presents it is no less divided than the plot lines and contributes to the mixed but potent effect of his book. We have seen how he was divided between British and Arab loyalties throughout *Seven Pillars.* But this is only the most prominent of the divisions in himself that he shows to the reader. These lines from Whitman's *Song of Myself* might serve as the motto for Lawrence as he appears in *Seven Pillars:* "Do

I contradict myself? / Very well then I contradict myself, / (I am large, I contain multitudes)." In the chapter "Myself" he writes that he "was a standing court martial on myself, inevitably" (*S*, 565), and after the Deraa beating he found himself dividing into parts.

The parts are contradictory, and Lawrence in the course of the revolt and later—in addition to the British-Arab conflict—experienced at least four contrary desires: to lead and to be led, to be active and to be introspective, to deny his body and to give in to it, and to reveal and yet conceal his feelings and problems.

He tells us on the one hand that "Always in working I tried to serve" and "I followed, and did not institute" (*S*, 564–65), yet he reveals a very dominant leaderly attitude when he tells his commander Gilbert Clayton after the capture of Akaba that Akaba "had been taken on my plan by my effort. The cost of it had fallen on my brains and nerves. There was much more I felt inclined to do, and capable of doing—if he thought I had earned the right to be my own master" (*S*, 323).

Similarly, he writes that he was an intellectual, who "felt mean, to fill the place of a man of action, for my standards of value were a wilful reaction against theirs, and I despised their happiness" (*S*, 277), but he shows again and again that he was a very capable man of action, who had been "in motion" for more than a year, "riding a thousand miles each month upon camels with added nervous hours in crazy aeroplanes, or rushing across country in powerful cars" (*S*, 502), often beating the Bedouin at their own game as well as planning strategy and leading his men into battle. He tells us that he was not a soldier but then adds that he had read almost everything that was available about strategy.[6]

A very powerful internal conflict arises from Lawrence's attempt to suppress his sexual urges. He writes that the "disgust of being touched revolted me more than the thought of death and defeat," that he "reverenced my wits and despised my body" (*S*, 532), and that "There was no flesh" (*S*, 564), yet he speaks approvingly of Arabs "quivering together in the yielding sand with intimate hot limbs in supreme embrace" (*S*, 30) and admits to "a delicious warmth, probably sexual" (*S*, 445) swelling through him after his beating at Deraa. Lawrence's sexual conflict has been related to his political conflict by some recent writers.[7]

Perhaps most of all, he wants to tell all concerning his inner nature and some of the military events in which he was involved and yet was unable to do so. He indicates experiencing a pleasure in pain but does not admit in any version of *Seven Pillars* to voluntarily practicing flagellation, although he was doing so during the very period when he was writing the book. He writes a very sensual poem to "S. A." but does not tell us his identity. He tells us that he took a trip behind Turkish lines but not what he did there.

In these basic conflicts, as in the division between his British and Arab loyalties, we have the essence of Lawrence's character in *Seven Pillars*. His biographers and interpreters have tried to present him as either a puritan or a sadomasochist, a great captain of war or a pretentious talker, an important leader or only a follower who exaggerated his role, a man admitting painful truths or only a liar. The truth is that Lawrence as a character in *Seven Pillars is* his contradictions—both self-revealing and self-concealing, attracted to homosexual and masochistic feelings but also repelled by them, a man of action who thinks more than most men of action, and a capable leader who envied the follower's freedom from responsibility. Lawrence can give us only his self-divisions as he saw them, not impose any smooth order or interpretation on them. He felt himself to be, and presented himself as, both monument and ruin, and in that eternal contradiction lies his charm for the reader.

Other Characters

Where we would judge a novelist by his ability to project himself into the many roles and minds of his characters, we expect the author of an autobiography to project his own personality and to place the mark of that personality on all characters and events in his book. Lawrence clearly recognized this aspect of autobiography, writing that "Doughty's book mirrored Doughty as much as it mirrored Arabia."[8] We want to open an autobiography to any page and sense the author's personality infusing every sentence on that page, every event, and every character.

Lawrence's characters become aspects of *his* personality, they are fit into the pattern of *his* sensibility, and he does not pretend to be inside their heads, like a novelist. Therefore, they cannot be the deeply realized characters of a modern novel who stand on their own feet or photographically true images of the real figures on which they are based. In other words, as these characters appear in *Seven Pillars*, they reflect only those aspects of the real figures that struck Lawrence and that he wanted them to reflect. Thus he refused to change his depictions of Hubert Young and Richard Meinertzhagen despite protests by both that his portraits were not mirror images of themselves. In *Seven Pillars*, Allenby's brilliant and ruthless intelligence chief Meinertzhagen appears as an archsadist who enjoyed "spattering the brains of a cornered mob of

Germans one by one with his African knob-kerri" (*S, 384*). About this, Meinertzhagen states that "I told him I had been considering what he said about me in his book and begged him to expunge it as the first part was not true and put me in a false light. Then he started. He surprised me by saying that little of his book was strict truth, though most of it was based on fact."[9] In making this "admission," Lawrence simply certified that he was an autobiographer rather than a historian. He did not want to understand Young or Meinertzhagen in depth on the basis of numerous interviews and documents or suppositions about their thoughts but only recorded his own subjective view of their personalities. A mild Meinertzhagen probably never appeared to Lawrence's eyes. Similarly, Auda may or may not have been a heroic (and occasionally greedy and treacherous) Homeric warrior, but the modern Lawrence saw him as such and has portrayed him that way in *Seven Pillars*.

While they reflect only his personal view of the participants and contain no pretense of novelistically showing the characters' own thought processes, Lawrence's portraits of the main characters are often complex. This fact has been overlooked when he has sometimes been accused of creating racist stereotypes of the Arabs. Feisal, for instance, is heroic, yet weak; Lawrence admires him, yet pities him; the British betray Feisal through the Sykes-Picot Treaty, and Feisal thinks of betraying the British, even late in the war, by "making separate peace with Turkey" (*S, 554*). The result is that Feisal emerges as a man, not a stereotype. If Lawrence's characterization of Feisal were only heroic, then he would be the mere propagandist for the revolt that Aldington and Elie Kedourie have claimed he was; if on the other hand his portrait of Feisal were purely negative, Lawrence might be the straw-man Western racist that Edward Said posits. Neither view gives Lawrence credit for the complexity of his literary vision, which applies to others as well as to himself. But ultimately this is Lawrence's book alone, and his personality pervades it completely not only because of his powerful portrayal of his own divided self but also because of his control of the most important and all-pervasive aspect of any literary work: its style.

Lawrence's Stylistic Aesthetic

If style—"proper words in proper places," according to Jonathan Swift—is important in fiction, it is particularly and even more so in poetic autobiography. Here the author's *primary* concern is not the presentation of an exciting plot or the depth psychology of a group of characters but rather the forceful exposition of the author's own personality, which he does not fully understand. The poetic autobiographer reveals himself to the reader most clearly not by recording inner and outer events, the significance of which he does not always fully grasp himself, but through his manner of self-expression. This manner implies what the author really thinks about the events he describes and therefore tells us what kind of person he is. And in fact poetic autobiographers, like Thoreau, Whitman, Yeats, and Henry James (to name only a few), are all masters of style.[10]

As R. P. Blackmur correctly noticed, the true unity of Lawrence's *Seven Pillars* lies not in the military framework, which only superficially holds the book together, but in Lawrence's own sensibility, that outlook that makes him who he is and not someone else: "Wholeness, for Lawrence, lay in the sensibility; so far as its elements could be expressed, they would make a unity that might be taken as complete if taken at all: the unity of obsession."[11] In a letter to Ede of 25 December 1928, Lawrence stated his realization of the use of style to express his personality:

I find that my fifth writing (after perhaps fifteenth reading) of a sentence makes it more shapely, pithier, stranger than it was. Without that twist of strangeness no one would feel an individuality, a differentness, behind the phrase. Unless it stays long enough in your thinking box to catch your likeness, it will not be demonstrably yours: and if anybody else could have written it, then it's no good.[12]

Lawrence's feeling of the necessity for every sentence to be his grows naturally out of the literary philosophy of his Victorian masters, Pater, Ruskin, Doughty, and Morris. For them, even descriptive or analytical essays on scientific topics would have to be written in individual styles by means of which the reader could instantly recognize the writer (Doughty, for instance, fortunately refused permission to both the Royal Geographical Society and the Cambridge University Press to revise his brilliant but idiosyncratic English for publication). Today, authors of essays, reports, and even autobiographies strive to write a clear, objective prose in which their individuality can be recognized only with difficulty. Written as it was in the 1920s, when the period of personalized prose was already passing, *Seven Pillars* appeared to be a throwback in style as well as in heroic content and found its greatest acceptance among older writers such as H. G. Wells and Arnold Bennett, who were able to appreciate its virtues independently of current fashions. Thus, Wells is reliably reported to have referred to Lawrence's book as "the finest piece of prose that has been written in the English language for 150 years,"[13] while Bennett compares T. E. favorably to D. H. Lawrence and finds T. E. "a better writer than Winston Churchill. He is one of the best prose writers living, but . . . doesn't always know when to stop. He thinks in separate words. Seemingly he has passed through a world bristling with cliches."[14] John Buchan, author of the thriller *Thirty-Nine Steps,* wrote Lawrence that "When you do not get inundated with adjectives you are the best living writer of English prose."[15] But the younger school of writers of the 1930s also found Lawrence a model not only of heroic ambiguity but also of style. One of its outstanding representatives, novelist and poet Rex Warner, himself acknowledged as a master of style, wrote that "The only modern novelist I like is Kafka, but the best prose I have read is by T. E. Lawrence." In the end, Lawrence based his own assessment of *Seven Pillars* on its style: "However, granted that the *Seven Pillars* is not wholly contemptible, as prose. I can concede that much, I think" (*L,* 586).

Although Lawrence's letters reveal a concern with the temporal and spatial shape of his book, his most interesting and detailed comments relate to the art of style. His method of styling his work was first to write down his sentences quickly and spontaneously, as we see in his claim that book 6 "was written entire between sunrise and sunset" (*S,* 21) and that 95 percent of text 2 was written in 30 days. Then he would go over the sentences again and again, making sure that each captured his individuality. So Lawrence's style has both a romantic spontaneity, a very deep expression of his feelings at the moment of writing, *and* a very deliberate and conscious polish. Lawrence indicates this balance between spontaneity and polish not only in the Ede letter recently quoted but also in a longer statement to Vyvyan Richards, which also clarifies his stylistic intentions:

> [P]rose depends on a music in one's head which involuntarily chooses & balances the possible words to *keep tune* with the thought. The best passages in English prose all deal with death or the vanity of things, since that is a tune we all know, and the mind is set quite free to think while writing about it. Only it can't be kept up very long, because of the mortal weakness and the wear and tear of things, & the function of criticism, revision & correction (polishing) seems to me to be either
> (i) *putting* a thing into thought
> (ii) [putting] thought into rhythm

(iii) putting expression into meaning
It seems to me that if you think too hard about the form, you forget the
matter, & if your brain is wrestling with the matter, you may not have
attention to spare for the manner. Only occasionally in things constantly
dwelt upon, do you get an unconscious balance, & then you get a *spontaneous* and perfect arrangement of words to fit the idea, *as the tune.* Polishing is an attempt, by stages, to get to which should be a single combined
stride. (*L,* 318)

Thus, Lawrence works toward a perfect matching of form and content,
expression and subject, which should appear spontaneous. In his choice
of a musical analogy for style, he reveals his debt to late nineteenth-
century critical theory, in which this analogy is often employed.

In fact, the result of Lawrence's polishing is highly complex, sophisticated, artificial (in the sense of being unlike normal speech) prose rather
than a Mozart-like purity, simplicity, and clarity. Although Lawrence felt
that "Simplicity is as often the mark of a first-class work as complexity is
of second-class work,"[16] he also felt that "so spiced and tormented a generation as ours can hardly be expected to find a simplicity which does
not ring false: so perhaps it is better to admit our complexity, and
develop it to the nth."[17] He also believed that his own complex style
grew naturally out of his personality and experiences and thus suited the
post-World War I age even as it appeared to be a throwback to the nineteenth century.

In the end, Lawrence approves stylistic complexity and artificiality.
One should not play at appearing simple if one has complicated things
to say: "I'm sorry for the sophisticated simplicity. That's decadence. If a
man is not simple by nature he cannot be simple by art, and if he tries
he only achieves a falseness. You can only (if complex) get simplicity by
my 'third degree': by distilling a scene into quintessential action" (*L,*
377). Therefore, *Seven Pillars* is "too elaborate and conscious a construc-
tion to admit simplicity—or rather, if I were limpid or direct anywhere
people would (should) feel a false stillness" (*L,* 371). Lawrence chooses a
complicated style to reflect his own complicated personality.

Lawrence's complaint about the styles of both Homer and Doughty is
that they try for "sophisticated simplicity," a false effect of primitivism.
About Homer, he writes in his translator's preface that "Wardour-Street
Greek like the *Odyssey's* defies honest rendering . . . the tight lips of
archaic art have grown the fixed grin of archaism." Doughty's book,
according to him, suffers from the same fault: "This inlay of strange
words into a ground-work of daily English is a mistake. The effect is

fussy, not primitive, more peasant art than peasant."[18] Yet when Lawrence describes not himself but Auda, Feisal, Tallal, and Nasir, for instance, the same "sophisticated simplicity" that he learned from Homer, Doughty, and Morris and that became a part of his own vision of the world comes out in chivalric parallel phrases and inversions: " 'What is upon you, Tafas?' said I" (*S*, 82); "the splendid leader, the fine horseman, the courteous and strong companion of the road" (*S*, 633). Despite Lawrence's condemnation of similar effects in Doughty and Homer, the fact is that this style of neomedievalist "sophisticated simplicity" of the Arab portraits in Lawrence as in Doughty is anything but simple to achieve; it is a conscious, artificial, complex effect.

Part of Lawrence's complexity is that fact that *Seven Pillars* is written in more than one style, as E. M. Forster points out:

> Book being lengthy, you have rightly several styles, one for R.E. 8s [airplanes], and that sort of thing, another for normal narrative, another for reflections, another for crises of emotion or beauty. The criticism I'd offer is that your reflective style is not properly under control. Almost at once, when you describe your thoughts, you become obscure, and the slightly strained sense which then (not habitually) you lend words, does not bring your sentence the richness you intended, imparts not colour but gumminess.[19]

In this fact of many styles, as in the fact of the military and spiritual plot lines of the book, we have the key to the confusion of the critics noted in chapter 1 of this work. Some critics stress the military story and thus see the book as highly structured; others, following without understanding the story of the two veils or of Lawrence's other personal conflicts, see only fluctuating confusion. Some critics stress the limpid style of the narrative sections, whereas others decry Lawrence's writing as involved or muddy because they emphasize the "gummy," reflective style. The end to this confusion lies in the realization that *Seven Pillars* is the autobiography of a man who seems always to be falling apart but never does so; and that Lawrence's poetic autobiography as a whole, with its two plot lines, complex self-characterization, and many styles, accurately and brilliantly reflects his personality.

All of Lawrence's styles in *Seven Pillars* have in common a high-powered complexity, the response Lawrence found most suitable for his own personality and the age and which reminds us of his love of powerful motorcycle, motorboat, and airplane engines. The whole of the "Strangeness and Pain" chapter is written in a prose influenced by the throb of air-plane engines, as Lawrence tells us himself.[20] Yet its total effect remains esoteric, Eastern as well as Western, and not of the modern age.[21] Describing "English Prose between 1919 and 1939," E. M. Forster notes that "The best work of the period has this esoteric tendency. T. E. Lawrence, though heroic in action, retreats into the desert to act."[22] In literature, Lawrence retreated into the exotic land of an art-prose owing much to the neomedievalism of the nineteenth-century romantic move-ment and earlier periods.[23] His concern with alliteration and assonance, with the rise and fall of his paragraphs, with keeping in tune with his subject, and with producing the 1926 Subscriber's Edition as a "book beautiful" appears more in line with the poetry of Keats and Swinburne, the prose of Thomas Traherne and Sir Thomas Browne, and William Morris's Kelmscott Chaucer than with the art of his own century. That Lawrence is extremely sensitive to style and aware of the great prose tra-dition is clear from the several pages of minute stylistic criticism that he wrote on Henry Williamson's *Tarka the Otter,* among which this remark appears: "almost fit, for its wonder, to be put next to Traherne's 'orient wheat,' as one of the finest passages of English prose."[24] Vyvyan Richards informs us that "Lawrence himself observed that his paragraphs seemed to rise and rise in a climax and then descend to their finish; and that the culminating point of the climax was commonly marked by the word 'all.' He constantly so analyzed his work as he went along."[25]

We have proof that Lawrence was aware of the straining of his prose after effects of all kinds. Sometimes he is unkind to himself in his assess-ment of this technique: "I wrote this thing in the war atmosphere, and believe that it is stinking with it. Also there is a good deal of cruelty, and some excitement. All these things, in a beginner's hands, tend to force him over the edge, and I suspect there is much over-writing" (*L,* 362). Sometimes he justifies it: *"The purple passages even when they are meant to be purple.* I suspect every purple passage is intentional. In my experience purple things are a conspicuous straining upward of the mind."[26] *Seven Pillars* becomes "to my mind, redhot with passion, throughout" (*L,* 542), according to Lawrence, but this is not quite true. Although his personality is reflected in every style in the book to a greater or lesser degree, it is his romantic Arab veil that is "redhot with passion, throughout," whereas his cooler, more analytical, British veil is some-times overrational and calm. By arranging his styles across a spectrum according to the amount of personality they contain, we see the full range of Lawrence's psyche and ability as a writer.

Styles

When we speak of the "amount of personality" in each of Lawrence's styles, what we mean is the *degree of involvement* of Lawrence in his subject that the reader detects by observing stylistic features. If the prose is highly complex, involuted, and gummy (to use Forster's term), Lawrence is too deeply involved in his topic to view it objectively—and this is the case with his chapters on his own personality: 99, 100, and 103. If the prose is full of obsessively observed details but seems clear and clinically detached in tone, we have the strange mixture of involvement and detachment that we get in scenes of horror, like the beating at Deraa and the Turkish military hospital, and the earlier execution of Hamed. If, on the other hand, the prose is calm, lacking in highly colored adjectives, and composed of a few relatively simple elements rather than many interlocking parallel elements, then we have the analytical distance of the Lawrence who considers military alternatives, describes details of topography, or views the Arab Revolt only as a tool for British victory. Even in these instances of technical detachment, however, we should notice that some amount of involvement, of personality, is always present. Lawrence did not write a single sentence that did not indicate some kind of involvement, at least in *Seven Pillars*. We can call those styles exhibiting a relatively high degree of involvement Lawrence's "Arab veil" styles, and those that reveal distance and detachment, his "British veil" styles. Arranged in a spectrum, the styles look like this:

Maximum Involvement and Introspection

Lawrence's Arab Veil[27]
1. Reflective: chapters 99, 100, 103—Lawrence's personality
2. Romantic: "S. A." poem, "Strangeness and Pain," heat of Arabia, death of Ferraj, charge of Tallal, introductory portraits of Feisal and Auda
3. Horrorific: torture at Deraa, massacre at Tafas, Turkish hospital at Damascus, execution of Hamed
4. Action Narrative: blowing up railway, rush on Akaba, battle of Tafileh

Lawrence's British Veil
5. Patriotic: British desire to better world (Oxford text introductory chapter); portrait of Allenby; capture of Jerusalem
6. Descriptive: desert flora and fauna, seasons
7. Strategic: chapter 33, "House of War"
8. Historical-Analytical: Syria in chapters 4 and 58; criticism of Feisal, Arab Revolt, and British commanders before Allenby

Minimum Involvement and Introspection

By closely examining small samples of Lawrence's styles, beginning
with the total involvement of style (1) and ending with the relative cool-
ness and detachment of style (8), we will see exactly how Lawrence projects his personality in *Seven Pillars of Wisdom*.

Style 1: Reflective

> True there lurked always that Will uneasily waiting to burst out. My
> brain was sudden and silent as a wild cat, my senses like mud clogging its
> feet, and my self (conscious always of itself and its shyness) telling the
> beast it was bad form to spring and vulgar to feed on the kill. So meshed
> in nerves and hesitation, it could not be a thing to be afraid of; yet it was
> a real beast, and this book its mangy skin, dried, stuffed, and set up
> squarely for men to stare at. (*S, 564*)

This gummy style indicates that Lawrence cannot describe himself
because he does not understand himself fully; he is too close to his
own personality to see it objectively. From this passage, one understands that Lawrence fears his tendency toward domination but feels
that it is healthily impeded by some inherent timidity or lack of
nerve. But, despite his use of some recognized philosophical terms
like "will," "brain," and "senses," it remains difficult to grasp his division of his personality, and the striking simile of the wild cat does not
help much. By using it, he implies that "Will" is the same as "brain"
(or intellect), yet he also implies that they are different. How, exactly,
do his "senses like mud" slow down his brain and/or his will to domination? Is *Seven Pillars* the "mangy skin" of the cat of his brain or his
will or both? We cannot see the cat through the bag of his confused
and confusing style. Lawrence's use of violent metaphor and simile—
always in evidence in the "Arab veil" styles—has run away with itself,
and the paragraph remains lively and tensed if not fully understandable. In this veil, Lawrence seeks always to excite and unseat the
reader, to force the reader's mind to make unfamiliar connections.
Sometimes it does not work, but the reader always receives a definite
sense of Lawrence's own dislocation. Lawrence's literary allusiveness
is also present in this passage, where his use of the word *beast*
inevitably calls to mind Kipling's story "The Mark of the Beast," in
which an Englishman is possessed by the spirit of a wolf as punishment for desecrating native gods. Another possible allusion is
Henry James's "The Beast in the Jungle," in which the protagonist
discovers that the "beast" he has been waiting for is in his mind rather

than outside of it.[28] The metaphor of the mangy skin also recalls Michelangelo's Sistine Chapel self-portrait of himself as a flayed skin.

Style 2: Romantic

The everlasting battle stripped from us care of our own lives or of others'. We had ropes about our necks, and on our heads prices which showed that the enemy intended hideous tortures for us if we were caught. Each day some of us passed; and the living knew themselves just sentient puppets on God's stage: indeed, our taskmaster was merciless, merciless, so long as our bruised feet could stagger forward on the road. The weak envied those tired enough to die; for success looked so remote, and failure a near and certain, if sharp, release from toil. We lived always in the stretch or sag of nerves, either on the crest or in the trough of waves of feeling. This impotency was bitter to us, and made us live only for the seen horizon, reckless what spite we inflicted or endured, since physical sensation showed itself meanly transient. Gusts of cruelty, perversions, lusts ran lightly over the surface without troubling us; for the moral laws which had seemed to hedge about these silly accidents must be yet fainter words. We had learned that there were pangs too sharp, griefs too deep, ecstasies too high for our finite selves to register. When emotion reached this pitch the mind choked; and memory went white till the circumstances were humdrum once more. (*S,* 29–30)

Here we see Lawrence's full romantic identification with the strangeness, pain, and adventure of the Arab Revolt. A microcosm of the structure of the book as a whole, this paragraph keeps the reader moving from peak to trough to peak of waves of emotion. Numerous rhetorical devices make this passage "redhot with passion, throughout" despite a strangely passive attitude on the part of the humans described in it. Ellipsis, or a condensation of sentence structure by omission of conjunctions and pronouns, operates everywhere to give a breathless effect of overpowering movement: "We had ropes about our necks, and on our heads [there were] prices . . . "; "and the living knew themselves [to be] just sentient puppets"; "Gusts of cruelty, perversions, [and] lusts. . . ." Parallel, balanced elements ("our taskmaster . . . our bruised feet"; "merciless, merciless"; "of nerves . . . of waves of feeling") in every sentence are piled on one another to illustrate the accumulation of perceptions that floods the mind. Extreme adjectives and adverbs ("everlasting battle," "hideous tortures," "bruised feet," "pangs too sharp, griefs too deep, ecstasies too high") enforce the effect of heights and depths of waves of feeling. The images are similarly extreme: men with ropes around their necks, a "merciless, merciless" taskmaster, the stretch and sag of nerves, gusts of cruelty, perversions, lusts. The basically iambic (with one or two anapaestic substitutions) rhythm combined with the use of parallel phrases within this sentence creates a rising and falling music that works well with the idea of wave crests and troughs: "We lived al / ways in / the stretch / or sag / of nerves, / either on / the crest / or in / the trough / of waves / of feel(ing)." Other sentences, too, have a definite rhythm of stressed and unstressed syllables to emphasize this idea. If we count the number of heavy caesuras in the sentences of this paragraph of nine sentences, we find the following pattern: 0–1–5– 4–1–3–4–3–1. Thus, the first two, the fifth, and the last sentences of the paragraph represent rest stops, troughs, in the building, forward movement, and final breaking of the wave of the paragraph, when the mind "chokes" and memory goes "white" on the material provided by the senses. Through it all, the men are acted upon rather than active themselves: The battle strips from them care of their lives; the taskmaster (God?) forces them on; impotence makes them live only for the seen horizon. The accumulation of perceptions and powerful feelings runs out of their control, beyond their ability to register. All grows out of the evil "inherent in our circumstances" (S, 29), and enforces the writer's idea that the forces of circumstance and environment were too powerful to act against, that the men were blown "like dead leaves in the wind" (S, 29). (This last phrase is Lawrence's translation of a line of Paul Verlaine, showing once again Lawrence's ever-present literary allusiveness.) Totally identified with the adventure, unable to resist the pull of the Arab veil, which involves romantic death and heroism as well as homosexual love and masochism, Lawrence "gives himself" to "be a possession of aliens" (S, 31) at the end of this chapter. Even as he warns us against doing what he has done, Lawrence's attraction to and involvement in the Arab veil show clearly in his romantic style.

Lawrence's romantic style has earned him more blame than praise. No doubt it is "purple" and "overwritten" by contemporary standards, perhaps by any standards, but *beautifully* so. Very few writers could achieve Lawrence's powerful romantic effects, and if he sometimes overshoots the mark, so does F. Scott Fitzgerald. We would agree, I believe, that the passage from *The Great Gatsby*, another neoromantic product of the 1920s, in which Nick Carraway steps into Daisy Buchanan's house to find that "A breeze blew through the room, blew curtains in at one end and out the other like pale flags, twisting them up toward the frosted wedding-cake of the ceiling, and then rippled over the wine-coloured rug, making a shadow on it as wind does the sea"[29] is also rather top-heavy with colored adjectives. But I think we would also agree that we would not want it changed under any circumstances. And the same goes for Lawrence's romantic style. In my experience, few students and casual readers—as opposed to critics—have not been charmed by it. In the end, we have a matter of personal taste rather than objective critical judgment on this point.

Style 3: Horrorific

> To keep my mind in control I numbered the blows, but after twenty lost count, and could feel only the shapeless weight of pain, not tearing claws, for which I had prepared, but a gradual cracking apart of my whole being by some too-great force whose waves rolled up my spine till they were pent within my brain, to clash horribly together. Somewhere in the place a cheap clock ticked loudly, and it distressed me that their beating was not in its time. I writhed and twisted, but was held so tightly that my struggles were useless. After the corporal ceased, the men took up, very deliberately, giving me so many, and then an interval, during which they would squabble for the next turn, ease themselves, and play unspeakably with me. This was repeated often, for what may have been no more than ten minutes. Always for the first of every new series, my head would be pulled round, to see how a hard white ridge, like a railway, darkening slowly into crimson, leaped over my skin at the instant of each stroke, with a bead of blood where the two ridges crossed. (*S*, 444)

Lawrence pays for destroying the Turkish railway with punishment that reminds him of that railway written across his back. In the closely observed, intense clinical detail the reader senses Lawrence's involvement as well as detachment from this event. He has both a tropistic, masochistic interest in the precise details of his pain and degradation, which he views as if it were happening to someone else, and also a very real and painful awareness of the destruction of his integrity, his wholeness, by this beating and disgust and repulsion from it.

Style 4: Action Narrative

> Out of the darkness came shattering crashes and long, loud metallic clangings of ripped steel, with many lumps of iron and plate; while one entire wheel of a locomotive whirled up suddenly black out of the cloud against the sky, and sailed musically over our heads to fall slowly and heavily into the desert behind. (*S*, 367)

In this passage of very clear and sensuous writing, the contrast between the soft *o* sounds and the sharp *r*, *t*, *l*, and *c* sounds provides a textbook example of Tennysonian orchestration of alliteration and assonance. We hear the sounds and watch the wheel falling, as if in an animated film. Only Lawrence's sensitive and artistic temperament could have caught this objective and powerful action so delicately and reported it in such an interesting, semicomical way. We feel the involvement of Lawrence's finely tuned senses and eye for the incongruous behind every phrase.

Style 5: Patriotic

> While I was with him, word came from Chetwode that Jerusalem had fallen; and Allenby made ready to enter in the official manner which the catholic imagination of Mark Sykes had devised. He was good enough, although I had done nothing for the success, to let Clayton take me along as his staff officer for the day. The personal Staff tricked me out in their spare clothes till I looked like a major in the British Army. Dalmeny lent me red tabs, Evans his brass hat; so that I had the gauds of my appointment in the ceremony of the Jaffa gate, which for me was the supreme moment of the war. (*S*, 453)

This is the "supreme moment" of the *British* war for Lawrence; he is happy to be at Allenby's side in conquered Jerusalem, but his matter-of-fact prose reveals that the formal British side of his personality is mundane and holds no special excitement for him. It is a very quiet "supreme moment" compared to the "supreme embrace" of Arab youths "quivering together in the yielding sand" (*S*, 30).

Style 6: Descriptive

> The trees and bushes stood somewhat apart, in clusters, their lower branches cropped by hungry camels. So they looked cared for, and had a premeditated air, which felt strange in the wilderness, more especially as the Tehama hitherto had been a sober bareness. (*S*, 79)

On one hand, this is good, clear, objective description that captures the look of lone trees in the Tehama region. On the other, only a sensitive temperament would have been able to feel and put into words the "strange" and "premeditated" air of the trees. The passage becomes subjective and disquieting to a certain degree while remaining primarily objective.

Style 7: Strategic
> In military theory I was tolerably read, my Oxford curiosity having taken me past Napoleon to Clausewitz and his school, to Caemmerer and Moltke, and the recent Frenchmen. They had all seemed to be one-sided; and after looking at Jomini and Willisen, I had found broader principles in Saxe and Guibert and the eighteenth century. (*S,* 188)

A textbook treatise on guerrilla warfare includes this almost biblical list that impresses the reader with the quantity of names dropped, and Lawrence's "tolerably read" suggests a flaunting of erudition. Lawrence's account of a rather dry subject is not at all tiresome because of the amount of sheer personality in it; Lawrence even turns his theory of warfare into a religious event: "Ours seemed unlike the ritual of which Foch was priest" (*S,* 190). As the chapter progresses, the reader increasingly credits Lawrence with a brilliant (and very influential) display of pure intellect and forgives him any pretentious airs.

Style 8: Historical-Analytical
> From childhood they were lawless, obeying their fathers only from physical fear; and their government later for much the same reason: yet few races had the respect of the upland Syrian for customary law. All of them wanted something new, for with their superficiality and lawlessness went a passion for politics, a science fatally easy for the Syrian to smatter, but too difficult for him to master. They were discontented always with what government they had; such being their intellectual pride; but few of them honestly thought out a working alternative, and fewer still agreed on one. (*S,* 335)

Lawrence writes a balanced, distinguished prose here, smooth but strangely muted considering his love of Syria, which makes him sick to think of Damascus burning at the end of the revolt. He cannot work himself into any enthusiasm, to play on all the keys of style that he reserves for the Arab veil. The comparative dryness of this paragraph indicates Lawrence's lack of identification with the subject and that his cold, clear, British veil is firmly in place.

Summing Up

Lawrence's two plot lines, self-characterization, and stylistic spectrum reveal much of the man as he saw himself during the period of the Arab

Revolt. But as much as he manages to project through the formal elements of *Seven Pillars,* a good part of Lawrence's personality remains veiled, hidden, and impervious to scholarly unraveling—just as he intended it to be. Lawrence created such a fascinatingly ambiguous and powerful self-image in *Seven Pillars of Wisdom* (and as we shall see, in its coda, *The Mint*), as well as such an intriguing canvas of characters and events, that he has provoked biographers and historians to seek out the real or historical Lawrence—as well as the real or historical Feisal, Auda, Storrs, and Meinertzhagen, for instance—ever since. But in the face of all the biographies and historical studies that will continue to be written about him, we may find that the closest we will ever come to the real man is the contradictory and teasing figure who comes across in *Seven Pillars* and *The Mint.* Readers must create their own Lawrence, perhaps after their own image, and this effect may be Lawrence's best achievement as an artist. Whichever Lawrence the reader takes away from *Seven Pillars of Wisdom* will be one of the greatest characters in all literature.

Chapter Seven

The Mint: Autobiography as Film

Like Lawrence's life after Arabia, when he joined the R.A.F. as an air-man, then the Tank Corps, and then the R.A.F. again, *The Mint* is an artistic and spiritual anticlimax. The story of recruit training and the new air force (Lawrence eliminated any reference to his Tank Corps experience in the interest of artistic unity) cannot equal in excitement and exotic appeal the fantastic tale of the Arab Revolt and the "two veils" contained in *Seven Pillars of Wisdom*. In *The Mint,* we have only the British veil—in plot line at any rate—and a more constricted one than in *Seven Pillars*. Instead of grand strategy, interesting descriptions of exotic scenery and equally exotic historical events and the pressures of war, *The Mint* contains only the daily hardship of basic training and Lawrence's feeling of the importance of air travel. Neither the men nor the events (internal and external) match the keyed-up excitement of the earlier book, and the deliberately antiromantic style of clipped sentences and abrupt chapters reveals the new straitjacketed constriction of the life of the narrator-protagonist. By joining the R.A.F., Lawrence deliberately forced himself into a "mint" that would amputate his will and hold his fragmented self together with external pressure. Unfortunately, as a literary character he is much more interesting when the pressure of strangeness, pain, and war causes his personality to come apart at the seams and when his struggle to hold himself together is embodied in a wide variety of styles and situations. *The Mint* follows a "hard act to fol-low"—*Seven Pillars*—and by contrast presents too attenuated and nar-row a view of life (despite the adventure of speed and air) to excite strong partisanship.

At the same time that we make this comparative artistic judgment, we should bear in mind that *The Mint* contains the important story of Lawrence's reintegration as a person and his reintegration into society (somewhat analogous to Henry Fleming's journey into himself in Crane's *Red Badge of Courage* and Ishmael's reconciliation with man and nature in *Moby-Dick* [1]). *The Mint* thus completes the process of alienation and detachment with a positive, if sporadic, fulfillment only rarely glimpsed in *Seven Pillars*.

Like *Seven Pillars, The Mint* is clearly a poetic autobiography in which we see some aspects of the narrator-protagonist's personality even more clearly than in the earlier book; ultimately, however, he remains a mystery. The central question of *why* he joined the R.A.F. as a simple airman is imperfectly answered, and the book thus contains an element almost as shadowy as the "S. A." and Deraa stories of *Seven Pillars*. Again like *Seven Pillars, The Mint* contains first and foremost the story of Lawrence's personality rather than that of recruit training or the development of the air force. All events in the book are seen through his eyes, filtered through his personality, and the reader's attention is fully drawn only to him.

As in *Seven Pillars*, the core of *The Mint* is a personal chapter (*M,* part 2, chapter 19), "Odd Man Out," in which Lawrence analyzes the elements of his character in clearer language than he does in the "Myself" chapter of *Seven Pillars*. We notice the same elements: a love of physical testing and a flirting with pain; the intellectual shyness and self-consciousness that make life in public a torture *and* the forcing of the self into public life, again as a test; fear of failing to live up to impossible, absolute physical and mental standards that only Lawrence could set for himself; a revulsion toward sexuality and touch that is to some degree resolved by the end of part 3; a fascination with pain and degradation, shown especially in the portrait of "Our Commanding Officer" (*M,* part 1, chapter 20); and finally an aestheticism that informs his whole view of his surroundings.

The difference in personal content between the two books is that *The Mint* presents an experiment, Lawrence's conscious attempt to "end his civil war and live the open life, patent for everyone to read" (*M,* 27). He wants to overcome his fears and fragmentation and largely succeeds by the end of the book. At first, Lawrence is worried about his ability to "plunge crudely amongst crude men" (*M,* 27) and to become their comrade and partner. By the end of the second section of the book, he cannot call his experiment a success even though he has been "In the Mill" with these men for a long time; his isolated, introverted nature persists: "For I have learned solidarity with them here. Not that we are very like, or will be. I joined in high hope of sharing their tastes and manners and life: but my nature persists in seeing all things in the mirror of itself, and not with a direct eye" (*M,* 195). He is still cut off from his own body as well: "Touch? I do not know. I fear and shun touch most, of my senses." (*M,* 127). In his typically puritanical "British veil" tone, which equates sexuality—both homosexual and heterosexual—with "beastliness," Lawrence states that he has not had voluntary sexual experience (*M,*

128). Thus his relationship with Dahoum may have been only idealized, rather than overt, and his journey into touch very limited. Until the last section of *The Mint,* Lawrence remains apart from nature. In *Seven Pillars,* nature was portrayed as a beautiful but essentially foreign and treacherous force that posed a continual threat to man:

> The crags were capped in nests of domes, less hotly red than the body of the hill; rather grey and shallow. They gave the finishing semblance of Byzantine architecture to this irresistible place: this processional way greater than imagination. The Arab armies would have been lost in the length and breadth of it, and within the walls a squadron of aeroplanes could have wheeled in formation. Our little caravan grew self-conscious, and fell dead quiet, afraid and ashamed to flaunt its smallness in the presence of the stupendous hills. (*S*, 351)

Even technology, the airplane, cannot place nature in a balance with man, and the comparison with Byzantine architecture (besides being very appropriate, for there are many ruined Byzantine cities in the desert, as *The Wilderness of Zin* demonstrates) actually emphasizes man's smallness. Lawrence, uncompromising in his search for the absolute in *Seven Pillars,* finds something humiliating and degrading in nature's ability to dwarf man. In *The Mint,* however, the R.A.F. allows Lawrence to feel that the airplane *can* forge a balance between nature and humanity. He uses technology for an attainable goal: "The darling partiality of Nature, which has reserved across the ages her last element for us to dompt! By our handling of this, the one big new thing, will our time be judged" (*M*, 218). Still, until the very end of *The Mint,* he clearly prefers technology to nature: "A skittish motor-bike with a touch of blood in it is better than all the riding animals on earth, because of its logical extension of our faculties, and the hint, the provocation to excess conferred by its honeyed untiring smoothness" (*M*, 245).[2]

In addition to the old divisions between man and nature, man and other men, and Lawrence and his body that persist until the very end of *The Mint,* we have Lawrence's most agonizing division as well, that between parts of his own mind:

> I watch, detachedly . . . judging myself now carried away by instinct, now ruling a course by reason, now deciding intuitively: always restlessly cataloguing each aspect of my unity. . . .
> There it goes again: the conflict of mind and spirit. . . . Man, who was born as one, breaks into little prisms when he thinks: but if he passes

through thought into despair, or comprehension, he again achieves some momentary onenesses with himself. And not only that. He can achieve a oneness of himself with his fellows: and of them with the stocks and stones of his universe: and of all the universes with the illusory everything (if he be positive) or with the illusory nothing (if he be nihilist) according as the digestive complexion of his soul be dark or fair. (*M,* 179)

As in *Seven Pillars,* Lawrence characteristically divides his mind into several parts. But there is something new here: his glimpse of the possibility of an almost mystical unity beyond all the parts. For the first time since the brief moments of mindless action recorded in *Seven Pillars,* Lawrence realizes that he has the chance, however temporary, to feel at one with nature, others, and himself.

This new opportunity is miraculously achieved in the last pages of *The Mint.* As the result of his R.A.F. experience, Lawrence can portray himself for the first and only time in his spiritual journey as a fulfilled and happy human being:

> We were too utterly content to speak, drugged with an absorption fathoms deeper than physical contentment. Just we lay there spread-eagled in a mesh of bodies, pillowed on one another and sighing in happy excess of relaxation. The sunlight poured from the sky and melted into our tissues. From the turf below our moist backs there came up a sister-heat which joined us to it. Our bones dissolved to become a part of this underlying indulgent earth, whose mysterious pulse throbbed in every tremor of our bodies. The scents of the thousand-acre drome mixed with the familiar oil-breath of our hangar, nature with art. . . . (*M,* 249)

Lawrence has learned to reach out, touch, and lose himself in nature and other men. He has been able to free himself (whether often or only occasionally), from the self-consciousness that plagued him up to this point.

The final passage of *The Mint* is a lyrical triumph in which Lawrence manages to work his austere self-deprivation and mystical sense of oneness with nature into a perfect synthesis:

> And airmen are cared for as little as they care. Their simple eyes, out-turned; their natural living; the penurious imaginations which neither harrow nor reap their lowlands of mind: all these expose them, like fallows, to the processes of air. In the summer we are easily the sun's. In winter we struggle undefended along the roadway, and the rain and wind chivy us, till soon we are wind and rain. We race over in the first dawn to the College's translucent swimming pool, and dive into the elastic water

which fits our bodies closely as a skin:—and we belong to that too. Everywhere a relationship: no loneliness any more. (*M, 249–50*)

This is the true conclusion of the long and hard spiritual journey that begins with the first page of *Seven Pillars* and continues to the last page of *The Mint*. In these passages, Lawrence indicates that especially toward the end of his life he was occasionally able to achieve F. H. Bradley's "Absolute," a state that the contemporary Oxford philosopher perceived as beyond thought and where all is reconciled in a blissful sense of oneness.[3]

Lawrence's success and happiness in Cadet College (part 3 of *The Mint*) have been questioned by skeptical critics.[4] His flagellation compulsion, which caused him to have himself periodically whipped by a service colleague, continued from 1923 until his death. Whether one takes it as Lawrence's medieval, ascetic self-punishment for having sexual feelings or as his only means of achieving sexual satisfaction, it certainly indicates that he did not completely resolve his felt division between body and mind. But this compulsive behavior of Lawrence's can be overemphasized in view of his oft-stated feeling of happiness during his later life. It does not prove that Lawrence is insincere in ending *The Mint* with statements of unity and joy.

The critic V. S. Pritchett locates the best (and therefore most sincere) writing in the book in its final 40 pages,[5] which contain Lawrence's statements of newfound happiness. The fact is that military service can offer the kind of comradeship and satisfaction that would be available in no other way to an intellectual like Lawrence. Through rest after hard work, simple living, physical exercise, and joint activity with a group of men, free of "thought," Lawrence (at least during these intervals and others like them) became one with his body, other men, and nature itself, instead of divided, solitary, and hostile to his surroundings. If we understand that Lawrence consistently attained the wholeness he claims for himself in the final passages of *The Mint* during those times of unintellectual activity or rest, we will be able to credit his statements as true and genuine, even as they apply to his own life and not merely as an "idea" or a good ending for his book. He seemed to achieve such experiences more often and in a quieter way in the R.A.F. than had ever been possible for him before. As his letters demonstrate, he was very reluctant to leave the service because he had become to a large degree the gifted but normal mechanic, free of most (if not all) of his former self-divisions, who wrote "A Handbook to the 37 1/2 Foot Motor Boats of the 200 Class." In a

fragment from a projected sequel to *The Mint,* he writes of his impending
retirement: "The wrench this is; I shall feel like a lost dog when I leave—
or when it leaves me, rather, for the R.A.F. goes on. The strange attraction in the feel of the clothes, the work, the companionship. A direct
touch with men, obtained in no other way in life" (*L,* 854).

Lawrence chose at the end of the autobiographical project that continues from *Seven Pillars* through *The Mint* to leave the reader with an
image of himself as happy and whole at last; undoubtedly he was closer
to this ideal in the R.A.F. than he had ever been before. But as we have
seen, this is not the whole story—there is also the implied despair of the
flagellation compulsion, which he kept secret. Lawrence leaves us then,
as always, with a contradiction, if in this case an unstated one, between
happiness and frustration. If he were an example of just one or the other,
he would perhaps not be as fascinating or as sympathetic as he remains
to us.

Technique and Form

In addition to the difference in content, *The Mint* displays two formal differences from *Seven Pillars:* its use of the present tense and its tight,
clipped style including brief, abrupt chapters. *Seven Pillars* was composed
under the pressure of immediate recollection, but apart from dialogue
it is written in the past tense. Since *The Mint* is transcribed directly
from notes written on the spot (in its first two sections) and from notes
and letters at a somewhat greater distance in time (in its third section),
Lawrence chooses present-tense narration throughout. For instance, he
writes "Every man in the hut, bar me, tries shamelessly or shamefully to
sing and hum and whistle" (*M,* 47), or "We grumble at the food" (*M,*
160), or "Tim is the Flight Commander. He's a jewel" (*M,* 215). Thus
The Mint is autobiography that tends in the direction of the diary, and as
a result it gains a certain immediacy. Lawrence learned photography from
his father early on and was sent to the R.A.F. school of photography at
Farnborough during the period in which he was contemplating and writing *The Mint.* Its strikingly etched, memorable scenes are not mirror
images of reality but rather photographs taken through the distorting
lens of his personality, and they have the immediate impact of photographs. At the same time, the narrator-protagonist takes a retrospective view of the process he has undergone when he writes "For I have
learned solidarity with them here. Not that we are very like, or will be. I
joined in the high hope of sharing their tastes and manners and life: but

my nature persists in seeing all things in the mirror of itself, and not with
a direct eye" (*M*, 195). Here, at the end of part 2, the narrator's consciousness has shaped all the preceding immediate photographs into a
pattern. This conscious retrospective shaping, usually lacking in *Seven
Pillars* except as the reader supplied it, actually makes *The Mint* a less
interesting book: The more Lawrence's character and process of change
are defined, the less reader participation that is necessary.

The effect of the stringing together of this series of distorted photos
and the summing up of their meaning, as Lawrence does in the passage
just quoted, is like that of a documentary film narrated from a certain
point of view, with a certain message to impress, very immediate but
restricted in content—like an unusually artistic military training film in
fact. This filmlike immediacy is also the result of the book's style of
writing. Clipped, abrupt, generally lacking in but not without rich diction, Lawrence's style in *The Mint* keeps us riveted to the surface of
proximate events rather than propelled to airy heights of thought or
tensed in involuted uneasiness. Lawrence chose this style deliberately to
express the new constriction of his self and his changed circumstances:

> I'd put the *Mint* a little higher than that: and say that its style well fitted
> its subject: our dull clothed selves; our humdrum, slightly oppressed
> lives; our tight uniforms: the constriction, the limits, the artificial con-
> duct, of our bodies and minds and spirits, in the great machine which the
> R.A.F. is becoming. I had to hold myself down, on each page, with both
> hands.
>
> A painted or sentimental style, such as I used in *The Seven Pillars,*
> would have been out of place in *The Mint,* except in the landscape pas-
> sages, where I have used it. (*L*, 596)

Within the basic attenuation, there is a certain amount of stylistic
variation in *The Mint*. Though clearer than similar passages in *Seven Pillars*, "gummy" reflective statements sometimes appear. Also, his aesthetic temperament continually shapes his surroundings in its own
expressionistic image: "So the beams and ties of the roof-trusses are
tonight futurist and mysterious, being pendent with all our equipment,
slung up there to dry stiff, after scrubbing" (*M*, 48). He is as good at
describing action as ever, and the first short sentences help:

> A glance at the speedometer: seventy-eight. Boanerges is warming up. I
> pull the throttle right open, on the top of the slope, and we swoop flying
> across the dip, and up-down up-down the switchback beyond: the

weighty machine launching itself like a projectile with a whirr of wheels into the air at the take-off of each rise, to land lurchingly with such a snatch of the driving chain as jerks my spine like a rictus. (*M*, 242).

His dialogue is very fine and rings true: " 'Do you know what happened to me, tonight? I met a girl . . . or she wasn't a girl, really . . . and we . . . clicked and went off together. Remember that dollar I borrowed off you, Monday? Well that just did it' " (*M*, 223–24). But the powerful, colored, high romantic touch is gone, and we miss it very much, as we do the whole Arab veil of adventure and strangeness.

Obviously, this book of "notes" has taken much work to polish—as the British Library manuscripts of *The Mint* prove—and it is an artistic autobiography, in which we feel what it was like to be T. E. Lawrence-Ross-Shaw in his new situation. The fact that this new situation is not nearly so interesting as the old and that Lawrence's personality is less pressured and consequently less divided and mysterious for us should not blind us to an interesting experiment in autobiographical form. For *The Mint* is poetic autobiography but in the form of a documentary film, complete with distorting lenses and a series of sharp frames (or chapters) moving past us, rather than a rich deep mysterious self-portrait in oils. As Lawrence pointed out in a letter (now in the British Library collection) to Mrs. Shaw, neither *The Mint* nor *Seven Pillars* owes anything to Joyce. But in its fast-moving immediacy, as in its paean to the air force, *The Mint* remains a tribute to twentieth-century technology. It is the first autobiography to meet the film on its own ground.

Chapter Eight

Further Arabians

Thanks to the diligent work of scholars, the extent of Lawrence's influence *as a character* on the literature of the twentieth century has been clearly established.[1] Numerous writers have based whole poems and novels on the Lawrence character. More writers have mentioned him tangentially in their work. This is actually a measure of Lawrence's literary ability, for most of these poems and novels have been influenced by the character Lawrence that he created in *Seven Pillars* and *The Mint* rather than by T. E. Lawrence the man.

T. E. Lawrence has proven to be one of the most fascinating self-created characters ever conceived, fully on a par with Henry Adams's Henry Adams, Norman Mailer's Norman Mailer of *The Armies of the Night,* and the Thoreau of *Walden.* Lawrence—or a reasonable facsimile thereof—has appeared in poems by W. H. Auden, Robert Graves, Archibald MacLeish, and Canadian poet Gwendolyn MacEwen, among others. In drama he has been the model for Ransom in Auden and Isherwood's *Ascent of F.6,* for Shaw's Private Meek and Saint Joan, and for Rattigan's Ross. He provided the impetus for Rudolph Valentino's "Sheik" and served more recently as the subject of the 1962 film *Lawrence of Arabia.*[2] Novelists have made even more use of Lawrence than have the poets, dramatists, and filmmakers. He has featured in thin disguise in James Aldridge's *Heroes of the Empty View,* Maurice Barrès's *Un Jardin sur l'oronte,* John Buchan's *Courts of the Morning,* André Malraux's *Walnut Trees of Altenburg,* Anthony West's *David Rees among Others,* and Hemingway's *For Whom the Bell Tolls.* C. Day-Lewis (who Lawrence early recognized as an important poet) made use of Lawrence's figure for a detective story, *Shell of Death,* and Matthew Eden in 1979 played on the public's taste for conspiracy theories with his novel *The Murder of Lawrence of Arabia.* Even D. H. Lawrence, the namesake who never reciprocated T. E.'s openly expressed admiration of him, makes some deprecatory remarks about a "Colonel C. E. Florence" in *Lady Chatterley's Lover.*

Although such evidence provides a tribute to Lawrence's creation of an interesting character—himself—it tells us very little about the direct artistic influence that Lawrence has had on later writers. Although these authors of poems, dramas, films, and novels obviously owe the inspiration for some of the characters in their work to Lawrence, we can scarcely say that he influenced the style or structure of any of their creations, including those in which he appears. Has his artistic influence then been confined to myth and nebulous inspiration, a father without any heirs in the direct line of descent, or has he in fact pointed the way for other literary artists to write their own work?

If we look to the writers in the tradition in which Lawrence himself wrote, we get a very clear answer to that question. All three of the best Anglo-Arabian travelers and travel writers after Lawrence are directly indebted to him for important bits of the content of their works, and at least one of them has been obviously and deeply influenced by his artistry. The fact that Bertram Thomas, Harry St. John Bridger Philby, and Wilfred Thesiger all held Lawrence in the highest respect as an authority on the desert and desert ways is a strong argument for the validity of his account of the Arabs' way of life in his time. After Doughty and Lawrence, the last great unknown in Arabian travel was the difficult desert area called the Rub al Khali, or Empty Quarter, which no European had ever crossed, so treacherous were its hardships for the traveler. In February 1931, Bertram Thomas became the first to accomplish this great feat and was closely followed in the same year by Philby, who took an even more difficult route. In 1946–1947 and 1947–1948, Wilfred Thesiger crossed the Empty Quarter twice, covering areas not explored by his predecessors.

Lawrence's introduction, generous in its praise of the explorer (for whom Lawrence tried to secure a knighthood [*L,* 714]), graces Thomas's *Arabia Felix.* In his own preface to that book, Thomas cites Lawrence as a "friend" to whom he turned for editorial reading. Philby scatters respectful references to Lawrence throughout his many books on Arabia, citing him more than 20 times in his *Arabian Days* (1948) alone. And Thesiger, in his brilliantly written *Arabian Sands* (Harmondsworth: Penguin, 1959), openly quotes Lawrence directly on several occasions as an authority on matters of Arab customs.

Although Lawrence respected both Thomas—who obviated Lawrence's own idea of surveying the Empty Quarter by airship—and Philby as explorers, he thought them inferior writers when compared to other "Arabians" like Palgrave, for instance. In a letter written in 1933, Lawrence classes Philby and Thomas as great explorers but calls Palgrave a great explorer *and* writer (*L,* 768). And in his foreword to

Thomas's book, he carefully refrains from praising Thomas's literary art, except for a suspect single sentence: "Thomas let me read the draft, and I then did my best to comment usefully; once remarking that the tale was good enough for his journey—no faint judgement, set against what I think the finest thing in Arabian exploration." This praise is faint indeed if we remember the extravagant praise that Lawrence lavishes on the artist Doughty in his foreword to *Arabia Deserta*. Thomas completed his journey in February 1931; he finished his book by December 1931, according to its preface. Philby wrote with journalistic ease and rapidity. If we recall that Doughty spent four years writing his manuscript and another several revising it, that Lawrence's book was the result of seven years of writing and revision, and that Thesiger's *Arabian Sands* appeared nine years after his travels, we have a clue to Lawrence's relatively negative assessment of the artistic merit of the Thomas and Philby books.

Lawrence thought Thomas the last great Arabian explorer because he had crossed the final barrier the country afforded, but Wilfred Thesiger proved him wrong by covering new territory within the Empty Quarter. Although Lawrence influenced Thomas and Philby in indirect ways, Thesiger remains Lawrence's direct artistic heir. Although there are important differences between Lawrence and Thesiger, Lawrence's influence on the form and content of Thesiger's book appears in several areas: (1) direct quotations used for authoritative support; (2) intense dissatisfaction with Western civilization and a desire to escape it; (3) a straddling of fences between Western and Arab identities; (4) a predilection for the austerity and physical test of the desert; (5) the use of highly colored style and dialogue; and (6) a creative literary use of characterization. Lawrence and Thesiger are not alone as twentieth-century travelers in feeling their Western identities weakened by the attraction of Arabia: Philby actually converted to Islam and served as King Saud's adviser. And all travelers, including Thomas, have been attracted to the physical challenge represented by the desert. But Thesiger remains Lawrence's true and most important heir because he alone of the three regards the travel book as primarily an artistic form and in *Arabian Sands* has created an enduring work of art.

In his book, Thesiger quotes or mentions Lawrence directly no less than five times; by contrast, Doughty is mentioned not even once. We learn that it was Lawrence's abridgment of *Seven Pillars*, *Revolt in the Desert*, that first "awakened" Thesiger's "interest in the Arabs" (39). The prologue of *Arabian Sands* includes a direct quotation from *Seven Pillars*,

"Beduin ways were hard, even for those brought up in them and for strangers terrible: a death in life." Thesiger's own comment on this quotation is that "No man can live this life and emerge unchanged. He will carry, however faint, the imprint of the desert, the brand which marks the nomad; and he will have within him the yearning to return, weak or insistent according to his nature. For this cruel land can cast a spell which no temperate climate can match" (15). On the Kissim Pass, Thesiger recollects and quotes approvingly Lawrence's parable about the lack of smell of the desert and the Arabs' comment on the desert wind: "'This,' they told him, 'is the best: it has no taste.'" In stating that "the Arabs are a race which produces its best only under conditions of extreme hardship and deteriorates progressively as living conditions become easier" (97), Thesiger quotes Lawrence for substantiation. The one footnote that he places on Lawrence's book is a clarification rather than a contradiction: "Homosexuality is common among most Arabs, especially in the towns, but is very rare among the Bedu, who of all Arabs have the most excuse for indulging in this practice, since they spend long months away from their women. Lawrence described in *Seven Pillars of Wisdom* how his escort made use of each other to slake their needs, but those men were villagers from the oasis, not Bedu" (125).

In almost all of these passages, as in his constant emphasis on the dangers of his journeys, Thesiger echoes Lawrence's own preoccupation with austerity and hardship. In fact, this seems to be his primary motivation: "I went there to find peace in the hardship of desert travel and the company of desert peoples" (278). He also reveals in himself a weakened Western identity and division between England and Arabia in his affections. Like Lawrence, he alternates between both ways of life; on an R.A.F. base in Arabia, he says

> It was a pleasant change talking English instead of the constant effort of talking Arabic; to have a hot bath and to eat well-cooked food; even to sit at ease on a chair with my legs stretched out, instead of sitting on the ground with them tucked under me. But the pleasure of doing these things was enormously enhanced for me by the knowledge that I was going back to the desert. (182)

Back in England, he cannot wait to return to Arabia: "In deserts, however arid, I have never felt homesick for green fields and woods in spring, but now that I was in England I longed with an ache that was almost physical to be back in Arabia" (203). Like the Lawrence caught between two cultures, Thesiger among Englishmen "knew that I stood apart from them and would never find contentment among them, whereas I could find it among these Bedu, although I should never be one of them" (184). Lawrence hated the idea that the consciousness of nationalism that he helped develop in the Arabs would destroy their traditional way of life. Thesiger writes that

> Today the desert where I travelled is scarred with the tracks of lorries and littered with discarded junk imported from Europe and America. But this material desecration is unimportant compared with the demoralization which has resulted among the Bedu themselves. While I was with them they had no thought of a world other than their own. They were not ignorant savages; on the contrary, they were the lineal heirs of a very ancient civilization, who found within the framework of their society the personal freedom and self discipline for which they craved. Now they are being driven out of the desert into towns where the qualities which once give them mastery are no longer sufficient. (11–12)

Thesiger merely chronicles the end of the process that Lawrence had foreseen 40 years earlier and that is underway in Israel today as well as in all parts of the Near East.[3]

Thesiger's style represents a more recent version of Lawrence's. He manages the feat of retaining the same tone of "Arabian" coloring that we noted in Lawrence's "Arab veil" writing but uses a basically contemporary English. Desert life evokes a lyrical, delicately chivalric style of parallelism expressed in contemporary diction: "I had learnt the satisfaction which comes from hardship and the pleasure which springs from abstinence; the contentment of a full belly; the richness of meat; the taste of clean water; the ecstasy of surrender when the craving for sleep becomes a torment; the warmth of a fire in the chill of dawn" (37). Subtly he attempts to capture the syntax and rhetoric of Arabic speech in very many passages, augmenting this lean bilingualism with Arabic names and words: "The Riqaishi gave his camel an angry blow and answered, 'You would not have brought the Christian here if you had wished to please me' " (318). Though less pronounced than Lawrence's Eastern linguistic touches, Thesiger gives us essentially an updated version of the same thing.

Perhaps most tellingly, he provides "A List of the Chief Characters on the Various Journeys" (332) at the end of the book. The use of the word *characters* instead of *people* or *personalities* gives a clear hint of Thesiger's literary intentions. Although less dramatized and spectacular than

Lawrence's Feisal and Auda, Thesiger's Salim bin Kabina and Salim bin Ghabaisha are in fact chief characters in a drama in which they emerge as vivid, fully rounded, and yet unusual central actors. The farewell between the three men, on the very last page of the book, remains as touching as any parting in Anglo-Arabian (or other) literature, and the entire story has been structured to emphasize this final message: "The lorry arrived after breakfast. We embraced for the last time. I said, 'Go in peace,' and they answered together 'Remain in the safe keeping of God, Umbarak.'. . . I was glad when Codrai took me to the aerodrome at Sharja. As the plane climbed over the town and swung out above the sea I knew how it felt to go into exile" (330). Ostensibly restrained, each carefully chosen word of colored dialogue carries a heavy emotional weight because we have watched the characters go through so much together and develop into human beings who come alive on the page.

Thesiger, in his own role as Umbarak and as narrator, never gives himself completely away. As in Lawrence's case, the reader feels that there remains a lot more for the author to say about himself if he cared to and that despite his stated explanation for going to Arabia, the real explanation—namely, what personality trait makes him so amenable to hardship—eludes us. Thesiger thus takes his place in the grand tradition of the Anglo-Arabian travel artist.

But despite these many spiritual and stylistic similarities, Lawrence and Thesiger differ in ways that once again illuminate Lawrence's uniqueness and appeal. Thesiger lives by a hunter's, warrior's, and aristocrat's code, whereas Lawrence never gave any indication of liking hunting, grew to hate fighting, and joined the R.A.F. as an airman in an ultimate renunciation of aristocracy and class. Although he wrote after World War II, when the dangers of such group stereotyping had become obvious, Thesiger thoughtlessly indulges in ethnic and national generalizations, insisting on the superiority of the Bedouin and (to a lesser degree) the British to all other peoples. Lawrence is unfortunately prone to making some group generalizations in Seven Pillars, but Lawrence wrote long before Thesiger, at a time when anthropology was a relatively new subject and people were not fully aware of the dangers of such stereotyping. Moreover, Lawrence (unlike Thesiger) entirely repudiated the idea that one national group was "better" than another. The result is that Thesiger, despite his artistry, already appears like a throwback in some ways, whereas the Lawrence who preceded him in time remains our contemporary.[4]

This quality of always being contemporary is what ultimately distinguishes Lawrence as a writer. His work belongs as much to our age of postcolonialism, cultural pluralism, changing sexual roles, terrorism, fast motorcycles, and the ever increasing prominence of literary nonfiction as it does to the time of late nineteenth-century aestheticism, World War I, and empire. Whenever relations between the Arabs and the West are mentioned, *Seven Pillars of Wisdom* is imitated, referred to, or quoted, as it has been in two of the most recent literary travel books, Jonathan Raban's *Arabia: A Journey through the Labyrinth*[5] and Christopher Dickey's *Expats*.[6] Moreover, Lawrence records not only a struggle for World War I military and political success but also for his own cultural and sexual identity, which makes his books immediately relevant today. His work also relates to the perennial philosophical problem of whether it is possible to attain both freedom and integrity. Lawrence's contradictory self-characterization is intriguing, complex, and unforgettable, and it is expressed in some of the best prose ever written. For all of these reasons, *Seven Pillars of Wisdom* and its sequel, *The Mint*, constitute one of the finest British autobiographical projects of the twentieth century. Lawrence's ever eroding and ever remaining monument to his own personality seems destined to be read not only in what is left of our century but also in centuries to come.

Notes and References

Chapter One

    1. See H. S. Gullett, *The Australian Imperial Force in Sinai and Palestine 1914–1918* (Queensland: University of Queensland Press and The Australian War Memorial, 1984), 394–400. Although obviously not filmed on location and less than fully detailed, the Australian film *The Light Horsemen* (1988; directed by Simon Wincer) nevertheless gives a convincing depiction of the World War I battle for Beersheba. British intelligence chief Richard Meinertzhagen's brilliant deception of the Turks paved the way for this battle. *Seven Pillars* also relates that story. For a history of the entire Palestine campaign, see *Military Operations, Egypt and Palestine*, 2 vols., ed. George MacMunn and Cyril Falls (London: H.M.S.O., 1928).

    2. T. E. Lawrence, *Seven Pillars of Wisdom* (Garden City, N.Y.: Garden City Publishing Co., 1938). All references are to this edition (hereafter cited in the text as *S*), except where I specifically cite the Oxford text of 1922 and other early manuscript forms. My edition is identical with the Subscriber's Edition of 1926 except for minor details, and I frequently refer to it as the "final edition." A history of the many texts of *Seven Pillars* begins my chapter 4.

    3. T. E. Lawrence, *The Mint* (New York: Norton, 1955); hereafter cited in the text as *M*.

    4. It appeared in a very limited edition in 1926.

    5. T. E. Lawrence, *Revolt in the Desert* (New York: Doran, 1927).

    6. T. E. Lawrence, *The Letters of T. E. Lawrence,* ed. David Garnett (London: Jonathan Cape, 1938), 513; hereafter cited in the text as *L*.

    7. R. P. Blackmur, "The Everlasting Effort: A Citation of T. E. Lawrence," in *The Lion and the Honeycomb* (New York: Harcourt, Brace, 1955), 108; originally published in R. P. Blackmur, *The Expense of Greatness* (New York: Arrow, 1940).

    8. Richard Aldington, *Lawrence of Arabia: A Biographical Enquiry* (London: Collins, 1955), 330.

    9. Malcolm Muggeridge, "Poor Lawrence," review of Anthony Nutting's *Lawrence of Arabia, New Statesman* 52 (27 October 1961): 604.

    10. "T. E. Lawrence: The Problem of Heroism," *Hudson Review* 15, 3 (Autumn 1962): 333–64.

    11. Several of these theses and dissertations have been published as books and can be found (albeit under different titles) in this volume's bibliography. The earliest thesis that I have found is James Leighton Bunnell's "T. E. Lawrence and Anglo-Arab Diplomacy, 1919–1922," (M.A. thesis, Vanderbilt

University, 1952), but then there is a gap until the 1960s, after which graduate works on Lawrence multiply rapidly: Lois Olive Gray, "Studies in T. E. Lawrence's *Seven Pillars of Wisdom*" (M.A. thesis, University of Florida, 1965); James C. Coates, "The Influence of T. E. Lawrence on British Foreign Policy in the Middle East 1918–1922" (M.A. thesis, McGill University, 1967); Stephen King, "Thomas Edward Lawrence in the City of Artisans" (M.A. thesis, Claremont Graduate School, 1969); Thomas J. O'Donnell, "The Dichotomy of Self in T. E. Lawrence's *Seven Pillars of Wisdom* (Ph.D. diss., University of Illinois at Urbana-Champaign, 1970); Stephen E. Tabachnick, "T. E. Lawrence's *Seven Pillars of Wisdom* as a Work of Art" (Ph.D. diss., University of Connecticut, 1971); John Saul Friedman, "The Challenge of Destiny: A Comparison of T. E. Lawrence's and André Malraux's Adventure Tales" (Ph.D. diss., New York University, 1974); Maurice Larès, "T. E. Lawrence, la France et les Français" (Doctorat d'État diss., presented to the University of Paris III, 1976; printed by the University of Lille Thesis Reproduction Service, 1978); Robert Warde, "T. E. Lawrence: A Critical Study" (Ph.D. diss., Harvard, 1978); John A. Hamilton, "Epics of the Lone Will: A Study of *Travels in Arabia Deserta* and *Seven Pillars of Wisdom* (Ph.D. diss., Harvard, 1979); Malcolm Allen, "The Medievalism of T. E. Lawrence ('of Arabia')" (Ph.D. diss., Pennsylvania State University, 1983); Victoria Carchidi, "Creation out of the Void: The Making of a Hero, an Epic, a World—T. E. Lawrence" (Ph.D. diss., University of Pennsylvania, 1987); Timothy Barclay, "T. E. Lawrence and the Arab Revolt: Innovation and Irregular Warfare" (M.A. thesis, Central Missouri University, 1991); Robert Davies, "Warriors and Gentlemen: The Occidental Context of the Arabian Travel Narratives of Burton, Blunt, and Lawrence" (Ph.D. diss., Loughborough University of Technology, 1991); Mohammed Nour Naimi, "T. E. Lawrence and the Orientalist Tradition" (Ph.D. diss., University of Essex, 1991); Paola Daniele, "*The Mint* di T. E. Lawrence come Documente e come Confessione" (Thesis di Laurea, Istituto Universitario Orientale, Naples, 1992); Joel Hodson, "Transatlantic Legend: T. E. Lawrence and American Culture" (Ph.D. diss., George Washington University, 1992); Celeste Renee Snyder, "The War within the Warrior: An Autobiographical Study of T. E. Lawrence in *Seven Pillars of Wisdom*" (M.A. thesis, University of Wisconsin, Eau Claire, 1993); Maren Ormseth Cohn, "T. E. Lawrence and Odysseus: A Study of Translation, Identity, and Heroic Action" (Ph.D. diss., University of Chicago, 1995).

    12.   *The Wounded Spirit: A Study of "Seven Pillars of Wisdom,"* (London: Martin Brian & O'Keeffe, 1973), 11.

    13.   *Lawrence of Arabia: The Literary Impulse* (Baton Rouge: Louisiana State University Press, 1975), xii–xiii.

    14.   *The Confessions of T. E. Lawrence* (Athens: Ohio University Press, 1979), 181.

    15.   Keith Hull, "*Seven Pillars of Wisdom:* The Secret, Contestable Documentary," in *The T. E. Lawrence Puzzle,* ed. Stephen E. Tabachnick (Athens: University of Georgia Press, 1984), 113–14.

16. *The Medievalism of Lawrence of Arabia* (University Park: Pennsylvania State University Press, 1991), 196.

17. *Lawrence of Arabia and American Culture* (Westport, Conn.: Greenwood Press, 1995), 79.

18. For the personal relationship between Lawrence and Hardy, see R. D. Knight, *T. E. Lawrence and the Max Gate Circle* (Weymouth: Bat and Ball Press, 1988).

19. Quoted in Stanley Weintraub, *Private Shaw and Public Shaw* (New York: George Brazillier, 1963), 113–14. This book provides an excellent account of the personal and literary relationship between Lawrence and Mr. and Mrs. G. B. Shaw and was a pioneering academic work in Lawrence studies.

20. "T. E. Lawrence" in *Abinger Harvest* (London: Edward Arnold, 1936), 170.

21. *Lawrence and the Arabs* (London: Cape, 1927), 407.

22. This letter appears in *Letters to T. E. Lawrence,* ed. A. W. Lawrence (London: Cape, 1962), 155.

23. Ibid., 213.

24. Ibid., 67.

25. L. P. Hartley, "A Failed Masterpiece," *The Listener* (April 14, 1955): 658–59.

26. V. S. Pritchett, "Ross at the Depot," in *The Living Novel & Later Appreciations* (New York: Random House, 1964), 288–90.

27. "T. E. Lawrence: The Mechanical Monk," in *The T. E. Lawrence Puzzle,* 133.

28. See *Letters to T. E. Lawrence,* 66–69 (Forster), 96–98 (E. Garnett), and 82–85 (D. Garnett).

29. Anonymous, "The Mint," *Kirkus* 22 (15 December 1954): 830.

30. 2 vols. (London: Golden Cockerel Press, 1936). The most recent edition, with an introduction by Denys Pringle, is Oxford: Clarendon, 1988.

31. Konrad Morsey, "T. E. Lawrence: Strategist" in *The T. E. Lawrence Puzzle,* 185–203.

32. See Philip O'Brien, *T. E. Lawrence: A Bibliography* (Boston: G. K. Hall, 1988), 427–29.

33. See J. M. Wilson, *Lawrence of Arabia: The Authorized Biography of T. E. Lawrence* (New York: Atheneum, 1990), 1054–55, and many other passages.

34. On this phase of his career, see Aaron Klieman, "Lawrence as Bureaucrat" in *The T. E. Lawrence Puzzle,* 243–68.

35. *The Odyssey of Homer,* trans. T. E. Shaw, intro. Sir Maurice Bowra (London: Oxford University Press, 1955), xvi.

36. Aldington's book, *Lawrence of Arabia: A Biographical Enquiry,* was first published in French in 1954 and appeared in English only in 1955.

37. For a review of the major print and film biographies from 1924 through 1986 and their relation to the politics of their times, see Stephen E.

Tabachnick and Christopher Matheson, *Images of Lawrence* (London: Cape, 1988), 37–91. See also Graham Dawson, *Soldier Heroes: British Adventure, Empire and the Imagining of Masculinities* (London: Routledge, 1994), particularly 208–30. For the most important print biographies appearing since (as well as before) 1986, see the bibliography in the present volume. Lowell Thomas's *With Lawrence in Arabia* (1924) is the model of the heroic biography; Richard Aldington's *Lawrence of Arabia: A Biographical Enquiry* (1955) began the second, revisionist phase in which Lawrence is seen as too pro-Arab; and Phillip Knightley and Colin Simpson's *The Secret Lives of Lawrence of Arabia* (1969) ushered in the third phase, in which in some biographies Lawrence is portrayed as a rampant British imperialist. Lawrence James's *The Golden Warrior: The Life and Legend of T. E. Lawrence* (1990) also charges Lawrence with imperialism. Strongly opposing such viewpoints are John Mack, in his *Prince of Our Disorder: The Life of T. E. Lawrence* (1976) and J. M. Wilson, in *Lawrence of Arabia: The Authorized Biography of T. E. Lawrence* (1989).

38. See John Mack, *A Prince of Our Disorder: The Life of T. E. Lawrence* (London: Weidenfeld and Nicolson, 1976), 179–85, 204–9; Jacob Rosen, "Lawrence in Arabic," *T. E. Lawrence Centennial: Presentations from the T. E. Lawrence Symposium held May 20–21, 1998 at Pepperdine University—Malibu, California* ([Pepperdine University, 1989]), 136–47; and, for instance, Edward Said's *Orientalism* (New York: Pantheon, 1978) as well as the Essex University Ph.D. dissertation by Naimi, listed in an earlier endnote.

Chapter Two

1. William L. Howarth, "Some Principles of Autobiography," *New Literary History* (Winter 1974): 363–81.

2. T. E. Lawrence, foreword to Bertram Thomas, *Arabia Felix* (London: Cape, 1932), xvii–xviii.

3. Dated 21 October 1925 in the Houghton Library series of 73 letters to Robert Graves.

4. In *T. E. Lawrence by his Friends,* ed. A. W. Lawrence (New York: McGraw-Hill, 1963), 343.

5. *The Home Letters of T. E. Lawrence and his Brothers,* ed. M. R. Lawrence (Oxford: Basil Blackwell, 1954), 207.

6. T. E. Lawrence, introduction to Charles M. Doughty, *Travels in Arabia Deserta* (New York: Dover, 1979), 1:28.

7. Michael Foss, "Dangerous Guides: English Writers and the Desert," *The New Middle East* 9 (June 1969): 39.

8. Beginning in the 1960s, a sizable literature offering the responses of non-Europeans to views of them by Europeans has emerged. The following works have particular relevance to the Near East: Rana Kabbani, *Europe's Myths of Orient: Devise and Rule* (London: Macmillan, 1986); Sari Nasir, *The Arabs and the English* (London: Longman's, 1976); Edward Said, *Orientalism* (New York:

Pantheon, 1978); and Muhammed Nasser Shoukany, "Orientalism and the Arab Literary Responses: Studies in Ahmad Faris Al-Shidyaq, Charles M. Doughty, Joseph Conrad, Jabra I. Jabra and Tawifiq Yusuf Awwad" (Ph.D. diss., University of Texas at Austin, 1990). Although valuable as a corrective to past one-sided European viewpoints, Said's book, for instance, has a polemical edge, as Arab reviewers themselves have noticed: See Emmanuel Sivan, "Edward Said and His Arab Reviewers," *The Jerusalem Quarterly* 35 (Spring 1985): 11–23. For a balanced discussion of attempts by both Westerners and Arabs to understand the Arab world, see Dale F. Eickelman, *The Middle East: An Anthropological Approach*, 2d ed. (Englewood Cliffs, N.J.: Prentice-Hall, 1989), particularly chapters 1 and 2. For a review of some attempts by Arabs to understand the West, see Bernard Lewis, *The Muslim Discovery of Europe* (New York: Norton, 1982). Two excellent works offering the perspectives of Arabs on nineteenth-century British literature dealing with the Near East are Muhsin Jassim Ali, *Scheherazade in England: A Study of Nineteenth-Century English Criticism of the Arabian Nights* (Washington, D.C.: Three Continents, 1981) and Issam Safady, "Attempt and Attainment: A Study of Some Literary Aspects of Charles Doughty's *Arabia Deserta* as the Culmination of Late-Victorian Anglo-Arabian Travel Books to the Levant" (Ph.D. diss., University of Kentucky, 1968). Studies of Lawrence by Arabs also began appearing in the 1960s: See Suleiman Mousa's *T. E. Lawrence: An Arab View* (1962 in Arabic; 1966 in English) and Subhi al-Umari's *Lurans Kama 'Araftuhu [Lawrence as I Knew Him]* (1969).

9. Jean Béraud Villars, *T. E. Lawrence or the Search for the Absolute,* trans. Peter Dawnay (London: Sidgwick and Jackson, 1958), 296. Originally published in French in 1955.

10. D. G. Hogarth, *The Life of Charles M. Doughty* (Garden City: Doubleday, Doran, 1929), 132.

11. Excellent histories of European-Arabian exploration and writing include Thomas J. Assad, *Three Arabian Travellers: Burton, Blunt, Doughty* (London: Routledge and Kegan Paul, 1964); Robin Bidwell, *Travellers in Arabia* (London: Hamlyn, 1976); Peter Brent, *Far Arabia: Explorers of the Myth* (London: Quartet, 1979); Robin Fedden, *English Travellers in the Near East,* Writers and Their Work, no. 97, ed. Bonamy Dobrée (London: Longman's, Green, 1958); Zara Freeth and H. V. F. Winstone, *Explorers of Arabia from the Renaissance to the End of the Victorian Era* (London: Allen & Unwin, 1978); David G. Hogarth, *The Penetration of Arabia* (New York: Frederick A. Stokes, 1904); R. H. Kiernan, *The Unveiling of Arabia: The Story of Arabian Travel and Discovery* (London: Harrap, 1937); Jacqueline Pirenne, A *la découverte de l'Arabie: Cinq siècles de science et d'aventure* (Paris: Amiot-Dumont, 1958); Kathryn Tidrick, *Heart-Beguiling Araby* (Cambridge: Cambridge University Press, 1981); and Richard Trench, *Arabian Travellers: The European Discovery of Arabia* (Topsfield, Mass.: Salem House, 1986).

12. Alexander W. Kinglake, *Eothen* (Oxford: Oxford University Press, 1982).

13. Iran Banu Hassani Jewett, "Kinglake and the English Travelogue of the Nineteenth Century, *Dissertation Abstracts* 25 (1964), 2961–62. See also her excellent *Alexander W. Kinglake* (Boston: Twayne, 1981).

14. In his *Abroad: British Literary Travelling Between the Wars* (Oxford: Oxford University Press, 1980), Paul Fussell claims that to be considered literary, a travel writer must demonstrate an interest in writing as well as in traveling.

15. New York: E. P. Dutton, 1917.

16. Letter dated 6 November 1928 in the Houghton Library series to Graves.

17. *T. E. by his Friends,* 331.

18. Robert Hamilton, *W. H. Hudson: The Vision of Earth* (Port Washington, N.Y.: Kennikat, 1970), 111.

19. This review first appeared in *The Bibliophile's Almanack* (1928), 35–41. Reprinted in Herbert Read, *A Coat of Many Colours* (London: Routledge, 1945), 24–26.

20. See Hogarth, *The Life of Charles M. Doughty,* 204.

21. For a detailed analysis of Doughty's incredible (and often misunderstood) style, which is one of the few examples of genuine multilingualism in English literature, see Robert A. Fernea, *"Arabia Deserta:* The Ethnographic Text," in *Explorations in Doughty's "Arabia Deserta,"* ed. Stephen E. Tabachnick (Athens: University of Georgia Press, 1987): 215–19; Edward A. Levenston, "The Style of *Arabia Deserta:* A Linguistic Analysis" in *Explorations in Doughty's "Arabia Deserta,"* 90–110; Annette Marie McCormick, "The Origin and Development of the Styles of Charles M. Doughty's *Travels in Arabia Deserta"* (Ph.D. diss., University of London, 1951); Stephen E. Tabachnick, *Charles Doughty* (Boston: Twayne, 1981), 53–63; and Walt Taylor, "Doughty's English," S.P.E. Tract, no. 51 (Oxford: Clarendon Press, 1939). See Tabachnick's *Charles Doughty,* 101–5, for an analysis of the Ibn Rashid court episode as tragedy.

22. Albert Cook, *"Seven Pillars of Wisdom:* Turns and Counter-Turns," in *T. E. Lawrence: Soldier, Writer, Legend,* ed. Jeffrey Meyers (New York: St. Martin's, 1989), 93.

23. In "The Changing East," an article originally published anonymously by Lawrence in *The Round Table* 40 (September 1920): 756–72; reprinted in *Oriental Assembly,* ed. A. W. Lawrence (New York: Dutton, 1940), 73. See M. D. Allen, *The Medievalism of Lawrence of Arabia* (University Park: Pennsylvania State University Press, 1991) for an enlightening discussion of all aspects of Lawrence's medievalism, which however scants the important influence upon him of Doughty—for whom Chaucer and Spenser were the two greatest authors.

Chapter Three

1. See Jeffrey Meyers, *The Wounded Spirit,* chapter 6, "Nietzsche and the Will to Power," and Thomas J. O'Donnell, "The Assertion and Denial of

the Romantic Will in *Seven Pillars of Wisdom* and *The Mint,*" in *The T. E. Lawrence Puzzle,* ed. Stephen E. Tabachnick (Athens: University of Georgia Press, 1984), 71–95; and O'Donnell's book, *The Confessions of T. E. Lawrence* (Athens: Ohio University Press, 1979).

2. *T. E. Lawrence by His Friends,* 240.

3. See Stephen E. Tabachnick, "A Fragmentation Artist," in *The T. E. Lawrence Puzzle,* especially pages 14–23, for a discussion of Lawrence's position on this important philosophical problem, including Telesio's theories.

4. Vyvyan Richards, *A Portrait of T. E. Lawrence* (London: Jonathan Cape, 1936), 29–30.

5. T. E. Lawrence, *T. E. Lawrence to His Biographer, Robert Graves* (New York: Doubleday, Doran, 1938), 56. See also Geoffrey Syer, "Morris Was a Giant: The Quest of T. E. Lawrence," *Journal of the William Morris Society* 10, 4 (Spring 1994): 48–52.

6. Robert Graves, *Lawrence and the Arabian Adventure* (New York: Doubleday, Doran, 1938), 134.

7. T. E. Lawrence, comp., *Minorities,* ed. J. M. Wilson (London: Jonathan Cape, 1971). For the connection between the poems that Lawrence read in his *Oxford Book of English Verse* and events during the course of the revolt, see Wilson's notes. The poems Lawrence read during the revolt were Arthur O'Shaughnessy's "Ode," John Davidson's "Song," William Watson's "The Great Misgiving," Henry Cust's "Non Nobis," Kipling's "Dedication," and Clough's "Say Not the Struggle Naught Availeth."

8. *T. E. Lawrence by His Friends,* 240.

9. M. D. Allen, *The Medievalism of Lawrence of Arabia,* 131.

10. James A. Notopoulos, "The Tragic and the Epic in T. E. Lawrence," *Yale Review* 54 (Spring 1965): 338.

11. Maren Ormseth Cohn, "Ambiguity and Fame: Lawrence's Odyssean Nature," paper read at the third American T. E. Lawrence conference, which was devoted to the topic "The Creation of Fame: Lawrence of Arabia," The Huntington Library, 19 May 1995, 27. See also her Ph.D. dissertation, noted in the bibliography in this volume.

12. Avraham Feinglass, "T. E. Lawrence and the Heroic Narrative Mode" (B.A. honors paper, Ben-Gurion University of the Negev, 1974).

13. See L. Robert Morris and Lawrence Raskin, *Lawrence of Arabia,* for an account of the making of this influential if in some ways biographically inaccurate film. And see the article by Michael Anderegg, also listed in the bibliography in this volume.

14. Quoted in Feinglass, 4.

15. For other interviews with Bedouin concerning Lawrence, see John Mack, *A Prince of Our Disorder,* 180–83.

16. See Phillip Knightley and Colin Simpson, *The Secret Lives of Lawrence of Arabia* (New York: McGraw-Hill, 1970), 180–86, for a discussion of Beaumont's testimony and the whole "S. A." question. The most reliable biogra-

phers to follow Knightley and Simpson accept this identification of "S. A." as Dahoum, which was hinted by Lawrence himself as early as 1922, correctly assessed by Robert Graves (despite Lawrence's attempt to cloud the issue) during the 1920s and accepted by Lawrence's brother A. W. as well. See Mack, *A Prince of Our Disorder,* 310–11, and Wilson, *Lawrence of Arabia,* 672–73.

17. He says this not only on page 128 of *The Mint* but also in a letter of 6 November 1928 to Robert Graves. See Malcolm Brown, ed., *The Selected Letters of T. E. Lawrence,* 389.

18. Wilson, *Lawrence of Arabia,* 127–28.

19. Mack, *A Prince of Our Disorder,* 425.

20. See for instance Jeffrey Meyers, *Homosexuality and Literature 1890–1930* (Montreal: McGill-Queen's University Press, 1977), 114–30; Kaja Silverman, *Male Subjectivity at the Margins* (New York: Routledge, 1992), 299–338; Donald H. Mengay, "Arabian Rites: T. E. Lawrence and the Erotics of Empire," *Genre* 27, 4 (Winter 1994): 395–416; and Daniel Wolfe, *T. E. Lawrence* (New York: Chelsea House, 1995). Graham Dawson discusses Lawrence in depth in the context of "modernist masculinity" in his *Soldier Heroes: British Adventure, Empire and the Imagining of Masculinities* (London: Routledge, 1994), 167–230.

21. On a graduate paper ("A House Divided: The 'Crisis of Belief' in T. E. Lawrence's *Seven Pillars of Wisdom*") that I wrote for a course that he taught at the University of Connecticut in 1970. Spender went on to comment more generally that "Lawrence was a very courageous man and experienced doubtless much of what he described, but he was not finally self-revealing and there was something about him which flirted with destiny. He is somewhere a bit false and capable of falsification."

22. Quoted in J. M. Wilson's edition of *Minorities,* 50.

23. Andrew Rutherford, *The Literature of War: Five Studies in Heroic Virtue* (New York: Harper and Row, 1978), 54.

24. Eugene Goodheart, "A Contest of Motives": T. E. Lawrence in *Seven Pillars of Wisdom* in *T. E. Lawrence: Soldier, Writer, Legend,* ed. Jeffrey Meyers (New York: St. Martin's, 1989), 123.

Chapter Four

1. E. M. Forster, *Abinger Harvest* (London: Edward Arnold, 1936), 165.

2. See Meyers, chapter 3, and O'Donnell, *Confessions,* passim.

3. See Philip O'Brien, *T. E. Lawrence: A Bibliography* (Boston: G. K. Hall, 1988) for a detailed bibliographical description of the many editions of *Seven Pillars of Wisdom.*

4. For a detailed account of the publication of this edition, see V. M. Thompson, *"Not a Suitable Hobby for an Airman"—T. E. Lawrence as a Publisher* (Long Hanborough: Orchard Books, 1986). Thompson and O'Brien are now conducting a complete census, or bibliographic survey, of the individual books

in this edition, each of which has its own binding. See also J. M. Wilson, "T. E. Lawrence and the printing of *Seven Pillars of Wisdom,*" *Matrix* 5 (Winter 1985): 55–69.

   5.   For a superb account of the artwork used in this edition and an assessment of the success or failure of the edition as a whole, see Charles Grosvenor, "The Subscribers' *Seven Pillars of Wisdom:* The Visual Aspect" in *The T. E. Lawrence Puzzle,* 159–203.

   6.   In Houghton Library MS Notebook fMS eng 1252 (356), Lawrence counts 217 copies; in Bertram Rota, "Lawrence of Arabia and *Seven Pillars of Wisdom,*" *Texas Quarterly* 5, 3 (Autumn 1962): 49, the figure of 211 copies is given. Lawrence's mysteries never cease!

   7.   In 1986 the *Arab Bulletin,* nos. 1–36, ed. Robin Bidwell, was published in four volumes by Archive Editions, Gerrard Cross, Buckinghamshire, England.

   8.   See the volumes of correspondence edited by David Garnett, M. R. Lawrence, and more recently Malcolm Brown (*T. E. Lawrence: The Selected Letters,* New York: Norton, 1989). In addition, a useful and well-annotated collection is *Lawrence of Arabia: Strange Man of Letters: The Literary Criticism and Correspondence of T. E. Lawrence,* ed. Harold Orlans (Rutherford, N.J.: Fairleigh Dickinson University Press, 1993).

   9.   This analogy is William Howarth's.

   10.   For the creation of this media image and the specifically American contribution to it, see Joel Hodson, *Lawrence of Arabia and American Culture: The Making of a Transatlantic Legend* (Westport, Conn.: Greenwood, 1995).

   11.   In *The T. E. Lawrence Puzzle,* 213.

   12.   See Elie Kedourie, "The Capture of Damascus, 1 October 1918," in *The Chatham House Version and Other Middle Eastern Studies* (Hanover: University Press of New England, 1984): 33–51, and J. M. Wilson, *Lawrence of Arabia,* 1105–6.

   13.   Robert Graves, *Lawrence and the Arabian Adventure,* 360.

   14.   Robert Payne, *Lawrence of Arabia: A Triumph* (New York: Pyramid Books, 1962), 159.

   15.   *Secret Despatches from Arabia,* foreword by A. W. Lawrence (London: Golden Cockerel Press, 1939), 17. This *Arab Bulletin* report of 18 November actually describes the meeting with Feisal that took place on 23 October.

   16.   Ibid., 37.

   17.   See, for instance, Jeffrey Meyers, *The Wounded Spirit,* 56.

   18.   Ronald Storrs, *Orientations* (London: Nicholson & Watson, 1943), 171.

   19.   Ronald Storrs, "Lawrence of Arabia," *Listener* 53 (3 February 1955), 188–89.

   20.   See Phillip Knightley and Colin Simpson, *The Secret Lives of Lawrence of Arabia* (New York: McGraw-Hill, 1970), 102.

   21.   Despite J. M. Wilson's attempt to do so in *Lawrence of Arabia,* 1083–84. Although Wilson is unconvincing about why Lawrence concealed the

apparent fact that the Bey identified him, he is very good when refuting the fanciful claims of some writers that the Deraa incident never occurred at all. The fact that Lawrence wrote a report about it already in 1919 and then a letter about it to Mrs. George Bernard Shaw in 1924 seems to show that it was no fantasy.

22. Knightley and Simpson, *The Secret Lives of Lawrence of Arabia,* 244.
23. Charles M. Doughty, *Arabia Deserta,* 2:406.
24. *Lawrence and the Arabian Adventure,* 357–58.

Chapter Five

1. See Joseph Conrad, *Lord Jim* in *The Complete Works of Joseph Conrad* (Garden City, N.Y.: Doubleday, 1924), 338–39.
2. E. M. Forster, *A Passage to India* (New York: Harcourt, Brace, 1952), 322.
3. In *T. E. Lawrence by His Friends,* 289.
4. Knightley and Simpson, 177–79.
5. See, for instance, Bernard E. Dold, *T. E. Lawrence: Writer and Wrecker,* Quaderni dei Nuovi Annali, Facolta di Magistero dell'Universita di Messina, 13 (Rome: Herder, 1988); and John M. Mackenzie, "T. E. Lawrence: The Myth and the Message," in *Literature and Imperialism,* ed. Robert Giddings (New York: St. Martin's Press, 1991). Although his monograph was published in 1988, Dold seems caught in a time warp in which very little serious Lawrence scholarship written after about 1970 seems to exist.
6. For a full discussion of this complex issue, see Stephen E. Tabachnick and Christopher Matheson, *Images of Lawrence,* 129–39.
7. T. E. Lawrence, *T. E. Lawrence: The Selected Letters,* ed. Malcolm Brown (New York: Norton, 1989), 111.
8. Hannah Arendt, *The Origins of Totalitarianism* (New York: Harcourt, Brace, 1951), 218.
9. Albert Memmi, *The Colonizer and the Colonized* (New York: Beacon, 1967), 124.
10. Dennis Porter, *Haunted Journeys: Desire and Transgression in European Travel Writing* (Princeton: Princeton University Press, 1991), 227.
11. T. E. Lawrence, *Shaw-Ede, T. E. Lawrence's Letters to H. S. Ede, 1927–35,* ed. H. S. Ede (London: Golden Cockerel Press, 1942), 11.
12. Lawrence is sometimes attacked for having supported the Hashemites rather than ibn Saud. See *Images of Lawrence,* 133–34, for the reasons for his choice of the Hashemites and the entire chapter in that book entitled "The Diplomat" for the full complexity of the Near Eastern political issues surrounding Lawrence.
13. Vyvyan Richards, *A Portrait of T. E. Lawrence* (London: Jonathan Cape, 1936), 186.

14. R. P. Blackmur, *The Lion and the Honeycomb: Essays in Solicitude and Critique* (New York: Harcourt, Brace, 1955), 123.

15. *Shaw-Ede,* 11.

16. Vyvyan Richards, *Portrait of T. E. Lawrence,* 186.

17. T. E. Lawrence, introduction to *Arabia Deserta* (New York: Dover, 1979), 1:20.

18. Dated 4 May 1927 (British Library). Quoted in O'Donnell, *The Confessions of T. E. Lawrence,* 78–79.

19. Dated 10 June 1927 (British Library); quoted in O'Donnell, ibid., 79.

20. But see Stephen Tabachnick, *Charles Doughty* (Boston: Twayne, 1981), 48–52 and 77–83 for a discussion of Doughty's attitudes that gives him considerably more credit for flexibility and tolerance (on matters other than religion or British patriotism) than Lawrence does. Along similar lines, see also Janice Deledalle-Rhodes, "The True Nature of Doughty's Relationship to the Arabs" in *Explorations in Doughty's "Arabia Deserta,"* ed. Stephen Tabachnick (Athens: University of Georgia Press, 1987), 110–29, and Robert A. Fernea, "*Arabia Deserta:* The Ethnographic Text" in ibid., 201–19.

21. *Arabia Deserta,* 1:33.

22. Ibid., 2:406.

23. Ibid., 1:448.

24. Richard F. Burton, "Mr. Doughty's Travels," *Academy* 34 (28 July 1888), 47–48. For a full discussion of Burton and Doughty's literary relationship, see Stephen Tabachnick, "Burton's Review of Doughty's *Arabia Deserta,*" in *In Search of Sir Richard Burton: Papers from a Huntington Library Symposium,* ed. Alan Jutzi (San Marino: Huntington Library, 1993): 47–59.

25. See Tabachnick, *Charles Doughty,* 81.

26. Albert Memmi, *The Colonizer and the Colonized,* 85.

27. Dennis Porter, *Haunted Journeys: Desire and Transgression in European Travel Writing,* 227.

28. Albert Memmi, *The Colonizer and the Colonized,* 45.

29. Knightley and Simpson, *The Secret Lives of Lawrence of Arabia,* 70.

30. Originally omitted from the final edition upon the advice of G. B. Shaw but now included in most American and British editions.

31. Joseph Conrad, *Heart of Darkness,* in *Conrad's Heart of Darkness and the Critics,* ed. Bruce Harkness (Belmont, Calif.: Wadsworth, 1962), 36.

32. Knightley and Simpson, *The Secret Lives of Lawrence of Arabia,* 83.

33. Joseph Conrad, *Heart of Darkness,* 31.

34. Alan Sandison, *The Wheel of Empire* (New York: St. Martin's, 1967), 128.

35. Quoted in Sandison, 122.

36. Forster, *Abinger Harvest,* 169.

37. Quoted in Knightley and Simpson, *The Secret Lives of Lawrence of Arabia,* 245.

38. As I explained in my chapter 4, even though Lawrence wrote in his secret report of 1919 that the Bey did identify him as Lawrence, which contradicts the Deraa account in *Seven Pillars* where he states that the Bey did not identify him, it is not clear when in the course of the torture Lawrence might have learned that the Bey knew who he was; perhaps it was only after the torture was over. If so, thinking that the Bey did not know who he was, he would have tried to conceal his true identity by continuing to speak only in Arabic throughout the torture. Or even if the Bey revealed that he knew who Lawrence was during the torture, Lawrence might have tried to deny it and continue speaking only in Arabic. But this idea, like most others about this incident, must remain speculative. Terence Rattigan's theory, in his play *Ross* (1960), is that the Bey knew who Lawrence was, deliberately assaulted him to break his spirit, and then deliberately let him go, thinking that Lawrence would no longer be a good commander. In light of Lawrence's report of 1919, published only by Knightley and Simpson in the late 1960s and therefore presumably unknown to Rattigan, this is a much more plausible theory than it once seemed to be. Yet the truth remains unknown.

39. Conrad, *Heart of Darkness*, 51.
40. Memmi, *The Colonizer and the Colonized*, 59.
41. *Letters to T. E. Lawrence*, 62.
42. E. M. Forster, *A Passage to India* (New York: Harcourt, Brace, 1952), 149.
43. Ibid., 286.
44. Ibid., 311.

Chapter Six

1. As Meyers and O'Donnell point out.
2. For further information on this interpretation, see T. E. Lawrence, *T. E. Lawrence to His Biographer, Liddell Hart* (New York: Doubleday, Doran, 1938), 130.
3. MS Eng 1252, 355.
4. Robert Payne, *Lawrence of Arabia: A Triumph*, 152.
5. Keith Hull, "*Seven Pillars of Wisdom*: The Secret, Contestable Documentary," in *The T. E. Lawrence Puzzle*, 96–114.
6. See Kingsley Widmer, "The Intellectual as Soldier" in *T. E. Lawrence: Soldier, Writer, Legend*, 28–57, for an excellent exploration of this conflict in Lawrence.
7. Both Kaja Silverman and Donald Mengay, like Thomas O'Donnell before them, make an interesting if speculative connection between Lawrence's sexuality and his attitudes toward colonialism. If psychoanalytical theory is applied to Silverman's own work, her unintentional mistake of using the title *Three Pillars* instead of *Seven Pillars* at one point in her essay (318) may indicate an overemphasis on sexuality (of which the number three is a well-known sym-

bol) as the exclusive "key" to understanding *Seven Pillars*. In her favor however is Lawrence's own placement of the "Deraa" chapter at a central point in the book's structure and its obvious importance for him. Mengay's discussion, which makes some interesting suppositions about the relations between Feisal and Lawrence, does not sufficiently distinguish between Arabs and Turks, an important distinction for Lawrence.

8. T. E. Lawrence, *Men in Print: Essays in Literary Criticism* (London: Golden Cockerel, 1940), 43.

9. Richard Meinertzhagen, *Middle East Diary, 1917–1956* (London: Cresset Press, 1959), 31–32.

10. For an interesting attempt to connect style and personality in several writers, including T. E. Lawrence, see A. Kingsley Weatherhead, "The Styles and the Men," *CEA Critic* 51, 1 (Fall 1988), 129–41.

11. Blackmur, *The Lion and the Honeycomb,* 106–7.

12. T. E. Lawrence, *Shaw-Ede,* 27.

13. *T. E. Lawrence by His Friends,* 131.

14. Houghton Library MS Eng. 1252, 362.

15. *Letters to T. E. Lawrence,* 21.

16. *Men in Print,* 43.

17. Ibid., 52–53.

18. Ibid., 43.

19. *Letters to T. E. Lawrence,* 60.

20. In an annotation on the inside front cover of his personal copy of Robert Vansittart's *Singing Caravan* (in the Houghton Library).

21. M. D. Allen has shown how Lawrence was influenced by the *Moallakat,* a pre-Moslem Arabic work that he read in W. S. and Lady Anne Blunt's English translation, *The Seven Golden Odes of Pagan Arabia, Also Known as the Moallakat* (London: Chiswick, 1903).

22. In his *Two Cheers for Democracy* (London: Edward Arnold, 1951), 291.

23. See M. D. Allen, *The Medievalism of Lawrence of Arabia,* for a detailed look at additional influences acting on Lawrence's style and outlook.

24. *Men in Print,* 48.

25. Richards, *A Portrait of T. E. Lawrence,* 186.

26. Quoted in Richards, *A Portrait of T. E. Lawrence,* 186.

27. See Meyers, *The Wounded Spirit,* 85, for a description of 10 styles in *Seven Pillars.* I thank Dr. Zev Bar-Lev for suggesting that Lawrence's styles could be arranged on a chart.

28. I thank Mrs. Noah Ben Porat, a student in my spring 1980 "Neglected Literature" seminar at the Ben-Gurion University, for pointing out the possible allusion to Henry James in Lawrence's passage.

29. F. Scott Fitzgerald, *The Great Gatsby* (Harmondsworth: Penguin, 1972), 14.

Chapter Seven

1. For a full comparison of Lawrence, Ishmael, and Ahab, see Stephen Tabachnick, "T. E. Lawrence and *Moby Dick*," *Research Studies* 44, 1 (March 1976): 1–12. See also Weintraub and Weintraub, *Lawrence of Arabia*, 48–51.
2. For Lawrence's love of machinery, see the chapter "The Mechanic" in *Images of Lawrence*, 141–51. See also Rodelle Weintraub, "T. E. Lawrence: Technical Writer" in *The T. E. Lawrence Puzzle*, 137–56.
3. See Stephen E. Tabachnick, "A Fragmentation Artist" in *The T. E. Lawrence Puzzle*, especially pages 14–23, for a detailed discussion of Lawrence's evolving position on the mind-body problem and the problem of unity. A serious student of philosophy, Lawrence was deeply influenced by Bernardino Telesio, Spinoza, F. H. Bradley, and Bertrand Russell, among others.
4. Including, among others, Jeffrey Meyers and Thomas O'Donnell. See Meyers's essay, "T. E. Lawrence: The Mechanical Monk" in *The T. E. Lawrence Puzzle*, 124–36.
5. V. S. Pritchett, *The Living Novel and Later Appreciations* (New York: Random House, 1954), 290.

Chapter Eight

1. See, for instance, Stanley Weintraub, "Lawrence of Arabia: The Portraits from Imagination, 1922–1979" in *The T. E. Lawrence Puzzle*, 269–92, and the bibliography in the second edition of Jeffrey Meyers's *The Wounded Spirit*.
2. See Joel C. Hodson, *Lawrence of Arabia and American Culture: The Making of a Transatlantic Legend* (Westport, Conn.: Greenwood, 1995) for a discussion of these and other manifestations of Lawrence in American (and British) popular culture.
3. And not just in the Near East. The situation of Native Americans in the United States and South America has involved a similar shift.
4. On these and other points, see Ian Baruma, "Wilfred of Arabia," *The New York Review of Books* (30 June 1988): 13–15; and Stephen E. Tabachnick, "Wilfred Thesiger: The Man Who Would Be Last," *Contention*, 2, 1 (Fall 1992): 181–96.
5. New York: Simon and Schuster, 1980.
6. New York: Atlantic Monthly Press, 1990.

Selected Bibliography

Philip O'Brien's *T. E. Lawrence: A Bibliography* (Boston: G. K. Hall, 1988) supersedes all previous Lawrence bibliographies and is the essential descriptive listing of works by and about Lawrence through 1987.

PRIMARY SOURCES

Manuscript Collections

Bodleian Library, Oxford.
British Library.
Harry Ransom Humanities Research Center, University of Texas.
Houghton Library, Harvard University.
Huntington Library.

Lawrence's Principal Works

Carchemish: Report on the Excavations at Djerabis on Behalf of the British Museum. 3 vols. Coauthors C. Leonard Woolley, T. E. Lawrence, D. G. Hogarth, and P. L. O. Guy. London: British Museum, 1914, 1921, and 1952.
Crusader Castles. 2 vols. London: Golden Cockerel Press, 1936.
Crusader Castles. Introduction by Denys Pringle. Oxford: Clarendon Press, 1988.
The Diary of T. E. Lawrence MCMXI. London: Corvinus Press, 1937.
Evolution of a Revolt: Early Post-War Writings of T. E. Lawrence. Ed. Stanley and Rodelle Weintraub. University Park, Pa.: Pennsylvania State University Press, 1968.
The Home Letters of T. E. Lawrence and His Brothers. Ed. M. R. Lawrence. Oxford: Basil Blackwell, 1954.
Lawrence of Arabia, Strange Man of Letters: The Literary Criticism and Correspondence of T. E. Lawrence. Ed. Harold Orlans. Rutherford, N.J.: Fairleigh Dickinson University Press, 1993.
The Letters of T. E. Lawrence. Ed. David Garnett. London: Jonathan Cape, 1938.
Men in Print: Essays in Literary Criticism by T. E. Lawrence. Ed. A. W. Lawrence. London: Golden Cockerel Press, 1940.
Minorities. Ed. J. M. Wilson. Preface by C. Day Lewis. London: Jonathan Cape, 1971.

153

The Mint. Note by A. W. Lawrence. New York: W. W. Norton, 1955.

The Mint. Preface by J. M. Wilson. Harmondsworth: Penguin, 1978.

[T. E. Shaw, trans.]. *The Odyssey of Homer.* Introduction by Sir Maurice Bowra. London: Oxford University Press, 1955.

Oriental Assembly. Ed. A. W. Lawrence. New York: Dutton, 1940.

Revolt in the Desert. New York: George Doran, 1927.

Secret Despatches from Arabia. Foreword by A. W. Lawrence. London: Golden Cockerel Press, 1939.

Seven Pillars of Wisdom: A Triumph. Garden City, N.Y.: Garden City Publishing Co., 1938.

Seven Pillars of Wisdom: A Triumph. Harmondsworth: Penguin, 1987.

T. E. Lawrence: The Selected Letters. Ed. Malcolm Brown. New York: W. W. Norton, 1989.

T. E. Lawrence to His Biographers Robert Graves and Liddell Hart: Information about Himself in the Form of Letters, Notes, Answers to Questions, and Conversations. New York: Doubleday, Doran 1938.

The Wilderness of Zin. Coauthors C. Leonard Woolley and T. E. Lawrence. London: Palestine Exploration Fund, 1915.

SECONDARY SOURCES

Since the first edition of this book was published in 1978, the growth of serious Lawrence research has been explosive. What follows is an attempt to describe for the reader some of the most important recent and older works dealing with Lawrence's life, writing career, and status as a cultural symbol. The American newsletter *T. E. Notes* and the British *Journal of the T. E. Lawrence Society* should be consulted for current research.

Biographies

Aldington, Richard. *Lawrence of Arabia: A Biographical Enquiry.* London: Collins, 1955. A negative point of view that remains important in Lawrence studies as a counterbalance to hagiography.

Graves, Robert. *Lawrence and the Arabian Adventure.* New York: Doubleday, Doran, 1928. Inaccurate biography but highly perceptive literary and character criticism.

Grosvenor, Charles. *An Iconography: The Portraits of T. E. Lawrence.* Pasadena: Otterden Press, 1988. Expert presentation of an important and otherwise neglected aspect of Lawrence biography.

Hyde, H. Montgomery. *Solitary in the Ranks: Lawrence of Arabia as Airman and Private Soldier.* London: Constable, 1977. Very sensible history of Lawrence's postwar life in the ranks that answers some of the wilder speculations about him.

Kedourie, Elie. "The Real T. E. Lawrence." *Commentary* 64 (July 1977): 49–56; (October 1977): 10–18. A valuable skeptical reading of John Mack's positive claims for Lawrence. Accuses Lawrence, among other things, of having romanticized terrorism.

Knightley, Phillip, and Colin Simpson. *The Secret Lives of Lawrence of Arabia.* New York: McGraw-Hill, 1970. Aggressively presents Lawrence as an imperialist but contains many valuable biographical documents and discoveries, including the first relatively full account of Lawrence's flagellation.

Lawrence, A. W., ed. *T. E. Lawrence by His Friends.* London: Jonathan Cape, 1937. One of the best biographical sources and full of valuable opinions concerning Lawrence's work.

Liddell Hart, Basil. *"T. E. Lawrence": In Arabia and After.* London: Jonathan Cape, 1934. Close to uncritical idolatry but still an important assessment of the military side of Lawrence's career, informed by personal knowledge of Lawrence.

Mack, John E. *A Prince of Our Disorder: The Life of T. E. Lawrence.* London: Weidenfeld and Nicolson, 1976. The best overall presentation of Lawrence's life to date, in part because of Mack's professional insight into Lawrence's psychology.

Mousa, Suleiman. *T. E. Lawrence: An Arab View.* Translated by Albert Butros. New York: Oxford University Press, 1966. Questions Lawrence's accuracy and the importance of his role in the Arab Revolt.

Orlans, Harold. "The Many Lives of T. E. Lawrence: A Symposium." *Biography* 16, 3 (Summer 1993): 224–48. Instructive discussion revealing the difficulty of arriving at any consensus regarding Lawrence's life, character, and career.

Richards, Vyvyan. *A Portrait of T. E. Lawrence.* London: Jonathan Cape, 1936. Excellent source of information about literary influences on Lawrence.

Tabachnick, Stephen E. Review of J. M. Wilson, *Lawrence of Arabia: The Authorized Biography. English Literature in Transition: 1880–1920,* 89–93. Detailed critique revealing not only the problems in Wilson's book but also those that all serious T. E. Lawrence biographers face.

Tabachnick, Stephen E., and Christopher Matheson. *Images of Lawrence.* London: Jonathan Cape, 1988. Centenary volume that surveys all major biographies of Lawrence in book, drama, and film format through 1986 and assesses Lawrence's career as an archaeologist, intelligence agent, guerrilla leader, diplomat, mechanic, and writer. With numerous photos.

Thomas, Lowell. *With Lawrence in Arabia.* New York: Century, 1924. A combination of showmanship and hagiography that began the "Lawrence legend" but nonetheless contains authentic details and impressions stemming from Thomas's personal knowledge of Lawrence.

Villars, Jean Béraud. *T. E. Lawrence, or the Search for the Absolute.* Translated by Peter Dawnay. London: Sidgwick and Jackson, 1958. Takes the position

that Lawrence was too pro-Arab and presents him as the forerunner of
political writers such as Malraux, Koestler, and Sartre.

Weintraub, Stanley. *Private Shaw and Public Shaw*. New York: George Brazillier,
1963. Excellent account of Lawrence's friendship with Mr. and Mrs.
G. B. Shaw. Contains very good work on the composition of *Seven Pillars*
but gives Shaw too much credit for revisions.

Wilson, Jeremy. *Lawrence of Arabia: The Authorized Biography of T. E. Lawrence*.
New York: Atheneum, 1990. Leaves some important questions about the
Deraa incident, the battle of Tafileh, and Lawrence's personal life unanswered but provides the fullest and most accurate account of the chronology and facts to date.

_____. *T. E. Lawrence*. London: National Portrait Gallery, 1988. Catalogue of
the centenary exhibition, including many excellent illustrations of the
Lawrence artifacts on display.

Wolfe, Daniel. *T. E. Lawrence*. Lives of Gay Men and Lesbians, ed. Martin
Duberman. New York: Chelsea House, 1995. Lacks footnotes and therefore proof of some of its assertions but nonetheless provides many fresh
insights, including an interesting comparison of *Seven Pillars* and E. M.
Forster's *Passage to India*.

Full-Length Critical and Cultural Studies

Allen, Malcolm. *The Medievalism of Lawrence of Arabia*. University Park, Pa.:
Pennsylvania State University Press, 1991. A very detailed discussion of
Lawrence's debt to medieval sources and of his transformation of those
sources.

Cohn, Maren Ormseth. "T. E. Lawrence and Odysseus: A Study of Translation,
Identity, and Heroic Action." Ph.D. diss., University of Chicago, 1995. By
far the most detailed discussion of Lawrence's translation of the *Odyssey* to
date, showing how his personality was expressed in his translation.

Hodson, Joel C. *Lawrence of Arabia and American Culture: The Making of a
Transatlantic Legend*. Westport, Conn.: Greenwood, 1995. A useful survey
of the contribution of Lowell Thomas and other Americans to the creation and study of the "Lawrence legend."

Knight, Ronald D. *T. E. Lawrence and the Max Gate Circle*. Weymouth: Bat &
Ball Press, 1988. Chronicles in detail Lawrence's friendship with Thomas
and Florence Hardy.

Lawrence, A. W., ed. *Letters to T. E. Lawrence*. London: Jonathan Cape, 1962.
The best source for detailed, penetrating criticism of Lawrence's work by
Forster, the Garnetts, Buchan, and others.

Meyers, Jeffrey. *The Wounded Spirit: A Study of "Seven Pillars of Wisdom."* London:
Martin Brian & O'Keeffe, 1973; New York: St. Martin's, 1989. A pioneering literary and psychological study of Lawrence, including compar-

isons of Lawrence with Doughty, Tolstoy, and Nietzsche, among others. The second edition contains an updated and expanded bibliography.

_____, ed. *T. E. Lawrence: Soldier, Writer, Legend*. New York: St. Martin's, 1989. Seven original, high-quality essays by experts in literature, translation, and Near Eastern history.

Morris, L. Robert, and Lawrence Raskin. *Lawrence of Arabia: The Thirtieth Anniversary Pictorial History*. New York: Doubleday, 1992. A thorough history of the making of the David Lean/ Robert Bolt film that, despite its inaccuracies, is now recognized as a classic work of art in its own right.

O'Donnell, Thomas J. *The Confessions of T. E. Lawrence: The Romantic Hero's Presentation of Self*. Athens, Ohio: Ohio University Press, 1979. Sophisticated analysis linking Lawrence's sexuality and politics and classifying him as a late representative of the nineteenth-century literary tradition of the divided self.

Tabachnick, Stephen E., ed. *The T. E. Lawrence Puzzle*. Athens: University of Georgia Press, 1984. Original essays by 13 Lawrence experts from five countries analyze all aspects of Lawrence's career and testify to his importance as a topic of academic discussion.

T. E. Lawrence Centennial: Presentations from the T. E. Lawrence Symposium held May 20–21, 1988, at Pepperdine University—Malibu, California. Includes 13 abstracts and papers from the first-ever Lawrence conference.

Thompson, Valerie. *"Not a Suitable Hobby for an Airman"—T. E. Lawrence as Publisher*. Long Hanborough: Orchard Books, 1986. An admirably detailed account of the publication of the 1926 Subscriber's Edition of *Seven Pillars of Wisdom* as a "book beautiful."

Weintraub, Stanley, and Rodelle Weintraub. *Lawrence of Arabia: The Literary Impulse*. Baton Rouge: Louisiana State University Press, 1975. Semibiographical introduction to Lawrence the writer.

Articles and Parts of Books

Anderegg, Michael. "Lawrence of Arabia: The Man, the Myth, the Movie." *Michigan Quarterly Review* 21 (Spring 1982): 281–300. A study of the film in the light of historical truth and Lawrence's cultural symbolism.

Blackmur, R. P. "The Everlasting Effort: A Citation of T. E. Lawrence." In *The Lion and the Honeycomb: Essays in Solicitude and Critique*, 97–123. New York: Harcourt, Brace, 1955. Pioneering attempt to apply the "new criticism" to Lawrence, and still one of the most perceptive critiques of the book ever written. Blackmur taxes Lawrence with "forced writing," including strained metaphors and flat characterization but places him among the "writers of magnitude" in English literature.

Cunningham, Virginia. "T. E. Lawrence and Malraux, 1929–1946." *Mélanges Malraux Miscellany* 16 (May 1984): 2–30. One of the most detailed and perceptive studies of Lawrence's influence on French writer and man of action André Malraux.

Dawson, Graham. "The public and private lives of T. E. Lawrence: The imperial adventure hero in the modern world." In *Soldier Heroes: British adventure, empire, and the imagining of masculinities*, 167–230. London: Routledge, 1994. A thorough, jargon-free "cultural studies" discussion of Lawrence as an exemplar of the changing British perception of military heroes in the context of changing perceptions of masculinity itself.

Forster, E. M. "T. E. Lawrence." In *Abinger Harvest*, 165–71. London: Edward Arnold, 1936. Excellent criticism of *Seven Pillars*, informed by personal knowledge of Lawrence. Notes that "when he analyses himself it is as a spiritual outcast, on the lines of Herman Melville's Ishmael."

————. "English Prose between 1918 and 1939." In *Two Cheers for Democracy*, 280–91. London: Edward Arnold, 1951. Presents Lawrence as a refugee from industrialism: "[I]t was not by the spear of an Arab but by a high-powered motor-bike that he came to his death."

Hoenselaars, Ton, and Gene Moore. "Joseph Conrad and T. E. Lawrence." *Conradiana* 21, 1 (Spring 1995): 3–20. A fine scholarly study of the one meeting between Lawrence and Conrad and its artistic and other ramifications.

Hopkins, Chris. "A Source for Rex Warner's *The Aerodrome*." *Notes and Queries*. 40, 1 (March 1993): 68–69. Speculates on the possibility that *The Mint* influenced Warner's outstanding fictional fantasy published in 1941.

Howe, Irving. "T. E. Lawrence: The Problem of Heroism." In *A World More Attractive*, 1–39. New York: Horizon, 1963. Presents Lawrence as a representative man of our century.

Hull, Keith. "Lawrence of *The Mint*, Ross of the RAF." *South Atlantic Quarterly* 74 (Summer 1975): 340–48. *The Mint* as biography and art.

————. "T. E. Lawrence's Perilous Parodies." *Texas Quarterly* 2 (Summer 1972): 56–61. Tafileh seen as Lawrence's parody of a battle and a battle report.

Kaplan, Carola M. "Conquest as Literature, Literature as Conquest." *Texas Studies in Literature and Language* 37, 1 (Spring 1995): 72–97. A careful approach claiming that although Lawrence regarded *Seven Pillars* "as an artistic failure . . . recounting a military success," it is really "an artistic success . . . documenting a personal failure" and holds together in spite of its appearance of disintegrating. Lawrence finds freedom only in the space between British and Arab cultures.

Malraux, André. "Lawrence and the Demon of the Absolute." *Hudson Review* 8 (Winter 1956): 519–32. *Seven Pillars* is "not a great narrative," is lacking in characterization, and ends anticlimactically but is the product of a great religious spirit whose true portrait was "written in the margin."

Martin, B. K. "Ezra Pound and T. E. Lawrence." *Paideuma* 6, 2 (1977): 167–73. Covers the main points of the relationship between the two writers.

Meyers, Jeffrey. Review of Edward Said's *Orientalism*. *Sewanee Review* 88 (Spring 1980): xlv–xlviii. Balanced critique of Said's polemic, which is relevant to Lawrence.

Notopoulos, James A. "The Tragic and the Epic in T. E. Lawrence." *Yale Review* 54, 3 (Spring 1965): 331–45. Thorough explication of Homeric parallels in *Seven Pillars* in the light of Lawrence's *Odyssey* translation. Lawrence was a "modern figure who experienced the Homeric delirium of the brave and wrote of it with the requisite magic of literature, yet was condemned to tragic frustration by the anachronism of the heroic act in our times."

Payne, Robert. "On the Prose of T. E. Lawrence." *Prose* 4 (1972): 91–108. One of surprisingly few detailed studies of Lawrence's style.

Porter, Denis. "Political Witness: T. E. Lawrence and Gide." In *Haunted Journeys: Desire and Transgression in European Travel Writing*, 223–35. Princeton: Princeton University Press, 1991. A defense of Lawrence's position between the veils rendered in "cultural studies" terms.

Pritchett, V. S. "A Portrait of T. E. Lawrence." In *Books in General*, 37–42. London: Chatto and Windus, 1953. Reviews David Garnett's *Essential T. E. Lawrence* and constructs a portrait of Lawrence from his writings: "Hardly classical in manner (for that was 'out' in the Twenties and writers were looking for manners which would bring home their nervous singularity) *Seven Pillars* is the solitary classic of the self-conscious warrior, as Doughty is the great self-conscious traveller."

Rutherford, Andrew. "The Intellectual as Hero." In *The Literature of War: Five Studies in Heroic Virtue*, 38–63. New York: Harper & Row, 1978. Views Lawrence as a tragic hero who achieved much but at enormous cost to himself.

Said, Edward. *Orientalism*. New York: Pantheon, 1978. Scattered superficial remarks on Lawrence, but Said gives some insight into the creation of Western stereotypes of the Arabs in the course of a shrill polemic against Western "Oriental" scholarship.

Shaheen, Mohammad. "Pound and T. E. Lawrence: Two Self-Crowned Laureates of the Time." *Paideuma* 17, 2–3 (Fall-Winter 1988): 223–38. Detailed discussion of the Pound-Lawrence relationship based on correspondence, some of it previously unpublished.

Silverman, Kaja. "White Skins, Brown Masks: The Double Mimesis, or With Lawrence in Arabia." In *Male Subjectivity at the Margins*, 299–338. New York: Routledge, 1992. Presents a linkage of Lawrence's sexuality and politics in the context of a "cultural studies" analysis heavily dependent upon psychoanalytical theory. Takes the position that what really happened at Deraa matters less than Lawrence's "fantasizing" about it.

Tabachnick, Stephen E. "T. E. Lawrence and *Moby Dick*." *Research Studies* 44, 1 (March 1976): 1–12. Lawrence's personality seen in terms of Ahab and Ishmael.

_____. "The T. E. Lawrence Revival in English Studies." *Research Studies* 44, 3 (September 1976): 190–98. Contemporary review of the origin of Lawrence studies as an academic discipline.

_____. "Unexplored Realms of Gold: Teaching Travel Literature." *Readerly/ Writerly Texts* 1, 1 (Fall/Winter 1993): 187–210. Presents many ideas for introducing travel writers, including T. E. Lawrence, into the university curriculum.

Tidrick, Kathryn. "The Great War and the Arabists"; "Hail and Farewell." In *Heart-Beguiling Araby*, 163–219. Cambridge: Cambridge University Press, 1981. One of the best critiques of the whole Anglo-Arabian writing tradition. Lawrence is presented as striving to regain his lost aristocratic patrimony in Arabia.

Turner, June. "T. E. Lawrence." *American Imago* 48 (1991): 395–416. A sympathetic attempt to understand Lawrence's fixation on pain, largely on the basis of Freudian psychology.

Weatherhead, A. Kingsley. "The Styles and the Men." *CEA Critic* 51, 1 (Fall 1988): 129–41. Attempts a method of analyzing the styles of Lawrence, W. H. Auden, and Richard Nixon.

Wilson, Colin. "The Attempt to Gain Control." In *The Outsider*, 71–84. Boston: Houghton Mifflin, 1956. Important existentialist critique, in which Lawrence searches for his own identity with the help of Puritan discipline and pain, which show him the limits of his "moral freedom."

Index

The Author

Stephen E. Tabachnick is a professor of English literature at the University of Oklahoma. He received his Ph.D. from the University of Connecticut in 1971 and taught at an Israeli university from 1971 to 1984. He is the author of *Charles Doughty* (1981) and *Images of Lawrence* (1988) and the editor of *The T. E. Lawrence Puzzle* (1984) and *Explorations in Doughty's "Arabia Deserta"* (1987). He has recently completed a biography of his doctoral adviser, British novelist and classicist Rex Warner, and is now writing a T.E. Lawrence encyclopedia.

The Editor

Kinley E. Roby is a professor of English at Northeastern University. He is the Twentieth-Century Field Editor of the Twayne English Authors Series, Series Editor of Twayne's Critical History of British Drama, and General Editor of Twayne's Women and Literature Series. He has written books on Arnold Bennett, Edward VII, and Joyce Cary and edited a collection of essays on T. S. Eliot. He makes his home in Sudbury, Massachusetts.